FEET OF THE CHAMELEON

FEET OF THE CHAMELEON

The Story of African Football

IAN HAWKEY

PORTICO

For Michael, my son.

First published in the United Kingdom in 2009 by
Portico Books
10 Southcombe Street
London
W14 0RA

An imprint of Anova Books Company Ltd

ISBN 9781906032715

A CIP catalogue record for this book is available from the British Library.

10 9 8 7 6 5 4 3 2 1

Printed and bound by Athenaeum Press, Ltd., Gateshead, Tyne & Wear

This book can be ordered direct from the publisher at www.anovabooks.com

A note on names:

Countries are identified throughout by their names during the period described. Belgian Congo was the state that became Congo (1960), Zaïre (1970), Democratic Republic of Congo (1997). Likewise, French Congo/Congo-Brazzaville (1960), Dahomey/Benin (1975), Rhodesia/Zimbabwe (1980) and Upper Volta/Burkina Faso (1984).

The Maghreb is the region made up by Morocco, Algeria, Tunisia and the enclaves of Ceuta and Melilla.

CONTENTS

PROLOGUE

On the morning of 15 May 2004, Nelson Mandela woke early, as usual. It was a habit he had formed young and rigorously maintained during 27 years in South African prisons. Overnight, Mandela had been thinking back over details of the first period of that incarceration. He would later share some of them in a short speech about life on the notorious Robben Island, where leaders in the struggle against apartheid had been isolated.

Mandela was in Zurich. He had travelled there against the advice of doctors concerned at the taxing schedule of global diplomacy pursued by the ex-president of South Africa even in his 86th year. Mandela felt his presence in Switzerland might help sway a decision of great importance. The 24-man executive committee of Fifa, football's world governing body, would vote on who should host the 2010 World Cup and South Africa had spent six of its ten years as a democracy in determined and costly lobbying. Their delegation had reason to be apprehensive about the process. A bid for the 2006 tournament had ended in narrow and controversial defeat at the poll when a meek Fifa member abstained, enabling Germany, by a single vote, to stage sport's most watched event in Europe. A World Cup had never been organised in Africa, seldom goes to the southern hemisphere, never to the developing world. So when Fifa guaranteed the tender for 2010 would be open only to Africans, nobody could rationally challenge the fairness of the idea. In the hours before the final, secret ballot, Mandela would eloquently put the case for sub-Saharan Africa against various Mediterranean states. The actor Omar Sharif had arrived to speak up for Egypt, the Gaddafi family to represent Libya's ambitious joint request with Tunisia. Morocco had a strong manifesto and lobbied shrewdly, appealing to those suspicious of African capabilities by emphasising its proximity to Europe with the help of a former prime minister of Spain.

In his suite at the Dolder Grand Hotel, Mandela dressed, putting on a colourful shirt: silk, with a racy design of flowers and ribbons on a background of gold. He had breakfast and, accompanied by his assistant, a blonde Afrikaaner woman named Zelda la Grange, they took the elevator down to the lobby. In the lift the pair would be joined by one of the vice-presidents of Fifa, an individual whose own vote might not only be decisive in what looked a tight run-off against Morocco but had the political clout to bring other delegates with him. Mandela bade the Fifa official a friendly good morning, and with the gentle ease anybody who has met Nelson Rolihlahla Mandela more than once would recognise, they settled into a small-talk that left the Fifa man with the gratifying sensation of Mandela's sincere delight at seeing him again, that they shared a special, informal intimacy which cut across hierarchy. When the lift doors opened, the man in the blazer assured Mandela South Africa could count on his vote and those of his allies. They wished each other luck.

Mandela soon found himself in the company of lifetime

acquaintances. Bishop Desmond Tutu had arrived in Zurich to lend more gravitas to South Africa's case, to remind Fifa that just in case all the country's hardware advantages – the stadiums, roads, hotels, a sophisticated tourist industry – seemed unpersuasive, their nation had saints and Nobel Peace Prizes in its line-up. When Mandela, charming and lucid, addressed the Fifa personnel in the final, formal presentations, he avoided sentimentality, but he did ask them politely to allow him a little nostalgia. He took them back to life on The Island, his prison off the Cape of Good Hope, and described the value he and other detainees had given the game of football. Their days there, Mandela recalled, had been filled by arduous physical labour in the lime quarry, their nights with regular humiliations. Among the rights prisoners lobbied hardest for had been to play and follow football. A Robben Island league had been established; another breakthrough had been the inmates' limited access to radio and newspapers. Keeping abreast of local football, of the fortunes of clubs like Orlando Pirates and Moroka Swallows had lifted spirits, Mandela told the men in blazers. 'On Robben Island,' he said, 'football was the only joyful release for the prisoners.' He went on to congratulate Fifa for its decision to expel South Africa from its membership in 1976, a boost to his movement's opposition to apartheid. He reminded its executives how the country had transformed since his release in 1990, and that it was now in their gift to celebrate the joyous transformation from white rule to Rainbow Nation with an event that would show off a renascent Africa, in the land with the continent's most developed infrastructure.

In Africa, people waited, impatient, expectant. Giant screens had been erected in Johannesburg and Cape Town to broadcast the announcement. State television in Egypt and Morocco cleared their schedules for live coverage of the ceremonial opening of the winning envelope. Presses had been readied to bring out exceptional, afternoon editions of South Africa's major newspapers. Architects had already designed a Nelson Mandela stadium for the city of Port Elizabeth.

• • •

In Zurich, Fifa said yes to South Africa 2010. In the auditorium where the decision was announced, Bishop Tutu hooted with delight and promised: 'I will buy all the Fifa executives first-class air tickets to heaven! But first, I shall go outside and dance.' Mandela, clutching the 18-carat World Cup trophy next to his gold shirt, declared: 'I feel like a young man of 15 again.' The president of Fifa, Sepp Blatter, trumpeted: 'This is Africa's right. It is a global game,' as if to answer in advance the next six years of intermittent scepticism from the rest of the world about Africa's capacity to steer the juggernaut that is a World Cup.

Of Africa's excellence at football, there can be no such scepticism. It is manifest in the ubiquity of its professional footballers in the theatres where the world's most popular sport reaches its biggest audiences, the competitions beamed by television to the rest of the globe. At the moneyed end of the game, in Western Europe, the sport scrambles for African talent rather as it scrambled for most of the continent's resources in the 19th century. It mines it as enthusiastically as it forages around the principal football cultures of South America, Brazil and Argentina, and does so because it finds something unique in the way Africans interpret the game. Across the vast space of the continent, it is perilous to generalise too boldly what that may be, except that, from Alexandria to Cape Town, you hear Africans stubbornly arguing for their favourite game's specific, African identity, a purity and daring they want preserved. In Africa, a certain generalisation is also encouraged. No continent aspires more often to gain strength from the shared experience of its 900 million people by promoting Pan-Africanism and there are not many activities which as regularly and cheerfully connect distant parts of the continent as football. Sometimes, it can seem like the only thing that brings together the people of the north of the continent and those below the great sandy frontier that is the Sahara.

The stories told here come from various territories, and make no claim to be an exhaustive history. There is a bias towards the areas that have taken most successfully to football. I draw on material gathered from over three dozen countries, from tough nations that rub up awkwardly alongside one another in the west, from desert lands and equatorial ones, from Cape Town on the opulent south-western tip, to Cairo in the north-eastern corner. Not much about Africa's rich football history has been written down, so most of what's here comes from talking to people, from knowing parts of Africa because I lived in them, and learning about others through reporting from them, usually about the continent's favourite, shared passion. I found the sport casts light here and there on how Africa works; or how it doesn't work. Africa fails sometimes and its shortcomings tend to command more news space than the areas at which it thrives. This is not a book about a continent doomed, or to be pitied. It's about something Africa enjoys, generously shares, and is very good at.

CHAPTER ONE

BIG GAME HUNTING

The call to prayer from the Muley El Mehdi mosque started just before kick-off, the sound carrying into the Alfonso Murube stadium just as the chief cheerleader for the home team took up his own chant through a loudspeaker. As it was carnival time in the Christian calendar, the man with the amplifier was dressed up, made up as a clown, face painted white, his hair a dark black curly wig. He was stirring up the partisans for their biggest home fixture of the season, the game the citizens of this sliver of Morocco's coastline call the North African derby. A few thousand had come to watch, so it was hardly Wydad Casablanca against Raja, or Cairo's Al Ahly versus Zamalek. Ceuta against Melilla is a peculiar sort of North African rivalry. The teams contesting it come from cities over 150 miles apart. The visitors, Melilla, had travelled more than twice that distance to be here, via a flight to Spain, a long bus ride through Andalucia and then a ferry back across the Mediterranean. 'The Moroccan roads are not good enough to go overland,' explained the Ceuta coach Carlos Orúe, as he beamed over the home side's 3-0 victory. It may be the only match in professional football where both clubs play their home games on one continent while belonging to a league from a different one. Ceuta and Melilla earn their professional living in the Spanish second division and take a plane or a boat every other week to honour their fixtures in Europe. The enclaves of Ceuta and Melilla are anachronisms, officially Spanish, the last European colonies on mainland Africa, two tiny tufts on the quiff of the continent.

Fewer than 150,000 people live in Ceuta and Melilla. Probably the most famous living citizen of the territories happens to be a footballer, a ceutí who played in derbies far bigger than his native city's showdown against Melilla and on stages far broader than the Alfonso Murube. His name is Mohammed Ali Amar, although few people address him as that. To his friends and his fans he is Nayim; in certain parts of North London, he would be better known by his full honorific, chanted title: Nayim From The Halfway Line. The song of those words is popular with supporters of England's Tottenham Hotspur and commemorates a spectacular goal Nayim scored in the final of the European Cup-Winners Cup in May 1995, for Real Zaragoza against Arsenal, a lob that he launched high into the sky from a point close to the halfway line and the right touchline of the Parc des Princes. It was struck with less than a minute remaining of the 120, the scores tied at 1-1. As the ball hung in the Paris night, there seemed an uncertainty into which arrondisement it might finally fall. By the time it dropped, the clock had ticked on significantly, the extraordinary trajectory of the shot taking it behind the back of the luckless goalkeeper, David Seaman, and into his goal. Zaragoza had won. If the strike was bizarre enough, the identity of the scorer made it a double blessing for enemies of Arsenal. Nayim had played for several years with Spurs, their principal London rivals.

A dozen years after his celebrated goal, Nayim happily tells the story of it, as he must have done hundreds of times. In Zaragoza there is a street called Calle Gol de Nayim. Nayim proudly tells me that in New York he was recently approached by a stranger who introduced himself singing Nayim From The Halfway Line and wanted to discuss the goal that fell down as if from orbit. Had Nayim struck it so high on purpose? Of course he had, he confirmed, adding that in his native barrio in Ceuta there were folk who could testify that as a child learning his football, he was forever trying ambitious stunts with the ball. Ceuta must have been an unusual place to grow up, I suggested. It was an unusual place, full stop, Nayim agreed: mosques and churches cheek to cheek, the sound of Arabic one minute, andaluz accents the next. Part of Ceuta looks like a twee, unspoiled Costa del Sol town, though with a markedly high proportion of men strolling around in army fatigues: Spain's rationale for owning these parts of Africa is military. Yet the interior of Ceuta could be an outskirt of Casablanca or Oran, densely populated, with a vivid street life. There you hear it called not Ceuta but Sebta, its Moroccan name, and see graffiti demanding the end of Spanish occupation. Ceutís like Nayim have grown up with a strange dual existence. 'I am proud to be African,' he says, 'and proud to be European.'

From the harbour in Ceuta, where the ferries criss-cross from continent to continent, you can see the outline of the rock of Gibraltar, so close that with a good breeze it seems no further away than a sturdy Nayim volley. As a child, Nayim boarded the boats that cross these Straits regularly, answering invitations to go and show his football talent in places like Seville. He was barely a teenager when he was selected to join Barcelona's youth system, and though he was born a Spanish citizen, and some notable North Africans had played successfully in Spain at that stage, he was aware he looked different from his contemporaries. Sometimes, a lout in the crowd at junior matches would shout 'Moro', a derogatory insult. After an English coach of Barcelona, Terry Venables, took Nayim to London and to Spurs, he encountered less casual racism. This was the late 1980s and, in Britain, foreign footballers counted as a small minority; footballers from the African continent made up a tiny fraction of them. Nayim was regarded as exotic and likes to think he brought a refined sort of skill and flair to the English first division.

After Nayim had shared some of these recollections, he gave me a short guided tour of his native enclave, and I went down to the frontier, where the daredevils, the desperados and the traffickers lurk. The peculiar political status of Ceuta, as with Melilla, means Africa has a land border with Europe, a short, heavily fortified one. Tens of thousands of Africans try to cross it illegally every year; the fences get built to tower up ever higher, cast-iron barriers to stretch further out into the sea, and the corkscrews of razor wire get tightened to look more and more menacing. The ingenious and the patient still look for ways through. Sometimes they wait for moments of inclement weather to make their surge into the perceived Promised Land that is a life in Europe. Or they wait for nights when they suppose the troops on the border might be distracted, watching television. When Spain played Italy at the European Championships in the summer of 2008, the attempted breaches were unusually high.

Some just keep trying, failing and trying again. Paul, who comes from equatorial Africa, did that. We'll call him plain Paul because he now lives in Spain and, having arrived there illegally, he prefers to give out pseudonyms for himself. He used to play football semi-professionally in his native country and earned a good living, between £200 and £300 a month, from the match-fees he collected for clubs in the top division. Still a young man, an able athlete, stocky, full of stamina and the kind of player who would galvanise the centre of midfield, Paul set off north one day, by bus and by hitch-hiking, and eventually he reached Morocco. Once there, he made his way to the frontier at Melilla. Thirteen times he tried to cross, to sail or to swim around the fence, and each time he was apprehended or had to retreat at various points of his escapade. The fourteenth bid worked. Once on Spanish territory, inside Melilla, he kept a low profile, encountered small kindnesses and people willing to pay for his cheap labour so that he had enough to pay his way by ferry to the mainland. There he scrapes by, and has found a benefactor in the shape of the president of a football club in Spain's lower divisions. Paul is one of the team's best players; he is playing at a standard well below what he was used to. Had he the right papers, he might be playing in a division of Spanish football where the matches are televised and the footballers handsomely salaried. As it is, he is grateful for the gig. The president of his suburban club 'looks after me when I need money,' he says, though there are days he would still appreciate a balanced meal. Nor would it be morbid to imagine that among those Paul encountered on his determined, intrepid journey, some may not have been as lucky as he was. Of the thousands of Africans who travel by raft, boat and canoe across the Mediterranean or via the Atlantic to Spain's Canary Islands, often paying a fee to an unscrupulous broker, most are eventually stopped, detained or deported. Many perish en route.

Among the African men and boys who try to enter Europe each year, a wildly disproportionate number do so in the belief their talent as footballers will hasten them through the red tape that distinguishes an illegal immigrant from a welcome one. They have, at an informed recent estimate, at least 2,000 reasons for believing: that's the number of Africans working as professional footballers in Europe. You can add another thousand who might be doing so semi-professionally. The figures have zoomed upwards in the 21st century.

When Nayim, the African proud to be a European, the Spaniard proud to be a Maghrebi, began his final season with Tottenham, he was one of just over a dozen first-team players in England's 22-club Premier League from outside the British Isles. By the middle of the 2008–09 English Premier League season, its 20 clubs were between them employing 44 African players. A schoolboy following British football from Africa need only glance at the leading goalscorers in the widely-broadcast Premier League to turn starry-eyed. One season, say 2006–07, the list would be led by the Ivorian Didier Drogba followed by the South African Benni McCarthy; the next a Togolese, Emmanuel Sheyi Adebayor, was heading the chart. That schoolboy need only glimpse a Monday newspaper in Francophone Africa to see that, on a typical weekend in France's championnat, one in every three of the footballers on a typical weekend there come from Africa, or their parents did. He could then turn to Spain's La Liga and see that when Barcelona score goals, the likeliest man to have done so was the Cameroonian Samuel Eto'o. Our schoolboy could have watched Sevilla winning back-to-back Uefa Cups, spearheaded by the strong, elegant Malian, Frédéric Kanouté. He might note that when Real Madrid spend vast amounts on a single transfer, it is no longer on a David Beckham or a Ronaldo but on a Mali midfielder, Mahamadou Diarra; that when Chelsea became the most prodigal spenders in professional football, they soon devoted a third of their matchday salaries to African footballers: to Drogba, to Ghana's Michael Essien, Nigeria's Mikel John Obi, to the Ivorian Salomon Kalou. African success stories in European football have just about as high a global profile as African success stories in any other profession. And unless you are in the top-salary band at a club in Egypt, Tunisia or South Africa, a job in Europe means a financial step up, even if the job is in Moldova, or the Bulgarian second division.

The dream, rags to riches, rough diamond to shimmering jewel, has become part of Africa's wishing-well, a motif in its cultural shorthand. You find it not only in the stories African footballers tell about themselves but in films like the Malian director Cheikh Doukouré's *Le Ballon D'Or*, which follows a boy living in a remote Sahel village, his adventures with his first ball, his dealings with the shifty businessman who sees in his talent opportunity, with the benevolent foreign aid worker who helps him; with the local mystic and the cheerful dwarf who advise him, with the challenges that await him when he reaches Europe on the cusp of his professional career. The story begins with villagers gathered around a broadcast of a Cameroon match at the 1990 World Cup and it has a cameo part for Mali's greatest footballer, Salif Keita, whose own odyssey created the prototype for such stories.

Keita was once the teenaged star who lit up the inaugural African Champions Cup final in 1965 playing for Stade Malien against Cameroon's Oryx Douala. Word of his delicate touch, lean frame and exceptional balance reached France. Keita stole away out of Mali one day in 1966. His route took him overland to Monrovia, Liberia, where in a storyline that would later be taken as an eerie premonition, he was housed not far from where, a few days later, George Weah was born. Keita had been offered a job at Saint-Étienne, in the French championnat; the Malian authorities were likely to have forbidden the flight of this national treasure, so he escaped in secret. Arriving in Paris, Keita stepped out at the airport and showed a taxi driver the address of the Saint-Étienne stadium. The cabbie told him it was 350 kilometres way. Keita insisted. The driver shrugged and an odyssey had begun. In 1970, Keita became the first African Footballer of the Year; his professional life thrived outside Africa, took him not only to

France, but to Spain, and Valencia, where nobody thought it politically risqué to call him La Perla Negra, The Black Pearl.

■ ■ ■

Cross the border from Ceuta into Morocco, sweep down the coast and you reach Casablanca. Here, professional football did some of its earliest panning for Africa's pearls. Here, in the melting-pot hub of what was then French North Africa, 'scouts looked under the stones in poor places.' So wrote Helenio Herrera, who grew up and played in Morocco in the 1930s, later to become one of the more influential coaches in football's history. Here, Africa's first global superstar, Larbi Ben Barek emerged, and came into the professional game just as celluloid and Pathé could bring his talents to a mass audience and emphasise his difference from others. Born in Casablanca sometime during the First World War – there is some doubt about the precise date – Ben Barek was the son of a boat repairer and grew up in the dense district of Ferme Blanche, close to the walls of the city's oldest Medina. An energetic boy, he played barefoot street football as a child, swam in the sea at Ain Diab, paid scant attention to his lessons at the Muslim école. His gifts, notably then his close-control dribbling and two-footedness, would be his living. The Moroccan club who first took him on gave him a job repairing petrol pumps and at weekends lined him up alongside players of Italian, Spanish and French roots as well as Maghrebi Muslims. Ben Barek stood out, not just because he would show himself a footballer of exceptional capability, but because of what reporters from France's *L'Auto*, increasingly excited by this young talent, would regularly refer to as his 'darker taint', his 'Senegalese aspect.' The scouts looking under stones had found their first Perle Noir, France had its 'Black Pearl'.

Ben Barek knew he was special. When Olympique Marseille offered him terms to cross the Mediterranean, he first said no, prepared to wait, sensing an auction would develop. By 1938, it had. He put on, according to his biographer, 'his smartest djellaba and his fez' and boarded a ship called the *Djenne*, to take him to Marseille. *Paris-Soir* anointed him 'the finest acquisition ever from North Africa' and regretted that he had only come to France a few months after the country had hosted a World Cup, in which he might have improved the fortunes of the national side. He embarked on a career with the Les Bleus, the France team, that would set a record for endurance, some 16 years passing between Ben Barek's first cap and his last. Herrera, his fellow Casablancan, then hired him at Atlético Madrid, paying a handsome sum. It seemed a daring move. Few French footballers crossed the border to work in Spain in that period, let alone an African, entering General Franco's republic. Quickly enough, Spanish football celebrated its 'Perla Negra', or as the paraphernalia produced by Atlético cast him, 'El Prodigio'.

What he had was something beyond the exotic. If his dribbling, full of feints and shimmies, had first caught the eye of the French, the footballer with whom Madrid was in thrall was a protean player, who could play in various positions in midfield and the forward line. Herrera, a sharp critic, struggled to find fault with Ben Barek and thought him as fine a footballer as he had or would work with in France, Spain, Italy or North Africa. Ben Barek had an ego, too: 'He improved once he came to Spain and that was because he saw the standard here was higher than he was used to,' wrote Herrera. 'He would never let himself feel bettered by anybody.' In Madrid, he seldom had to. Atlético won two league titles with Ben Barek. The France team were still calling on him as he approached 40 years old.

Europe's scramble for African talent turned catty in the 1960s.

Benfica and Sporting, the most powerful clubs and rivals in a Lisbon then flexing its muscles on the grand theatre of European football, fought one another all the way to the High Court for ownership rights to the son of an Angolan railway worker and a Mozambican mother. Eusébio da Silva Ferreira had been spotted in Lourenço Marques, in then Portuguese East Africa. In his teens he was The Phenomenon of Mafalala, the working-class district where he grew up; by his 20s he was The Black Panther. By 23, Eusébio had been voted Europe's Footballer of the Year and when Benfica won their second successive European Cup final in 1962, he was one of two Mozambicans and an Angolan who between them scored four of their five goals against Real Madrid. When Portugal went to the World Cup in 1966, half their outfield team were often players from Africa. Eusébio's combination of balance, a ferocious right foot, courage, stamina and speed made him as close to the ideal modern forward player as the game recognised. It put him, in many minds, on a par with his contemporary, the Brazilian Pelé.

Eusébio had not been long at the summit of local football when the Sporting-Benfica squabble broke out. Sporting assumed and argued Eusébio belonged to them by virtue of his having passed through their satellite club in Lourenço Marques. Through stealth, Benfica won a legal battle that had developed into quite a soap opera on two continents, animated by vivid descriptions in the pages of *A Bola* and *Record* of the exploits of the player. Sporting decried Benfica's 'kidnap'. Benfiquistas would over the next 15 years brag about the coup: Eusébio scored 473 goals in 440 matches for the club, he played in five European Cup finals and scored 40 times for Portugal.

■ ■ ■

In the new millennium, the 'search under stones' that unearthed Ben Barek assumes an almost industrial scale. In the scramble for African talent, tawdry fights still erupt between European juggernauts over the contracts of Africans. In 2003, Manchester United and Chelsea had a litigious spat over the teenaged Nigerian footballer Mikel John Obi. United's Mozambican assistant-coach Carlos Queiroz self-consciously evoked the Eusébio affair when he referred to Chelsea's 'kidnap' of the footballer.

Instances of the expatriated, exploited and vulnerable young African, chasing his dream abroad, are many. When the Senegal national team reached the 2002 World Cup quarter-finals, they did so with a squad entirely of footballers who worked abroad. African football celebrated their achievement; a few voices drew attention to another life they represented. 'Now the entire world knew that our sportsmen, busy recovering our national pride, live in France, how could we dissuade young people they ought to go and seek triumphs there?' asked Fatou Diomé in *The Belly of the Atlantic*, her moving novel about a boy who wants to be a footballer in Europe. 'Let our valiant players tell their supporters at home, the boys dreaming of European clubs, how they sit most of the time on the bench, or played out of position, so the senior players could thrive.'

Recruiting African players directly from Africa means they are cheaper than any others, and regarded as more dispensable. They are also more tolerant. Desperation breeds resourcefulness. Countless coaches working in the wealthier parts of Africa's football economy, in South Africa, Tunisia, Egypt or Morocco have been button-holed by players from the west or middle of the continent, and presented with a team-group photo which shows the face of the applicant alongside one or two recognisable players from his country. Sometimes, his own face has been superimposed. Or there's the flexible age, a notorious trick: the 20-year-old, say, who passes himself off as 16 to join a youth club with a strong record for getting good players the right connections to Europe. Nigeria were banned from a series of Fifa youth tournaments in the 1980s for irregularities over the ages presented by some of their players. It was not a one-off. Other countries have entered national teams into age-group tournaments in Africa with several players all registering exactly the same birthday on their official documentation. Players have turned up for a series of major tournaments in their careers and been accredited there with several different birthdays. A Cameroonian defender called Toby Mimboe gained a special fame for his Peter Pan paperwork as he pursued his varied career through clubs in South America, Turkey and the Far East; an odyssey that in turn began to fascinate Italian publishers who had set about the Herculean task of producing an accurate statistical annual for African football. They found Mimboe was officially 31 when he went to the 1996 African Nations Cup in South Africa. By the time he later joined Genclerbirligi of the Turkish first division, he was in his very early 20s. When accreditation staff at the next African Nations Cup, in 1998, took down Mimboe's details they noted the same birthday, 30 June, as the South Africans and Turks had seen, but a new year of birth entirely: not 1964, nor 1974, but 1970. He had aged rapidly since moving to Ankara, yet checked in rejuvenated from the man he was two years earlier.

Then there are the victims not of false paperwork but false promises. Take the story of Ayi Nii Aryee, a Ghanaian teenager, who in the summer of 2006, just over a month after the Ghana national team had reached the last 16 of the World Cup, set off for Singapore from Accra. He had been offered a professional contract in the relatively wealthy Singaporean S-League, a wage of US$1,000 a month. At 18 years old, it was an opportunity, perhaps a stepping-stone to elsewhere. On arrival in Singapore, it turned out the offer was a chimera. The club who had recruited him wanted him, but at $100 a month. He refused to sign. Without a return fare, he applied for a student visa that would enable him to stay in Singapore, where he thought he might renegotiate with the club or find another berth elsewhere. He had a friend in Manila, so he travelled there in the meantime. On trying to return to Singapore, however, he was detained at the airport, and deported to the Philippines, from where he had flown in. Surreally, Ayi Nii Aryee spent the next five months in the no-man's land of the airport terminal at Clark International airport in Manila, without a visa to proceed, without funds to go home, without diplomatic representation in the country in which he found himself stranded. He was like the Tom Hanks character in the film, *The Terminal*, dressed in a Juventus replica shirt, befriended by Filipino airport workers. And stuck.

The tale of Ghana's best-known teenage genius is a little less cinematic, but no less dramatic and ultimately sad. Nii Odartey Lamptey was registered as 14 years old when he went with the Ghana national under-17 team to the world championships in Scotland in 1989. At the next edition of the tournament, Ghana's Black Starlets won the championship, and the 16-year-old Lamptey outshone a teenaged Italian, Alessandro Del Piero, and a starlet Argentinian, Juan Sebastián Verón to be named the world's outstanding footballer of his age. From then on, his career would be a series of mishaps, fights over his ownership and personal tragedies. His childhood had been brutal, his father a violent alcoholic who used to punish his son by burning his skin with lighted cigarettes, his parents divorced. He says he often slept rough to avoid being at home. As a very young boy, he found himself in a religious dilemma, too, obliged, as he tells it, to convert from

Christianity to Islam in order to play his football for one of the youth clubs in Kumasi, where he grew up. He grew up tough, but naïve. 'I lacked education,' Lamptey recalls when he describes his odyssey and the unfulfilled career of a boy who was supposed to become the best African footballer of his generation.

His epic story began one day in Kumasi in 1989, and it started with an argument. Billeted in a Ghana national youth squad training camp, he clutched a business card given to him by the Nigerian national team captain of the time, Stephen Keshi. It had the name of a middleman in Lagos on it, an agent Keshi had recommended to Lamptey to facilitate Lamptey's move to the Belgian club, Anderlecht, where Keshi then played. Lamptey put it to the Ghanaian Football Association that he wanted to travel abroad to sort out his future. They forbade it and as they held his passport, he was stuck. So he ran away, collecting together the bonus money he had saved from his performances for the Ghana youth team, and negotiated with a taxi driver to take him to Lagos. It was a long drive, along the road to the Togo border, passing the forested villages where the wares made from local timber are put on show next to the highway and an eerily large number of coffin manufacturers tout their carpentry. At the frontier crossings at Lomé and either side of Benin, Lamptey concealed himself below eye level behind the driver's seat. Eventually, he found his new ally in Lagos and swiftly a Nigerian passport bearing his image was produced. It had him down as 'Stephen Keshi junior'. His fake dad eagerly embraced him. Together they boarded a flight to Brussels.

Lamptey told me this story in Accra, where he lives and runs a school, not a football academy like the hundreds dotted around that city but an institution he hopes will provide for Ghanaian children the education he feels very painfully he missed, the means he never had to control some of his own destiny. He smiles at the subterfuge he used to make his escape the day he fled Ghana but not because he feels proud of his artfulness. 'At first when I arrived at the training ground, Anderlecht were not sure I was the Lamptey they were looking for,' he remembers. 'On the TV screen they thought I looked bigger. They argued with Keshi and said "It's not him!" Everyone was there, board officials, the club president. I think my first two touches of the ball confirmed that it was the real Lamptey.' The real Lamptey is quite a short man, but the teenaged Lamptey was also lithe, fast and with a particular sweet sense of timing when he met a ball on the volley with his right foot. Those were the images that Anderlecht's coaches had seen on television and conformed with what they quickly saw from 'Stephen Keshi junior'.

The Ghanaian consulate in Brussels gave him a proper passport. Anderlecht had him sign a five-year contract. 'I don't remember what the money was, because it was so small. But I didn't even care. I just wanted to play football. When I really started to make money from football was when I signed a personal contract with adidas. That was 1991–92, after my first season with Anderlecht. My first season was very good.' Events the following summer, to the delight of his sponsors at adidas, promoted Lamptey still further. Ghana's under-23 team won a bronze medal at the Barcelona Olympics, the 17-year-old Lamptey dazzling in their midfield. The following year, Lamptey captained Ghana to second place at the world youth championship. European agents had also swooped on most of his contemporaries by then. The defender Sammy Kuffour would go to play at Bayern Munich, Germany's grandest club, for a decade.

Lamptey had by 1993 moved to Holland, and PSV Eindhoven, a step up from Belgian football. His upward rise seemed to be continuing. At PSV he scored 10 goals in 22 matches from midfield. After only a year there, he made a surprising move, initiated as he recalls, by the agent with whom he had signed a contract, an Italian named Antonio Caliendo, who in the early 1990s was given a 10-month suspended sentence by an Italian court for corruption. Lamptey transferred to Aston Villa in England and the next year to Coventry City. One detail of the negotiations sticks in his mind. 'I didn't even know I had a right to a signing-on fee. The manager [of Aston Villa], Ron Atkinson, told me, and in the club office they gave it straight to me. Two weeks later, my agent came over and I think he went to the club to get the money. They said they had given it to the player. He was very upset with me. So many things were happening behind my back ever since I was 16 and too young to sign papers so an agent came to Accra to get a signature from my parents. In the end there were so many people cheating me in my career, just looking after their own interests.'

By the time he reached England, Lamptey the athlete also showed symptoms of burnout. His prodigious talent had meant the demands on him by the Ghanaian Football Association were doubled. Eligible for their youth teams, he was also wanted by their first-team, two sets of commitments in between trying to fulfil the demands of his European clubs. In the English Premier League he was never consistent, and frequently injured, and his last season there would be interrupted by Ghana's commitment at the African Nations Cup of 1996. There he played his last competitive match for the Black Stars, aged just 21.

Lamptey finds people respond to him in two ways when they meet him now. 'Some of the players who have moved abroad thank me because they say I opened the doors to Europe,' he says. For others, his name is a parable for the exploitation of young African footballers. Tales like his led Fifa to prohibit the international transfer of players under 18. His own story teaches its lessons to the 400 students at the school he established in Accra. On the walls of the library are some of the press cuttings from his era as the game's child sensation: full-page features on the pink newsprint of Italy's *Gazzetta dello Sport*, articles in French and Spanish, panegyrics from the Barcelona Olympics. The classrooms in his school are each named after a country he worked in as a player: Belgium, the Netherlands, England. Then the tailspin years: Italy, Argentina, Turkey, Portugal, Germany, China, Saudi Arabia. Beholden to his agent, chasing a 25 per cent share of each new contract, Lamptey kept moving, year after year, his brilliance seldom recaptured for long enough to give him a sense of momentum. No longer the poster boy for a sportswear manufacturer, he started to feel cursed. While in Argentina, Lamptey and his wife lost a son, Diego, who died as an infant. In Germany, they lost another child. Lamptey's mind went back to the fights that raged around him when he was barely more than a boy. 'They say there is all this juju in football and I remember in Kumasi when some of the Muslim people I was with were angry with me and telling others: "We'll see if he plays for the national team again". And it came to pass. Since 1996, I have not played for Ghana. Sometimes I will be in my room and I will cry about it, that the great Pelé once said I was the player who would step into his shoes. It's really painful when you can see that there is something you can still do, but that thing has been taken away from you.'

■ ■ ■

If you drive now down the road that 15-year-old Lamptey travelled when he escaped to Nigeria, you'll pass signposts to 'Football Schools' or 'Soccer Academies', or some variant or other, occasionally misspelled, often claiming to work on behalf of the Lord. These are dream factories catering to young West Africans and the claims and promises of many are dubious. 'Football is totally a business in these places,' says Lamptey. 'If you want to take a kid into an academy, you probably have to spend a lot of money. They will chop your money and maybe not even give you what they are supposed to give you.' At the worst ones you might even disappear. In December 2006, 34 families in Ivory Coast discovered the dream of a professional career in Europe for their sons came with a nasty sting. They had enrolled the boys in a football 'academy' in Abidjan and, at a cost of around 300,000 CFA francs each, paid an intermediary what he called the costs of facilitating the teenagers' trip to Europe where, they had been told, a series of trials with leading clubs had been arranged with a high likelihood most would be taken on. Four months later, police in Sissako, a city in neighbouring Mali, found the 34 footballers, aged between 16 and 18, crammed into a house, many sleeping on the floor, many complaining of hunger.

Ghana has some genuinely inspiring places that, through football, enhance the lives and educational opportunities of hundreds of young West Africans, like the Right to Dream school just outside Accra. It also has a centre set up by a major European club, the Feyenoord Academy, which takes orders from Rotterdam and the principal interest of which is to find and train the best young footballers from the region, provide a sophisticated working environment for them and bring the very best to Holland or on to the European marketplace. France's Monaco had the idea earlier, investing in a football school in Dakar, Senegal, through which half a dozen of the players who represented the Senegal squad at the 2002 World Cup would emerge. Ajax Amsterdam bought out the franchise of a club in Cape Town, and renamed it Ajax Cape

Town, who are a competitive team in the South African Premier League, Africa's richest domestic league and every so often a productive talent factory for Holland's most famous football club.

Other European clubs have ventured to more remote sites. Head north out of Ouagadougou in Burkina Faso, and you used to see a small sign directing you off the tarred carriageway to somewhere called Planète Champion International. This was once the project of Paris Saint-Germain, PSG, who thought they would formalise the career trajectories that lead a number of African players out of the sub-Saharan region, to better salaries at a North African club, in Tunisia, Egypt or Morocco and then onto Europe. PSG took a stake in the Burkina Faso site, with its simple dormitories, schoolrooms and dry earth pitches and made arrangements with Espérance, a successful club in Tunisia, and Servette, of the Swiss league, to funnel players north, step by step, then welcome the best of them to Paris. It was all a little too schematic, and PSG's interest soon declined. But Planète Champion remained a beacon for young Burkinabe players, 13 of whom passed through its gates and onto professional careers in various places around Europe in its first decade of existence, a startling figure when you consider how seldom impoverished, remote, landlocked Burkina Faso registers on anybody's map of world football.

There is a barely disguised imperialism to these projects. One coach of Ajax Cape Town's first team had the feeling he was being controlled remotely from Amsterdam, when he received instructions on what formation to play from a Dutchman living 6,000 miles away. More and more, the notion that Africa's football exists in service to Europe's professional game dictates the type of athlete clubs, schools and academies promote. 'Sooner or later when you speak to a coach in Europe who might be interested in a young player,' says one scout employed to survey African talent for a leading British club, 'they ask you "So what's his aerial elevation like?" They want big, tall, strong players, first of all.' There is a prevalent stereotype among recruiters that the best sort of footballer to look for in Africa is the quick striker or the muscular defensive midfielder. In the European Champions League of 2008–09, Chelsea, Barcelona, Real Madrid, Juventus, Internazionale and Olympique Lyonnais all had West African-born players in the so-called 'holding' position. Europe's acquisitive eye shapes the very shape of an aspiring African footballer.

■ ■ ■

The most celebrated star factories in football in the 21st century tend to be the big institutions, those who invest heavily in recruitment, market themselves to parents and schoolboys. Manchester United's class of the 1990s would be a celebrated example, Barcelona's class of the noughties another. But not far behind ranks the Association Sportive des Employés du Commerce of Abidjan, better known as Asec Mimosas of Ivory Coast. Channel-hop across a weekend of football in the major leagues of Europe in early 2009, and you would find a dozen footballers whose careers began at Asec's Sol Béni Academy. There are two, Kolo Touré and Manu Eboué, playing for Arsenal, the team most praised for the stylishness of its football in the English Premier League; there's another at Chelsea, Salomon Kalou; another, Didier Zokora, at Spurs. At the top of the Spanish league, another, Yaya Touré, is in the midfield of Barcelona, and another, Ndri Romaric plays for Sevilla. In the French first division, there are a further three or four, including the prolific goalscorer Aruna Dindane and the Marseille striker Bakari Koné. There are Asec graduates in leading teams in the German Bundesliga, the Dutch Eredivisie and in Belgium, which at one point became the routine stop-off point for young Ivorians, following the super-highway to fame and fortune.

At Asec's headquarters in Cocody, Abidjan, they feel proud of their long list of alumni. It stretches back to the greats of the sepia era of African football. The club were founded in 1948, and in one of the long bungalow buildings that accommodates the young footballers practising, learning and living at their academy, pictures on the wall serve as a Hall of Fame. Next to the photographs of the many modern exiles who wore their bright yellow strip, are monochrome portraits of footballers like Laurent Pokou, whose exploits as a goalscorer at African Nations Cup tournaments – he contributed 14 goals – set a record that stood unbroken for nearly 30 years. Asec have a feisty city rivalry with Africa Sports, Abidjan's next strongest club, and a record of achievement in African club competition that, though eroded by the exodus of their best players to Europe, means it is still a rarity when they are not among the last 16 or eight in the African Champions League. They have spacious, enviable premises next to the Ebrié lagoon, from where storks and egrets glide into land on the grass football pitches and pick around hopefully in the shade under mango trees. To Asec's gates file a regular stream of young visitors, boys who have sometimes travelled across West African frontiers to try and find a place among the Asec academicals.

The president of Asec Mimosas is the urbane Roger Ouégnin, an Ivorian lawyer who had the idea in the early 1990s that Asec should attract the best Ivorian footballers not simply because they were the Real Madrid of the country but by offering the best facilities for them to develop and study there. Sitting on a terrace overlooking the club's premises, he told me how the story of African football's greatest modern star factory began with a single match. It was the African Super Cup final, in February 1999, a hot day in Abidjan, a contest between the winners of the previous year's African Champions Cup, Asec, and of the African Cup-Winners Cup, Tunisia's Espérance. The Tunisians had been considered outstanding favourites for the Super Cup on the basis of their experience and the fact that Asec's XI were so startlingly young, most of them 17 or 18. 'We had no choice but to field a team of kids,' recalls Ouégnin, 'because, of the side that had won the Champions Cup only a few months before, almost all the players had gone straight to Europe or to North African clubs on the back of that success.' Ouégnin grins at the recollection: 'I remember the Espérance goalkeeper, Chokri El Ouaer, who was quite a figure in African football at the time, looking at the kids in our line up and laughing with his team-mates and the Espérance coaches before the game. And I remember thinking how small a little guy like Bakari Koné must have looked to them. It really was men against boys.' Some Asec supporters, angered at the mass departures of so many senior players and fearful of the hiding their ingenu replacements might receive, boycotted the match.

They missed an epic. David struck the first blow against Goliath ten minutes before half-time, reward for the zippy and expansive football the Asec teenagers had played in the first 45 minutes. They hung on to the 1-0 lead given them by Zézé 'Zézéto' Venance deep into the second period, when their athletic central defender, Kolo Touré, excellent up until the 87th minute, conceded a penalty for a handball. El Ouaer, the Espérance goalkeeper, marched the length of the field from the opposite goal to take and convert it.

The match moved into extra time, Boys 1, Men 1. 'That next half-hour made the name of this academy,' reflects Ouégnin. 'I looked at the boys and they weren't rushing to the touchline to drink water. They were so fresh. I didn't see a worried look on their faces.' The Espérance team, a worldly mix of Tunisians who had played at a World Cup eight months earlier, and Nigerians in the forward line, wearied in the extra half-hour of tie-break football, sapped by the cool capacity of the teenagers to circulate possession, and surprise them with their changes of speed. The substitute Dindane put Asec 2-1 ahead just after the first period of extra time, and Zézéto, after two hours of darting and running in the forward line, scored his second goal just before the final whistle. 'News of that performance went around the world,' says Ouégnin.

The youthful Asec heroes, one by one, then two by two, and then by the half-dozen, duly boarded flights to Europe. Five years later, a bizarre sort of replay of Asec's famous Super Cup final took place in northern Europe. It was the Belgian domestic Cup final, and if the presence of the small provincial club Beveren at the annual showpiece of Belgium's domestic football excited some underdog sympathy, the make-up of their starting XI was the chief talking point. Ten of the Beveren XI were black. All but one of the team were Ivorians and not a single Belgian made the starting line-up. Some players, like goalkeeper Boubacar Barry, had been involved in the famous African Super Cup match between Asec and Espérance; several even younger men had passed through Asec Mimosas. The connection was a Frenchman, Jean-Marc Guillou who had coached the 1999 African Super Cup winners and two years later led a consortium that bought Beveren, a club in financial trouble. Guillou had overseen a shrewd piece of business. He knew he could recruit very good Ivory Coast players inexpensively, that Belgium had no restrictions on the number of foreign players in its domestic teams and that Belgian law made the country one of Europe's most generous and speedy places to acquire citizenship if you were an immigrant with a good professional standing. So

Beveren Football Club became a market stall for Ivorian players en route to other European clubs who in turn paid the sorts of transfer fees that would sustain the Belgian club. England's Arsenal, who, it later emerged had provided a loan to help Guillou's group establish themselves in Belgium, showed a special interest: they acquired two footballers, Kolo Touré and Manu Eboué, from Beveren in the subsequent four years.

Soon enough, Ouégnin and Guillou would fall out over the nature of the relationship between Guillou, the Abidjan club and some of the players who went directly to Beveren. 'I also understand that for Beveren, it was not so fair,' says Ouégnin, 'suddenly giving their supporters a team with a totally different identity.' The compensation for Beveren fans was that they played some of the most dashing football in the Belgian league. For Asec fans, it became wearily assumed that their favourites will go to Europe soon after their 18th birthdays. While the volume of trade between Asec and wealthier European clubs does bring money into Ouégnin's club, because a small percentage of the transfer fees accrued by players goes to the club that educated them, the drain of talent systematically weakens the Ivorian league, just as it does most leagues in sub-Saharan Africa. 'Sometimes, supporters have wanted to lynch me when our best players leave,' says Ouégnin, 'but you cannot stop a boy wanting to go and earn what seems fantastic money abroad and make a future there. It is all their dreams. If the local baker comes up to them and says "I can get you to Europe," they want to believe him and say yes.' Ouégnin doubts he will ever find the same concentration of talent as Asec had when they were African champions in 1999. They are in a competitive market. He reckons in Abidjan alone there are now some 450 sites calling themselves football academies, some run by little more than the local baker, some by big business, all promising to make of boys what Asec made of the Touré brothers, Kolo and Yaya, and dozens more. 'I think this club, Asec, has been at the vanguard of modernising Ivorian football,' says Ouégnin, 'but we also have to accept that the more successful you are, the more you have to cope with the exodus.'

CHAPTER TWO

THE WHITE WITCHDOCTOR

Football arrived in Africa with colonialism. Not too long after the English Football Association had drawn up the official rules for the sport, statesmen in Berlin, Paris and London, with epaulettes on their shoulders, medals on their chests and greed in their eyes, sat around large tables drawing up a set of lines across a map of Africa almost as if they were six-yard boxes, penalty areas and centre-circles. In the last two decades of the 19th century, almost the entire continent would be divvied up and appropriated by western Europe's major political powers, borders created on the basis of vague sketches and often little knowledge of the interior. The scramble for Africa happened swiftly, and civil servants, missionaries and merchants took their hobbies to a people they had come to exploit, to Christianise, to educate or to expatriate. France, Britain, Portugal, Belgium, Germany and, in pockets, Italy and Spain would lend out their sports with various conditions of strictness, sometimes suspicious if the natives started showing too much talent. As early as 1913, Baron Pierre de Coubertin, founder of the modern Olympics and an enthusiastic French colonialist, expressed his unease that a sporting 'triumph, even a light-hearted, friendly one, by the dominated race against the dominant one, could encourage rebellion.'

Football thrived earliest where Africa had its larger settler populations: the north and the south. A hundred years before the vast majority of Africa's states were hurtling towards independence, a match took place that pitched new arrivals against those proud of their established settler status. In Port Elizabeth, South Africa, a Colonial-Born XI, all white, dressed in slacks, long sleeves and variety of caps, bowler hats, bushy sideburns and beards, took on a Home Born XI, a team of recent migrants to the Eastern Cape. It was May 1862, so a strong, chilly wind likely blew across the bay. The score is not recorded, nor whether any of the local Xhosa population joined the crowd. This may have been Africa's first modern football match, though others like it were being played through the later 19th century around the continent's principal ports, kickabouts between soldiers, sailors and settlers. At the tip and the tail of Africa, clubs had been established by the beginning of the 20th century. A group of Pietermaritzburgers, inland from Durban, formed a football club seeking fixtures in 1879. In Oran, Algeria, where the French were spreading their language and their citizens, fixtures were taking place in the early years of the new century. On the Gold Coast, in a Cape Coast park overlooked by a bust of Queen Victoria, groups of Ghanaian students began to play XI against XI in 1903, under the guidance of a John Briton, a British teacher born in Jamaica. In Egypt, the game had put down strong enough roots by 1907 that Al Ahly could form and begin its journey to becoming the most successful football club in free Africa.

By the First World War, sport had its place on Africa's colonial curriculum. Gathering tension in Europe made it essential: fitness meant strong fighters. Britain and France conscripted half a million

Africans between them between 1914 and 1918 and after the Great War military service would become an obligation for many African men. Paris ordered civil servants in French West Africa to 'develop disciplined and hardened soldiers' through organised games. Between the two wars, a General Freydenberg, commander-in-chief of the colonial forces in French West Africa, noted his African troops 'practise most sports, but football attracts most and it attracts the most talented of them. The natives are drawn to sport, or rather to football.' Sport was godly, too. Missionaries lured young men to the Christian faith by offering the facilities for recreation. The saintly Marion Stevenson, a sort of female David Livingstone, set up a mission school in Kenya where, according to a devoted chronicler, 'one might wax lyrical over the part football has taken in attracting and educating the lads, and giving them an outlet for their energies, in place of fighting and bad dances.'

British Africa's governors imagined themselves by far the best qualified teachers of the young game. Being good at sport and armed with an Oxbridge education were deemed ideal recommendations for a stint in Africa; so much so that, in Whitehall, parts of west and east Africa were sniggeringly referred to as 'The Land of Blacks Ruled by Blues'; so much that for Africans the image of the sporty colonial officer perspiring under his pith-helmet as he explains the role of an inside forward and the values of Corinthianism became a caricature. The Nigerian writer Wole Soyinka tells a nice story about the Emir of Gwando, an apocryphal figure from northern Nigeria who regards all aspects of colonialism with a snooty disdain. Invited one day by the British District Commissioner to watch a game of football, the Emir turns to the Englishman after 20 minutes and wearily asks if he might be excused this 'pitiable spectacle, with these fellows all chasing one piece of leather around like drunks or madmen.' The Emir asks the district commissioner 'how many drunks and madmen are on the field?' He hears the reply and he turns to his treasurer: 'Make available to the man enough money to buy 21 more balls for these poor chaps, and another two for the men with flags who keep running up and down the sides.' The Emir of Gwando then addresses the District Commissioner: 'I realise it's your job to try and reduce us to infants, but, please, don't ask me to watch this absurdity again.'

Football's absurdities would become a part of life in Africa's cities, and in most of them, of lives lived separately. Broadly, there were two forms of the game: one for white settlers, played on better pitches in more comfortable arenas; the other for blacks. Mixing on the field remained unusual, frowned-upon, south of the Sahara. Sometimes, African teams would play each other on even, grassy surfaces as a curtain-raiser to the all-settler contests before crowds where the best seats were occupied mostly by whites. But African football had an audience. It had stars. In Brazzaville, French Congo, large crowds were watching and celebrating men like 'D'Artagnan' Goye, 'Show-Off' Momengo and 'Hammer' Makosso. Lagos had established a league in the 1920s and over the next decade and a half, in other Nigerian cities, even in the northern stronghold of the Emirs, spectators flocked to local competitions. By 1942, Dakar, the principal city in French West Africa, had 64 teams competing in leagues, the best of them playing against XIs from other cities, like Conakry in Guinea. Though football's appeal ahead of other sports owed something to its simplicity, that it could be played with a ball made of tightly-bound cloth, could bear a bumpy surface, with greater participation and higher standards, petitions to the authorities grew for better facilities: proper balls and graded terraces to accommodate the numbers who wanted to watch.

Very occasionally, a talented footballer from Africa would make his way to play for a club in Europe, though before the Second World War, he tended to end up there through privilege or because he had another skill. Arthur Wharton, born in Ghana, the grandson of an Asante princess, played in goal for Rotherham and Sheffield United just before the turn of the century. Eccentric – he would hang from the crossbar and make saves with his feet – he had been talked up for a place in the England team at the turn of the century. Hassan Hegazi, who would play for Egypt at the 1920 and 1924 Olympics, first arrived in London to study engineering, sponsored by his family, titled Nile valley landowners. The 'Djinn (genie) of the leather and wizard of wiles', as the *Athletic News* called him, Hegazi was recruited by Fulham and Dulwich Hamlet and set off a brief fashion for Egyptian players in Britain, like winger Tewfik Abdallah, at Derby County and after Africa's first, brief expedition to a World Cup in 1934, the Egyptian goalkeeper Mustafa Kamel Mansour at Queen's Park. Four years later, a West African named Raoul Diagne played for France at the World Cup. But he had not been plucked from a red-earth pitch in Dakar. Diagne was the son of a Senegalese diplomat who worked in Paris.

It was fascism in Europe which stirred the idea that good footballers from Africa might be corralled in colonial service. The other imperial powers had watched Germany swagger at the Berlin Olympics, and Mussolini's Italy beat its breast hosting and winning the 1934 World Cup. France, for one, began to wonder how it might better compete at these high-profile events. Struck by the achievements of Jesse Owens and other black athletes for the United States of America at the Berlin Games, the French wondered if, with a greater empire than Germany or Italy, the country could secure glory on the track or in the field by men from their overseas territories. In an enterprise to be repeated by thousands of scouts and agents over the next 70 years, the French sports newspaper *L'Auto* launched a mission: it volunteered to scour the African continent and find exceptional athletes. Led by Larbi Ben Barek, a parade of North Africans would wear the France jersey and turn out for championnat clubs through the 1940s and 1950s. A few came from south of the Sahara, like the Senegalese Boubacar Beye, who joined Monaco after serving in the French army during the Second World War. Ivorians arrived in groups – Sète FC recruited them in numbers – and a line of Cameroonians would be led by Eugène Njo Léa, the leading scorer for Saint-Étienne's champions of the late 1950s.

English football delved into its former colonies in South Africa, by then under white-minority rule. It had a long tradition of hiring white southern Africans, and spotted others across the colour bar being erected by apartheid. Bill Perry, a Johannesburger from a mixed-race background, scored the winning goal in the 1953 FA Cup final and won caps for England; the intrepid Steve 'Kalamazoo' Mokone, joined Coventry City, first stop on a picaresque adventure that would see him contracted by Barcelona in Spain, Torino in Italy, Marseille in France, Cardiff City in Wales, and, most successfully, with Heracles in Holland. Albert 'Hurry, Hurry' Johanneson, confined in his teens by the narrow restrictions of South Africa's 'Coloured' leagues, followed, offered a job at Leeds United in the late 1950s, where the fans made his exoticness an affectionate joke, singing: 'I'm not sure where he comes from but I think it's Timbuktu'.

But nowhere would the colonial link prove as fruitful to the mother country as in Portuguese Africa: Angola, Guinea-Bissau, the Cape Verde Islands, and Mozambique. The Lusophone idea of empire could be as brutal as anybody's and in Africa it was certainly as stubborn. Right-wing governments in Lisbon hung onto their colonies up until the mid-1970s, jealous of the oil and mineral resources in the west, and the agricultural riches in the east. At the same time, theirs could seem a more relaxed sort of colonialism, less pedantic about imposing and guarding the barriers between races, better at mixing. Portuguese men, in Africa as in Brazil, acquired a particular reputation in the colonial era for their wandering eye, siring children with African mothers, and while they were by no means unique for that among the colonials, they felt less obliged to be furtive about it. Portuguese settlers also shared space on the football field more willingly than most. In Mozambique, satellite versions of Lisbon institutions like Benfica and Sporting had been established after the First World War. An outstanding all-round Angolan athlete Guilherme Espirito Santo had played for Benfica in the 1930s and, shortly after the war, excited reports filtered back to Lisbon of one Sebastião Lucas de Fonseca, or 'Matateu', a striker from Lourenço Marques. By 24, he had been hoisted from a humble home in the black quarter of the city to the capital of Portugal, where he joined Belenenses. There he broke records – 268 goals in 209 matches – and in 1952 made his debut for the Portugal national XI. His performance in a victory over in England had *The Daily Sketch* proclaim him 'The King of Portuguese Football' and in a magnificent piece of linguistic fantasy, the paper translated 'Matateu' as 'The Eighth Wonder of The World'.

■ ■ ■

Matateu was the first of many. So when the grandees of Fifa, the world game's governing body, gathered for their 1956 Congress in Lisbon, they did not have far to look for a symbol of Africa's prowess in the sport they governed. Matateu of Belenenses was the talk of the Portuguese league at the time, having finished its leading goalscorer for two seasons, a household name. Africa was on Fifa's agenda, or at least it had a place in the margins. The colonial blanket across the continent had begun to fray and in the Portuguese capital's Avenida Palace hotel, a meeting of ambassadors from the pioneer states of independent Africa had just put the finishing touches to the constitution of their new body, the Confederation of African Football (Caf). Caf lobbied Fifa into acknowledging that the sport's government needed to become less Eurocentric, that Africa was on the threshold of dramatic change, that Africa deserved a seat on Fifa's high-table, its executive and that it merited a chance to compete at the World Cup.

They were a curious quartet, the founders of Caf. Egypt, as ever, stood in the vanguard. Members of Fifa since 1924, they sailed to the Lisbon summit on the breeze of Gamal Abdel Nasser's revolution. With them was Ethiopia, where Emperor Haile Selassie had become a prominent advocate of Pan-Africanism. There was Sudan, independent from British rule for some six months by the time of the 1956 Fifa Congress. Finally, there was the Union of South Africa, independent but decidedly, defiantly, determinedly undemocratic. On Caf's agenda was not only the right for independent Africa to have a voice in the running of the national game, but to stage its own showpiece. It was resolved that a first African Cup of Nations would be held in Khartoum, with a view to its growing as more countries threw off the chains of colonial rule, that the best footballers from the continent would not be wearing the jerseys of France or Portugal, but their native lands. But the planning of the debut Nations Cup hit an immediate snag. The man from the South African Federation awkwardly relayed to his Egyptian, Sudanese and Ethiopian colleagues the conditions under which his bosses in Pretoria would endorse participation. 'He was a chap named Fred Fell, not an Afrikaner but British,' recalled Abdel Halim Mohammed, the delegate from Sudan. 'We accepted him, we accepted South Africa. He accepted we would host the first African Cup of Nations in Khartoum the next February. Then we came to that "area". He said his government had told him "It is either a pure white team or a black team." We said we don't accept that. We want black *and* white.' South Africa got banned.

So then there were three: Egypt, Ethiopia and Sudan. In time, there would be many, many more. Between 1956 and 1962, free Africa swelled. In January 1960 British prime minister Harold Macmillan made his speech in Cape Town about the 'wind of change blowing through the continent, and whether we like it or not, this growth of national consciousness is a political fact.' France signed off on the independence of its chunk of the African mainland, Britain ceded its parts of the west and east and the map of the continent transformed. The Portuguese territories apart, Africa by 1964 no longer functioned as an imperial patchwork of pinks and maroons and blues. It was a place to raise the bright flags, striped in greens, yellows and reds of autonomous nations. The process took time to trickle into football. The early Nations Cups were contested only between Caf's founders, with South Africa excluded. Egypt would win it in 1957 and 1959, establishing a pre-eminence that was to return at the beginning of the 21st century. In 1962, for the third Nations Cup, the baton moved east. Ethiopia beat Egypt in the final and did so thanks in large part to the Vassalo brothers, Luciano and Italo, captain and leading scorer, two men who could hardly have been better invented to represent a sport that owed something to colonial legacy but would now be thrillingly reinterpreted by Africans. The Vassalos were the sons of an Italian soldier who had come to East Africa during Mussolini's aggressive Abysinnian adventures and married an Eritrean. By the mid-1960s, Luciano, with his deceptively pigeon-toed running style, his dexterity in curling a ball with the outside of his foot, would be dubbed the 'African Di Stéfano'.

Footage of the first African Nations Cups casts the events as a very distant relative to the 21st century equivalent, the 16-team festival broadcast across the globe. The pitches in Sudan and Ethiopia were poor, players kicking up dust with their shots. But look along the touchlines and on the benches, and there's a feature that independent Africa's first initiatives in international football seems to have maintained through 50 years. Look at the man giving the orders and calling many of the shots, and he tends more often than not to be an expatriate: he is no longer the District Commissioner, but he's still the boss.

■ ■ ■

It is tough for an African coach or manager to get a good job in football and even tougher for him to keep it. But it can appear very easy to get a good coaching job in African football if you are from Europe or South America. It may be hard to keep it for very long, but chances are there will be another one around the corner. And another one. And another one after that. Rather like an enlarged version of the way Italy's Serie A used to operate, where the same four or five Italians would play musical chairs around the prime coaching jobs, African football has a charmed circle of expatriates who get sacked and always re-employed. And it has a startling gap in its overall record when it comes to native managerial achievement. In the first 75 years of Africa's World Cup life, 28 teams from the continent have travelled to final tournaments: 10 of them have been coached there by Africans. Of the six times an African team has broken through the initial round, either a Brazilian, a Frenchman, a Dutchman, a Russian or a Serb was in charge, never an African. The first Nations Cup, Egypt's in 1957, was won by an Egyptian coach; the next two would be overseen by a Hungarian and a Yugoslav. In the first 50 years of Nations Cups, the majority of the titles were won by teams with a foreign head coach.

To find out why this should be, I made an appointment with the man they call Le Sorcier Blanc, or The White Witchdoctor. He is Philippe Omar Troussier and he lives in Rabat, the broad-avenued, rather sober capital of Morocco. He is not yet quite clear which of his two houses there, the cottage on the beach, or the large pink villa with bourgonvillias tumbling over its high perimeter walls he calls home, but approaching his mid-50s he seems pleased to at least have a city he calls home. Troussier has led an expatriate life, and calling himself 'a globetrotter' is to understate. As a football coach he has lived and worked in three continents, and held nine different jobs in Africa alone, five of them with national teams. When I called on him, Troussier was doing almost everything he could to apply a pause to his frenetic working life, putting down roots. He and his wife Dominique had recently adopted two daughters, both born in Morocco, and they had converted to Islam, Philippe with the name Omar, Dominique as Amina. Their house, the pink villa, was a study in home-making, a process into which Troussier had thrown himself with dangerous enthusiasm and characteristic energy. He answered the door on crutches, legacy of a nasty fall as he was erecting a giant cinema-sized screen that would pull down in front of some exquisite, 20-foot, carved, antique Moroccan doors he had fitted to one of the large salons in his home.

The Troussiers are hospitable, charming and they put on display their love for Africa. Theirs is, on a grand scale, a home with the eclectic mix of collectables you might find in the house of a career diplomat, or a veteran foreign correspondent. Besides the arabesque doors, you enter the hall to be confronted by a striking wooden figure from Ivory Coast, wide-eyed, round-mouthed, the size of a child. Waiting to be hung in a prominent place is a photograph of Troussier and Nelson Mandela. There are artefacts collected from Nigeria and elsewhere in West Africa, several curios from Japan, where Troussier worked with considerable success with the national team before he moved on, briefly, to France's toughest, most popular club, Olympique Marseille.

Troussier is a Parisian who had an unremarkable career as a professional footballer, and turned early to coaching. He was put in charge of the French national under-15 squad when he was 28, and acquired a reputation as innovative, enthusiastic, a little head-strong, and as he recalls it, 'a bit intellectual.' In his mid-30s his career was in a lull, when it was suggested to him that one of Francophone Africa's stronger clubs, Asec Mimosas, of Ivory Coast wanted a head coach. Troussier felt doubtful. 'In the 1980s,' he remembers, 'Africa did not have a good image in the French football world. It was a place where managers who had nowhere left to go would end up. That was exactly the situation I was in.' Asec offered him the post in spite of his utter ignorance of their city, the country. 'I had to check on a world map where Ivory Coast was located. As for black Africa, I had a primitive image in my head, as if it was like *Tintin in the Congo* and that in Africa they eat white men, and put them in a big cooking pot.' It sounded an unlikely sort of a blind date. As Troussier boarded his flight from Paris to Abidjan, he was called to the gate to take an urgent call from his employers-to-be. They asked him to make sure he was the last person to leave the aircraft on landing. He felt confused: 'Then it dawned on me. No one there had any idea what I looked like.'

Twenty-four hours later, Troussier was no longer Tintin in the

Congo; he was Karen Blixen in *Out of Africa*, a gushing romantic, overcome by a beautiful sunset and the lights shimmering off the lake as he surveyed Abidjan from the privileged position of a suite at the Hotel Ivoire. 'My eyes were like a baby's eyes, my imagination like a baby's,' he says. 'I wanted to discover everything.' Troussier still had some of that romanticism in him when I first met him in the early 1990s: he talked of 'the smells, the feel and the stimulation of Africa.' By then he had his passport across the continent, because at Asec he had worked some magic, taking the team to trophies and a scarcely precedented run of unbeaten matches. There he got his nickname, Le Sorcier Blanc, The White Witchdoctor of the touchline. He remembers the moment the moniker stuck. It was a simple decision, a lucky managerial hunch. 'We were maybe two minutes before the end of a match and the opponents were leading 2-0. I changed two players and we won. So they called me Le Sorcier Blanc because I did something that changed the story of the match. And we kept on winning, and winning after that.' He had discovered what he and most expatriate coaches working in Africa also say, that his communion with his public was more intimate than he had or would experience in Europe. 'It's not aggression in the physical sense,' explains Troussier, 'but it's an aggressiveness in the level of expectation. Everybody, the fan, the president, the journalist, wants to tell you what they feel and they want you to always win 5-0. I was very lucky when I began. I did not lose a match for practically three years.'

In Africa, Troussier's reputation was made. After Asec, he was offered the job in charge of the Ivorian national team, whom he very nearly led to a place at the World Cup in 1994. Le Sorcier Blanc's fame had spread by now, and he was taken on by another of the continent's most glamorous clubs, Kaizer Chiefs of

Johannesburg. There his methods caused some startled first impressions. He was too much the martinet. 'He thought we needed to be tougher,' recalls Lucas Radebe, the leading footballer at Chiefs at that time, 'and he went too far. One day he was dragging my team-mate "Bricks" Mudau around the ground by his feet.' Now, 'Bricks' was a big man, who had not earned his nickname for being flaccid. Troussier's first spell in Johannesburg lasted less than a year, although he would be invited back there, again and again.

Troussier's globetrot became a gallop after that. He coached two Moroccan clubs, CA Rabat and FUS Rabat, then the national team of Nigeria, whom he guided swiftly to a place at the 1998 World Cup finals. He would not, though, lead them there, because he left Lagos in a dispute over unpaid money. There were plenty more offers instead, and in an extraordinary 12 months, Troussier turned himself into the epitome of the quick-fix, hired hand. He took a three-month contract to coach little Burkina Faso when they hosted the African Nations Cup in 1998, and embellished the legend of Le Sorcier Blanc still further by taking the Burkinabe team all the way to the semi-finals in front of their own, delighted crowds. He had already agreed a contract to steer South Africa's national squad at the World Cup finals that year. Again, it meant a short-term deal: take over in March for a tournament beginning in June. So in the space of a year he had been in charge of three countries: Nigeria, Burkina Faso, South Africa.

The 1998 World Cup marked a nadir for the cause of African coaches. Africa went there with an increased berth of places, and all five teams were under foreign management. Troussier was one of three Frenchmen, and one of five Europeans. They were mostly old Africa hands, men forever riding on the whirligig of Africa's top management jobs. Claude Le Roy, the bespectacled Frenchman with a resemblance to the British actor Timothy Spall, took over Cameroon a matter of weeks before the finals, part of a CV that included several years in the 1980s with Cameroon's Indomitable Lions, and spells in charge of Senegal, the Democratic Republic of Congo and of Ghana. Henryk Kasperczak, a Pole with a French passport who coached Tunisia, was on the second of his five African countries. Like Le Roy, Kasperczak has coached Senegal. He also did a stint with the Mali national team. Morocco went to France '98 under Henri Michel, a former captain of France and a man of whom African Federations and club presidents never tire. In 1994, Michel oversaw Cameroon's World Cup campaign; in 1998, he was with Morocco; in 2002 with Tunisia; in 2006 with Ivory Coast. Michel, tanned and rather louche in appearance, can trump most of his contemporaries with the illustrious club jobs he has also compiled: Zamalek of Cairo, Raja Casablanca and Mamelodi Sundowns, the nouveau riche South Africans who pay high salaries.

The very least all this hopping around one another's old jobs suggests is that large parts of Africa find the pool of adequate head coaches rather small, and getting no larger. Ten years after Troussier, Le Roy, Kasperczak and Michel were off to a World Cup, three of the quartet had all taken charge of teams at the 2008 African Cup of Nations in Ghana. Troussier had turned down Benin and been approached by Cameroon in the lead-up to the event. Cameroon eventually took Otto Pfister, the German with a face like Erno Goldfinger, who has been barking orders from dugouts across Africa for decades. They were Pfister's eighth national team – after Rwanda, Upper Volta, Senegal, Ivory Coast, Zaïre, Ghana and Togo – and his 12th job in Africa. He has a way to go, though, to overhaul the extraordinary German, Rudi Gutendorf, who between taking charge of the Tunisian club US Monastir in 1961 and the Rwanda national team in 1999, had coached Ghana, São Tomé e Príncipe, Mauritius, Tanzania, Zimbabwe and Botswana in Africa, in addition to 15 other national teams in Asia, Australasia, the Caribbean and South America.

So what do all these white witchdoctors have, that a native coach does not? 'It's not a problem with colour,' insists Troussier. 'The problem is a political problem. And it's not so different from, say, Real Madrid, where things can be much more difficult if you are a Spanish coach than if you are a foreigner. It's an ethnic problem and an authority problem, because the local coach can be influenced by the atmosphere around a team, he can smell the feelings of people, he knows everything; whereas a foreign coach comes with nothing but his job. He doesn't know if player x comes from the north, south, east or west of the country. So, the foreign coach can be presented as a neutral man, who doesn't have a favourite tribe or region. He just picks the best 11 players, wherever they come from. In Africa, they want a foreign coach to neutralise the position.'

There is another issue, too, suggested Troussier, a by-product of the exodus of Africa's best players to Europe. 'There is a balance you have to achieve between discipline and freedom. You have to consider that in Africa boys playing football can take some decisions in the way they play that will not be a decision a European player takes. You can say with more truth that all European players play the same football: if a player there is on the right, he crosses; if he is on the left, he crosses. In Africa that is less likely to be the case. That background gives the player more freedom, and you need to hold onto some of that. But with national teams, I also saw what the players expect: they expect foreign coaches. The players working abroad often don't respect coaches coming from their own country. They are like a passenger in a plane and they expect the pilot must have a body of experience a little bit higher that theirs.' In short, if the height of a player's ambition is a job in European football, they want their boss to have a background in Europe. Thus did the former head coach of Nigeria and Togo, the Nigerian Stephen Keshi once explain to me some difficulties he had been having with a star Togo player: 'He is trying it on with me because he thinks I am his brother, a black person. That's why he wants to impose and do whatever he wants to do, because I am a black person.' The Algerian satirist, Rachid Taha, puts it as bluntly: 'Just as people always get the black or the Arab bouncer to break up a fight in a night-club, Africans go looking for a white man to coach their football teams.' And here's an answer I heard from the talented Nigerian full-back Celestine Babayaro when I asked him why he thought there was such high turnover of coaches in Africa, and why the first recourse always seemed to be foreigner? 'For us,' Babayaro replied, with disarming candour, 'it's important the boss has a big car.'

■ ■ ■

Sometimes, it's just important the boss has a car at all. You can go a long way down the hierarchy of football in Africa and find the cult of the foreign coach alive and well, visit remote stadiums where just a few hundred people are watching a lower-league or a schoolboy match, and there'll be one man in the stadium conspicuous for being an expatriate, for being white: he'll be the head coach. Sometimes, he'll be there on some sort of overseas aid programme, funded by a Football Association in Europe as part of their benevolent gift to a struggling economy. Or he'll be installed as part of the sponsorship package arranged with a kit manufacturer, usually a US or European corporation. Sometimes he may even have landed the post by accident, like the Englishman,

Ray Whelan, who realised he had been appointed national coach of Tanzania in the 1990s only when a journalist asked him about tactics at a press conference he thought he was giving to launch new administrative and marketing initiatives at the Tanzanian FA. Or the Austrian, Gerry Saurer, who found himself leading Kenya to the African Nations Cup in Senegal in 1992 and having to arrange cover for his hotel and restaurant businesses in Mombasa. Saurer's qualifications for the position of national head coach consisted of enthusiastically volunteering himself while working in the tourism and catering industry in the Seychelles. Moving to Nairobi he took his hobby with him, and ended up the manager of the Harambee Stars, Kenya's national XI. He did it well enough to take them to a tournament they do not usually reach. Then there was the Briton, Jeff Butler who came to the conclusion that in Africa, a voice turned hoarse with shouting, a gruff Yorkshire manner and an impression that you had grown up in the tough, admired world of English professional football could take you a long way. This Jeff Butler had achieved so highly with Al Ahly and Kaizer Chiefs that, when South Africa looked for its first national coach after the end of apartheid, they turned to him. Only then did it emerge that he had been travelling around the continent claiming as his own the English playing career of another man, a former player with Norwich City also named Jeff Butler, who was surprised to hear of this ingenious piece of identity-theft when contacted at his home in East Anglia.

This is the sort of slapstick Caf was anxious to put an end to, when, in late 2008, it launched a licensing programme that will insist on a level of professional qualification for anybody coaching professionally in African football. 'We have fallen behind in this,' says Abdel Moneim Hussain, Caf's development director and a former coach of Egypt's Al Ahly. 'Far too many coaches are working in Africa without the right qualifications. We have a lot of work to do in that because Africa has suffered for the last 50 years, and more, in terms of infrastructures, and administration. We have great, great players, but you can't get them to the top if they are riding there on a tram.' With the wrong tram-driver at the wheel, a team can lose its identity, cease playing to its strengths, adds Abdel Moneim Hussain. He is careful not to rehearse simplistic old arguments that suggest all Africans play football in much the same way, and to over-coach them or to impose an alien set of rigours is to lose the essence of their game, but he makes the point that a sensitivity to how Africa works should be part of the requirement for a coach taking authority over players there. 'Polishing talent is not an easy job. In Europe a talented player is a precious diamond; in Africa sometimes you have precious diamonds that are never discovered. We have to put into the federations a kind of stability that coaches can work in a relaxed way, not just come in for a few months to win important matches and then leave. We need to keep the coaches with the players for as much time as possible.'

He is preaching to an unforgiving constituency. The chief reason why Africa creates its ceaseless, circulating system of job opportunities for European coaches is that it sacks the incumbents so often. Nigeria changed their head coach 20 times between 1989 and 2009, South Africa 11 times in the decade after Troussier took them to their first World Cup; Ghana 16 times in the same period; Cameroon 16 times in the 19 years after their quarter-final appearance at the Italy World Cup of 1990. There is a routine within the apparent chaos, a cycle where a foreign coach gives way to a local man, who gives way to a foreigner. Quite often the man appointed, if he is a European, stipulates high up on his contract not specific clauses about practice facilities or fitness and nutritional support, but the number of air-tickets home that will be made available to him. More and more often the men in charge of national teams in the stronger West African countries choose not actually to live there, arguing that as most of their players are employed in European leagues, they should be based in Europe, and even adding, as the German Uli Stielike did during his time in charge of Ivory Coast, that while working with an African team was stimulating for him, Africa itself seemed rather too dangerous a place to reside.

There are indeed risky places in West Africa, a good deal more dangerous than Stielike's suite at Abidjan's Golf Hotel on Lake Ebrié. A long way down the rungs of the coaching ladder, there are some very able coaches. In Sierra Leone, where a brutal civil war disfigured the country in the 1990s, a set of teenagers nonetheless emerged strong enough to reach the under-17 World Cup final tournament in 2003. For Moosa Kallon, a former Sierra Leone player who spent much of his career in Europe's middling leagues, like Portugal and Turkey, the task of coaching the national youth team starts in the kitchen: 'My concern at the beginning of a day is whether or not these boys have been able to eat a piece of chicken or not in the week before we get together,' he says. In the Democratic Republic of Congo which, as Zaïre, once stood in the vanguard of black African football, war has changed the very morphology of the sport, says the Congolese Federation's youth coach, Guillaume Ilunga. 'Part of our strength historically was the players who came from the east of the country,' Ilunga explains, 'and the fighting there has disrupted everything. I notice that we don't see the players with the strength and stamina that used to come from that region.' When Frédéric Acosta sets out the practice drills for the best teenaged footballers in Niger, a country afflicted by terrible drought, he uses not bespoke traffic cones but the discarded triangular display units used to sell lollipops in roadside kiosks. His Niger players do their jumping and hopping exercises on tracks marked out by old inner-tubes from bicycle tyres. 'If I make little savings like these, we can eat better at meal-times,' Acosta explains. 'The job of coach in a country like mine, which is very poor has to be pastoral work too. I want to make these kids better footballers but also hope they can become good men. We have to make the best of what we have, and learn to be clever. That applies to the style of football we have to cultivate, too. In Niger, we tend not to be big and physically robust. We have to be quick, sharp-minded instead.'

Kallon, Ilunga and Acosta were among 25 junior coaches from across Africa I interviewed at the 50th anniversary of Caf, in 2007. I wondered how many of them, given the continent's predilection for appointing European or South Americans to the top job in charge of the senior team, anticipated rising all the way up the ladder. Many hoped they would, and most emphasised the importance of understanding the peculiarities of their specific jobs. I heard 25 different opinions on how the game in their country should be best developed; although they coincided in some areas, many agreed that the instinct to improvise remained a pronounced feature of African football. As many coaches said the young players they worked with were inspired by Jay-Jay Okocha as said their boys wanted to emulate Didier Drogba or Samuel Eto'o: in other words to be a slick trickster, albeit with a lesser global profile. The environments in which children pick up the game shape those priorities. Tom Vernon, an Englishman who lives in Ghana and scouts for talent in Africa on behalf of Manchester United, notes how the neighbours, Ghana and Ivory Coast, have emerged among the very best national teams at the end of the first decade of the new millennium with distinct strengths. He explains it like this: 'If you watch how children play in Ghana, they will set up a pitch, wherever they can, which is perhaps 20 or 30 yards long and with a pair of stones at either end two feet apart. There will be a gutter or a ditch maybe marking out the boundaries. It constricts the game into a tiny area, so the skill is all about receiving the ball and driving through the middle. Look at Ghana's senior team and its strength is the central midfielders, like Michael Essien and Ali Sulley Muntari.' He contrasts modern Ivory Coast's fortes: four or five strikers – Aruna Dindane, Salomon Kalou, Boubacar Sanogo, Arouna Koné and Bakari Koné – competing to partner Drogba. Go to Ivory Coast, Vernon adds, and you see many more goal frames painted on urban walls than you do in Ghana.

■ ■ ■

Fashions alter, but the expatriate on the touchline remains a fixture. Half a century ago, freshly independent, African football was eagerly looking at other countries' coaching systems to harness its own talents. In many cases, it aggressively rejected the governing systems imposed by colonial rule and turned against coaches from France, or Britain. So, some of the first white witchdoctors came from very red regimes, gifts from the Cold War, Russians and Eastern European technocrats sent as part of the Communist-block aid packages to sympathetic states in Africa. In Nigeria, a Yugoslav named Tihomir Jelisavčić, alias 'Fada Tiko', had a long influence. His compatriot Blagoje Vidinić led Morocco and Zaïre to the World Cups of 1970 and 1974; the Yugoslavs Rade Ognjanović and Vladimir Beara made an impact in Cameroon. Hungarian coaches, thanks to the revolutionary, passing football of the Magyar team were a fad, too, in West Africa and in Egypt, where Nándor

Hidegkuti, the centre-forward from the brilliant Hungary side of the early 1950s, coached Al Ahly for many years.

Brazil was, and remains an appealing model. Nejmeddine Belayachi, an Algerian coach and author of the intensely pedagogic *Style et Identité du Football Africain*, argued at the end of the 1980s that: 'The African footballer possesses a sense of creativity and he is drawn to improvisation as part of a carefully constructed and thought-out game. He detests football made up of long balls, thumping clearances and headers and incessant running and physical confrontation.' So, Belayachi concluded: 'The playing style that suits African footballers, the way they express themselves on the pitch and their instincts is indisputably that adopted by South Americans and notably Brazilians.' When South Africa appointed Carlos Alberto Parreira, coach of Brazil's 1994 World Cup winners, as the coach to prepare them for the 2010 World Cup, they were thinking along those lines, and asking of Parreira much of what Ghana had sought from him 40 years earlier, when as a young man Parreira had been sent from Brazil to oversee the Ghana squad of the late 1960s. Nigeria had the same idea with the appointment of Otto Gloria as their head coach in the 1980s. Morocco made history in 1986 in gaining a place in the last 16 of a World Cup under the Brazilian José Faria.

The instinct to entrust African talent to a foreign coach, usually a European, appears as strong as it was 50 years ago, perhaps stronger. At the African Cup of Nations finals in 2008, three-quarters of the 16 participating nations were coached by men from outside Africa. Ten years earlier in Burkina Faso, when Egypt had also won the tournament with an Egyptian in charge, just over half the teams had been under foreign management. For a further, forthright opinion on why, I turned to Jo Jo Bell, the former goalkeeper of Cameroon and one of the game's more strident voices. 'I wish someone could explain to me why, after 60 years of independence, 60 years of football, a child has not been born who has played football and is deemed to be able to understand football like a European,' says Bell. 'Of course they are there. But it's in the heads of the people who make the appointments that it has not yet happened. You always have these foreign coaches on almost every touchline. For me, they're imposters. They have no value. They don't offer or show anything. But usually one of them ends up winning, so it's taken as proof we need foreign coaches. Now think about this: in Italy, they change governments every six months. Because they keep changing, do they turn around and ask a German to come and run their country? No. Do they ask an American to come and take over? No. But we Africans, we don't put our own people in charge of our teams, we just put in another foreigner. We sack a white man and bring in another white man. And they, these imposters, they say: "Ah, there's work over there, we have to go and help each other."

Bell detects a wider issue. 'I understand it perfectly. In Africa, there is a fear of progress. That's the truth of it. If you are good in Africa, they don't need you. That's serious. Africa has not dealt with colonialism. In other areas of African life, it's the same, but you don't see it too much. Because football is popular, you see it. The men in charge don't have confidence in themselves or in each other. So they think that in order to stay in power they'd better be in service to a foreign state.'

CHAPTER THREE

FEET OF THE CHAMELEON

'Fare ye well on the field,' declared Bishop Vining of Lagos, quaintly, as 18 young men, dressed in smart blazers, filed on board the passenger ship *MV Apapa*, bound out of Nigeria. They included a number of the best local footballers, though there had been considerable local argument about whether they were genuinely the top dozen and a half that might have been selected. But the British organisers of the 1949 Nigeria tour of England had dual priorities. They carefully chose a group of men who would politely act as ambassadors for the benevolent aspects of the colonial regime in the state and the importance of their diplomatic role would be stressed to the players throughout, not least by the team manager, Captain DA Holley, an Englishman whose sense of formal decorum, according to the Nigerian journalist Samuel Akpabot, obliged him to wear a bow tie even while dressed in shorts. The attire of the players also drew attention to itself, even before the *Apapa* left the shoreline. 'Fare ye well,' announced Bishop Vining, 'boots or no boots.'

The naked feet of the first Nigerian team to set off on an overseas tour would continue to catch the eye, not just through admiration for their tough soles in all sorts of weather, but for the sensitive relationship these feet had in contact with the ball. At first, shoelessness was taken by their hosts as a primitive characteristic. That developed into another sort of appreciation. Soon after the boat docked in Merseyside, the *Liverpool Echo* welcomed 'the wizards in bare feet.' By the end of Nigeria's first match, The Barefoot Wizards had ceased to be a cliché. They beat Marine 5-2 in the opening fixture of a hectic schedule and the *Echo* cooed at the pace of their game and, bootless, the 'astonishing power of their kicking.'

The tour, mostly pitting the Nigerians against England's best amateur teams, drew good crowds and the visitors frequently outplayed their opponents. Once in London, the novelty of playing shoeless, with their ankles and the smalls of their feet bandaged, drew more precise analyses. The *Daily Graphic* reported: 'Their control is a form of caress, helped by the spreading of the toes.' British talent spotters became interested. Titus Okere, a left-winger from Railways Club, would be invited to join Swindon Town as a result of his performances. Tesilimi Balogun, aka 'Thunder', spent a productive season with Queen's Park Rangers. The captain Dan Anyiam would return to London for trials with Chelsea. The Nigerians drew comparisons with a dashing Dynamo Moscow team which had toured England not long earlier, and their one heavy defeat, when they shipped eight goals against a combined XI from the Athenian League, would be easily enough excused: it was a boots issue. The weather was foul, the pitch muddy, the debate at half-time vexed as the bow-tied Holley exhorted the majority of the players still without boots to put some on, to lace up, for the second half. He did so in a 'hectoring manner' noted the *News Chronicle*. But several of the footballers seemed genuinely to prefer to go without boots, as if the style they had developed, some of its subtleties and habits would be dulled by a coating of leather.

The 1949 Nigerians were not the first African footballers to be widely celebrated for their bootless ingenuity. Nor would they be the last. Images of African boys, shoeless, chasing balls on an unkempt surface has for decades been the staple assignment of visiting photojournalists exploring the main sport of the continent. Such pictures are easy to find, in any African city, village or track. Childhood stories told by the leading African footballers across generations almost invariably describe makeshift barefoot championships, constructed with vivid imaginations and scant resources.

Related games may even have existed before European settlers brought FA rules, touchlines, crossbars and studded soles to Africa. In Egypt, a country that likes to lay claim to almost any invention that shapes modern society, they make a case for having thought about football entirely on their own, in the pharaonic age, and point to a range of balls found in mausoleums of Egyptian royals and their families, colourful objects, made from leather hides or cotton-fibre, stuffed with dried palm or papyrus leaves. Then there are the etchings on the walls of tombs at Beni Hassan in Minya, pictures of upright figures juggling balls; others clutching sticks or bats ready to strike. Some lean forward, poised, preparing to kick at the balls with their bare feet. Beneath the Sahara, a 19th century study of the San of southern Africa reported a fast moving sport using balls crafted from the fatty hide of hippopotamuses' necks, material that lent a bouncy elasticity to the toys. From equatorial Africa emerged accounts of activities rather like hockey, using a wooden stick and a ball fashioned from bark, palm nuts or fruit; from the Sahel, a strip of arid land south of the Sahara, a stick-and-ball game played on the sand to mark the end of Ramadan. French anthropologists in the Congo region noted a pursuit whose object was to kick round objects – lemons, typically – past an opponent guarding an imaginary frontier. Save the shot and it would be the other side's turn: a sort of penalty shoot-out without the crossbars and posts.

As for boots, they became a divisive issue in the development of African football well before the barefoot Nigerian team toured England. In colonial Brazzaville in the Congo, the permission to use footwear to play the game led to a confrontation between Africans and French administrators in the 1940s. A Monsieur Benilan, President of the Federation, wrote in reply to native pleas for boots that 'shoes encourage the African players to use brutality rather than technique'. The authorities made barefoot football compulsory among the black population, as it was in neighbouring Belgian Congo.

A long way north, the most famous African feet of the time developed the dexterity of a pianist's hands without the hulking boots of the era. They belonged to Larbi Ben Barek. His legend turns on the day he lined up as a teenager in a friendly match in Casablanca against Union Sportive Marocaine, USM, one of the leading teams in North Africa, and scored two goals. He wore a pair of espadrilles. The rest of the players wore boots. That game led to his first transfer and from then on, the peculiar way he addressed the ball would intrigue his coaches. 'He almost always passed, shot and played the ball with the toe or with the outside of his foot,' noted Helenio Herrera, who recruited Ben Barek at Atlético Madrid and at Stade Français. 'Very seldom, even for short passes, did he use his instep. His timing of volleys was so good,' wrote Herrera, 'that it allowed him to strike a volley with his right foot to the right of an opponent, while the head was cocked towards the left. And there was his amazing way of taking penalties. He would shoot with the outside of his right foot, to the goalkeeper's left and, like a cannonball, into the top corner of the net, but just as he reached the ball, he would turn his body as if he was going to fire it the other side, just to confuse the goalkeeper.'

■ ■ ■

Eusébio, the next African great, describes barefoot epics of his early years on patches of ground in Mafalala, he and his friends assuming the names of contemporary Brazilians. In the vibrant football culture of Eusébio's Portuguese East Africa in the 1950s, a new, and detailed vocabulary was also developing for the African game. Words in Ronga, a language spoken in the area around and inland of Maputo, so evocatively described specific manoeuvres on the field that they were soon being borrowed by non-Ronga speakers, including Portuguese settlers. At least that was the case put forward in 1955 by just about the highest authority in the land on matters of language, the Mozambican poet José Craveirinha. Writing in *O Brado Africano*, Craveirinha listed a wealth of Ronga terms that had entered the game's lexicon. He did so to make a point: that just as language had enriched a new, Africanised form of a sport imported there by the Portuguese, it did so because African talent had created a superior creole of a game. Several of the terms describe special cunning, even slyness on the part of a player. A 'beketela' occurs when the man in possession, anticipating a challenge, slows the momentum of the ball in such a way that his opponent fouls him or, in a 'wandla', is caught, perhaps painfully, by the tip of the foot of his opponent as he aims for a ball which has not quite reached the spot the challenger imagined it would move to. Other words describe moments of crescendo: a 'pandya' is what English might call a '50-50', at the moment when two players both make contact with the ball simultaneously. A 'tchimbela' sounds nasty: it's a powerful drive or volley that smacks hard into an opponent's body. A tchimbela *is* nasty. Here's Craveirinha's translation in full: 'To shoot the ball directly at the opponent with maximum violence so that he is intimidated in later moves. Advantage can thus be gained simply by threatening to kick, which will almost always make the target turn his back to the ball, allowing him to be passed very easily.'

But football told in Ronga is not all intimidating or sneaky. On the lips of a supporter or a commentator, words like 'wupfetela', 'psetu' and 'pyonyo' sound cheerfully plosive. What they describe are moments of particular swagger, extravagant skill, touches that delight in their superfluity: a striker has performed a wupfutela when he humiliates a goalkeeper, perhaps dribbling around him in a duel and then hesitating before scoring to tempt the goalkeeper into another, doomed attempt at retrieving the ball. The word, explained Craveirinha, is borrowed from cooking, and means seasoning. A psetu is a manoeuvre that teases an opponent, a pyonyo might be the flourish with which a successful psetu concludes, the touch that finishes off the outwitted opponent. Craveirinha concludes, with his own flourish, that Mozambican football needed these terms in colonial times because the Portuguese had no vocabulary to describe the unique trickery that African footballers were bringing to the game.

Cross the border into South Africa, where Ronga becomes Tsonga, which in turn competes with another 10 official languages, and the same thing occurs. Words from one tongue are now recognised across many. A 'tsamaya', from the Sesotho language, serves for just about any eye-catching piece of skill to win a duel. What the British call a nutmeg, the slipping of the ball between an opponent's legs, is a 'shibobo', a term that jubilantly jived its way into the cultural mainstream when the South African national team scored their first goal at a World Cup, at the 1998 finals. It was converted by Benni McCarthy, a striker with an impudent streak, the Denmark goalkeeper Peter Schmeichel the victim of McCarthy's cool finish; a finish so cool the popular kwaito band TKZee invited McCarthy to join them in recording a hit single, 'Shibobo'. In South Africa commentators in most languages, including English, use shibobo and tsamaya and imagine all their audiences would recognise the terms. Listeners would likewise know what was meant when they said 'laduma'. It has come to mean 'goal', and the better the goal, the longer the man with the microphone will stretch out the u of its second syllable, as if he were drawing out a note on a hand-held concertina.

The figure who brought 'laduma' into football is Zama Masondo, the best known sports commentator in Zulu, and a man for whom calling football matches has opened up a variety of subsequent careers. We met one day in central Johannesburg, where Masondo runs a catering school, preparing young students for work in the country's large tourist industry. Masondo has a further sideline as an actor, a job that has come to him late in life, in his early 60s. He had lately been appearing in a popular soap opera, *Muvhango*, on the state channel, the SABC. He plays a serial womaniser, a lounge lizard named Malume Khumalo. Masondo says with a smile and a glint in his eye that he rather enjoys the role of an ageing rake, though insists it is nothing like the real Zama. Of the millions who watch the series, most may not have recognised the actor. As soon as he spoke they knew the voice: Zama Masondo is an institution, and he is inimitable. His voice sounds a little nasal, but it is so deep and so rich that it could never he heard as whiny. Before he became a commentator, Masondo had trained as a schoolteacher, and it can be assumed he brought an authority to the job, with his upright bearing and his basso profundo. Teaching in under-resourced classrooms in apartheid South Africa in the 1970s, he would have needed to be strict.

Masondo moved into broadcasting because he enjoyed sport and very obviously had a voice for it. He also had an imagination that he felt the commentators working in the country's African languages had suppressed in their work. And he could hardly help but notice what his contemporaries were saying. He recalls how in the early days of his career, covering big matches like Kaizer Chiefs against Orlando Pirates in Soweto, the commentators serving radio stations in their multitude of different languages – Xhosa, Sesotho, Venda, Ndebele, Shangaan, Tswana, Tsonga – would be corralled into a tiny, outdoor space somewhere along the touchline, all within earshot of one another. What Masondo heard too often for his liking, was 'everybody doing the same thing, just as if they were translating an English style of commentary into Zulu or whatever. It didn't work with the culture in a lot of cases. So I said to myself: "Let me differ".' The idea of a more evocative way of registering and celebrating a goal came to him spontaneously. 'I just said it "Laduuuma!". What it means, in Zulu, is something like "It has thundered." Initially I would sometimes say "it has thundered from the foot" or that sort of thing, but after a while everybody began to know that laduma means goal.' He added certain tics to his crescendos, sometimes borrowing from abroad. Visiting South America, Masondo enjoyed the excitable variations on the word 'gol': 'I like the way they say a long "Goooool!" or quickly shout "Golgolgolgolgol!" So I worked on some things I had picked up there.' His style is not that of a twenty-words-a-second chatterbox, so moving from radio to television did not plunge Masondo into the commentator's common trap of too much talk, excessive stating of the obvious.

What television did set was a challenge he needed to act on, and the way he did it became almost as famous as his coining the word

'Laduma'. Television only reached South Africa in the second half of the 1970s and was received with wonder. Slow motion replays came soon afterwards, and Masondo quickly learned that some of his viewers, particularly in rural areas, found them confusing. 'They thought this was real-time action, or that something had gone wrong with their TV sets at first,' he recalls. 'There was no sense in saying "Now for the replay", so I came up with a phrase that caught on. I said "Ngonyawo lo nwabu". It means: "Now let's see it again with the feet of the chameleon".' It is a lovely metaphor, taking a creature nature blessed with the wonders of technicolor, the ability to subtly alter its form and observing the purposeful languor with which the reptile moves its limbs along a branch. Zama Masondo had made slow-motion replays no longer alarming, but comforting for his viewers. His phrase stuck. 'I think of that as my other main coinage,' he says proudly.

Masondo enjoys word-play in his Zulu commentary, and he happily uses the vast range of nicknames that animate football not only in southern Africa but across the sub-Saharan states. He has bestowed a few of them himself, he says, but the most intriguing and fetching have been the invention of fans. The followers of Orlando Pirates, formed just before the Second World War, used to thrill to the goals of Sam 'Baboon Shepherd' Shabangu, a bearded forward. Masondo narrated dozens of matches of the Sowetan club Moroka Swallows when they sought goals from Thomas 'Who's Fooling Who' Hlongwane. He was pleased to celebrate the most important laduma in Orlando Pirates' history, the winning goal of the 1995 Champions League scored against Asec Mimosas in Ivory Coast, its scorer Jerry 'Legs of Thunder' Sikhosana, a centre-forward with, naturally, powerful thighs. Other footballers, nimbler ones, evoke sweeter sounds: Harold 'Jazzy Queen' Legodi used to be among Masondo's favourites.

You could compile a hefty encyclopedia of the monikers by which football in Africa tells its stories, makes its heroes, piques its villains. The highest form of flattery has often been to bestow scholarship. To play the sport with precision and spatial sensitivity is to play it 'scientifically'. Léopard de Douala in Cameroon are said to have had a footballer nicknamed 'D'Alembert' (after the French mathematician of the 18th century, no less) in the 1940s. South Africa had Mlungisi 'Professor' Ngubane. There have been plenty of Doctors, from Theophile 'Doctor' Abega, captain of Cameroon when they won their first African Nations Cup in 1984, to Theophilius 'Doctor' Khumalo, icon of Kaizer Chiefs in the 1990s. Reporters covering football in South Africa in the Doctor Khumalo era used to attend weekly press conferences organised by the league at the Soccer City stadium in Soweto, events designed to brief on the issues of the day but usually hijacked by the loquacious public relations officers of leading clubs. Kaizer Chiefs had a PRO named Louis Tshakoane, Mamelodi Sundowns had Alex Shakoane, alias 'Goldfinger' for the heavy jewellery he liked to wear. They would declaim at one another, like Tweedledum and Tweedledee, often in the language of high learning, competing for the right to be quoted at most length in the next morning's editions of *The Star* or *The Sowetan*. Our notebooks would be filled with phrases like: 'It's all a matter of geometry, Pythagoras and theorems,' from Tshakoane. 'The other teams just can't fathom out our angles.'

Nigeria's national team, then the Green Eagles, built much of their growing reputation in the 1970s and 1980s around Segun 'Mathematical' Odegbami, a nickname hastened into broad usage by the voice of Ernest Nkonkwo, the doyen of Nigerian commentators. Zambia's leading footballer from the 1970s became Alex 'Computer' Chola for similar reasons, given the moniker via the microphone of Dennis Liwewe, probably Africa's most widely recognised commentator, at least across the English-speaking parts of the continent. Liwewe contributed for many years to the BBC Africa service and his commentaries on Zambian matches were remarkable for their emotional range. Liwewe talked very fast indeed in the build-up to a goal, and would sound terribly morose if, calling a match involving the national team, Zambia had fallen behind. Liwewe's passion was sincere, corporeal. His son, Ponga, sometimes accompanied his father into the gantry, and remembers: 'It was almost like he was on the field. He'd be going on at hundreds of words a minute, sweat pouring off him. He'd even take off his shirt sometimes when he got really hot. He was passionate but he also had a real gift for language, and could transmit from the tone of his voice the state of the game, especially if it was the Zambian team against an opponent from somewhere else.' He was, without apology, biased: 'Compared to modern broadcast standards, my dad's work in the 1960s, 70s and 80s, had far less objectivity,' says Ponga Liwewe. 'He felt it was part of his job to rally behind the team.' Zama Masondo would share that instinct, to a degree. 'We are there to paint pictures with words, to inform and to educate,' says Masondo, 'but we are also praise-singers, and we come from a culture with a long tradition of that.'

■ ■ ■

In neighbouring Mozambique there lives a fan who not so much sings praises as wears them. Her name is Gina Matessane and her ritual on matchdays starts early. First, there's the foundation, a chalky base paint she applies to her cheeks, a few dabs to the chin and the forehead, to give her face a faintly ghostly look. There are thick strokes of dark make-up for around the eyes, and then various layers of cloth and hide she swathes around her small, slender frame in a particular order, depending on the weather conditions in Maputo or at wherever she may be heading. The journey may be hot and cramped. Usually she travels by minibus, and the trek from home to an away venue can be a long one. It may take her across borders, with their queues at customs, perhaps a small bribe demanded from the driver at the check-point and a whip-round among the passengers to collect it. Gina Matessane hopes for two or three big away trips a year supporting her beloved Desportivo de Maputo. She is often disappointed. Mozambican football is not what it was when Eusébio and his contemporaries were playing for Sporting de Lourenço Marques in the late 1950s, and Desportivo seldom make the later stages of the African club competitions that offer the most exotic away trips. Gina follows the national team, too, which guarantees some interesting voyages: north, to Tanzania or Malawi; west, around the Vumba mountains into Zimbabwe; or south into Swaziland or South Africa. Here, too, the journey and the dressing-up can seem more gratifying than the event. Mozambique rarely qualify for the finals of the African Cup of Nations, never for a World Cup. But Gina goes to support, though thick and through thin. 'I love it too much, this game,' she sighs, examining her elaborate costume. She travels to back her team and to draw attention to herself, to perform, just as her 11 favourites are performing for her on the pitch.

Among her various robes, the garment with the brightest colours is the one that marks her allegiance. It is a huge flag, five foot by two foot. Mozambique has an especially striking flag, wide horizontal stripes of dark green, black and red, separated by narrow channels of white. At the hoist, there's a red triangle into which are packed symbols of the country's recent history and its aspirations. There's the shape of a book, its white pages opened, framed by a big yellow star; superimposed on top are the black silhouettes of a hoe and a Kalashnikov sub-machine gun. Gina Matessane will set off well armed. She ties the cords of her large flag loosely around her neck. On top of the flag, Gina puts on a cloak made of animal skin, its fur a little worn in patches. She is now ready for the hat, a round half-sphere of stitched pale leather, into which have been sewn the tops of two curved horns of a Sanga cow, the cattle whose throats sag in low flaps of skin and whose horns can measure two feet long. Gina's horns reach up above her head about six inches, to form two-thirds of a crescent. It looks rather like a Viking helmet, although the overall effect of the costume, the ghostly make up, the hides, make her look something like an inyanga, a traditional healer in her part of the world. That effect, she laughs, is incidental. Gina reckons preparing herself for a match can take up to four hours. It sounds an exaggeration, but what with the black nail varnish that needs to dry, perhaps it does. There are rituals to be honoured, details to be remembered. And the tour de force is still to come. It's getting her companions into line that takes up most of the time.

The most unusual part of Gina's outfit is stored not in a wardrobe but a cage. It is her own little aviary, where her two live doves are kept. Hat on, robes tied, she attaches a string of just under a yard long to one of the legs of each bird, knots it tightly, just above the claw. The other end of each cord is then wrapped around her heavily bangled, beaded and braceleted wrists. One of the doves is jet black, the other virginal white. When they flutter up onto her shoulders or her hat, she looks like she's a puppet, being controlled from above. To sit too close to Gina Matessane at a match is to risk moments of alarm, white feathers or a black beak suddenly at your face. Though the birds calm and coo to Gina's touch, amid the applause, the song and the exclamations of a crowd, they flap their wings and dart this way and that. And when Desportivo attack, Gina ululates, raising her arms into the air, inviting her fellow, feathered travellers a little closer to the sky. As they fly in their small, haphazard circles, Gina Matessane looks like she might be carried up with them, the Mary Poppins of Maputo.

Africa puts obstacles in the way of travelling fans: distance, expense, bad roads and a shortage of long-distance trains. So some of those who do go far, like Gina, want to make the most of it, draw attention to themselves, become part of the show. Some start to belong to the team, portable cheerleaders, griots for the modern age. Ghana had a jester-cum-praise-singer who called himself Ajax Bukana when their national team began to conquer the continent. He wore outsized shoes, like a clown, had prominent and irregular teeth and was once arrested in Liberia where, travelling with the squad, he had been taken for a sorcerer. Some countries carry with them a sound to know them by instantly, like Nigeria's trumpets, tubas and trombones. You encounter a lot of unlikely creatures, too, wilder than Gina Matessane's doves. Nowhere else does the meeting of nations trail such a carriage of nicknames, such an expansive shorthand of birds and beasts. When Gina follows the Mozambique national side, she is supporting the Mambas, suspending for 90 minutes the knowledge that there is little venom in their bite. Two dozen of Africa's national teams have taken on animals as emblems for their teams, and for many, the monikers are used more widely than the name of the country. Ivory Coast are the Elephants. To be in Abidjan during any outing of the national team is to witness on television an endless parade of music videos featuring the bellowing roar of the great pachyderm as part of the chorus. Mention the Super Eagles, and the term needs no glossing for Nigerians, even if they spent years settling on the right sobriquet for their national XI: the Super Eagles used to be the Green Eagles, who were once the Red Devils. With maturity, a nickname can breed. Nigeria's under-17s are the Golden Eaglets. So Ghana's under-23 side are the Black Meteors, their under-20s the Black Satellites, their under-17s, the Black Starlets, the first XI having established themselves firmly in the popular solar system as the Black Stars.

In the north, where the mightier mammals of real-life wildlife tend to be scarcer, names honour geography and history. Egypt are the Pharoahs, Tunisia the Eagles of Carthage; Algeria, with its vast share of the Sahara, call themselves the Desert Foxes. Morocco are the Atlas Lions, though by no means the only kings of the plains. Senegal are Lions, Cameroon Indomitable Lions, christened in the early 1970s, occasionally called to answer for their presumption. 'Indomitable Lions,' the commentator Peter Essoka broadcast to the nation at one sad defeat, 'you have shamed the name.' The Democratic Republic of Congo, formerly Zaïre, are the Leopards. But to call yourself a devastating hunter cannot on its own inspire predatory excellence. Lesotho go by the term The Crocodiles: they seldom frighten when they bare their teeth. More comfortable with their nicknames are the not-so-heavyweight football nations who strive not for might but stealth. Gambia go by the sign of the Scorpions, as do the island footballers of Madagascar's national squad. Benin's Squirrels have recently done well by their zoomorphic choice: the squirrel may be small but he climbs fast. Benin, a narrow strip of West Africa, had never reached an African Nations Cup finals in the 20th century; qualifying for the tournament both in 2004 and 2008 showed how nimbly they have scuttled up the boughs of the continent's hierarchy. Rwanda, The Wasps, also made their first incisions on the final stages of a Nations Cup in 2004.

Grace is as attractive an aspiration as aggression. Angola, the Palancas Negras, take their moniker from the dark sable antelope, Botswana from the zebra. Burkina Faso are stallions. Animals roam domestic leagues, like Thohoyandou's Black Leopards in South Africa or Venomous Vipers of Ghana, partners in the enduring Cape Coast derby against Mysterious Dwarves. Club football in Africa is dotted with names that identify something far beyond locale. In several southern African countries, there is a Naughty Boys FC. One of Swaziland's more successful clubs is Eleven Men in Flight. Under the right circumstances, an African club competition could one day bring them a tie with Mali's Eleven Creators, or Ghana's Eleven Wise of Sekondi. The best names are a handy tool for fans dressing up in manes, wings or leopard skins, and for broadcasters. 'In African football, a squirrel can maul a lion and an eagle can frighten an elephant,' the Ghanaian commentator Michael Oti Adjei likes to tell his listeners.

The chameleon has a habit of cropping up in surprising places, too. Nature's cleverest reptile found its way to the 2006 World Cup in the Black Stars' talented midfield when Ghana's poet laureate, Atukwei Okai, composed a long epic in praise of the squad. Of their best footballer, he exhorted: 'Michael Essien! Swing your chameleonic foot!' The image is provocative: appreciators of Essien's dynamic football for the English club Chelsea tend to emphasise his stamina, his muscular power and his drive. Here, he was being admired for something quite distinct, less monochrome, but an equally important aspect of a very fine player's game: his stealth, his precise footwork, his versatility and perhaps something of the bulbous-eyed chameleon's amazing peripheral vision. Zama Masondo would forgive the breach of copyright.

CHAPTER FOUR

LEOPARDS SKINNED

Freedom from colonial rule set challenges for Africa, and they piled up quickly and suddenly. New states defining themselves within arbitrary borders found the national sport could genuinely unify, and it could mobilise. Leaders saw that to back football generously might be helpful to the image. Back it successfully, and a reflected glory was there for basking in.

In the most arduous struggles against minority, settler rule, football had often made a useful ally. Ahmed Ben Bella, the first head of state of an independent Algeria was never offended when the curiosity that he had once played for the distinguished French club Olympique Marseille was noted on his curriculum vitae, nor to add that he might have continued there were the overthrow of colonialism not his chief priority until 1962. The same year, the president of South Africa's African National Congress, the Nobel Peace Prize winner Albert Luthuli published his influential – and banned – autobiography. He identified a symptom of his young, firebrand years: 'The streak of fierce fanaticism which is looked for in presidents of the ANC showed itself in one way even then – I became a fanatical football fan. To this day I am carried away by the excitement of a soccer match. And I confess that when I watch matches between white South Africans and visiting teams I invariably want the foreigners to win. So do other Africans. I think that what had attracted me as much as the game has been the opportunity to meet all sorts of people, from the loftiest to the most disreputable.' His last observation applied to much of the continent. The football developed by Africans was largely urban, but it was inclusive, spread across class.

So a man like Benjamin Nnamdi Azikiwe, product of a privileged education, shrewd politician, media mogul, and future leader of a free Nigeria could seem just as proud of being a 'self-made soccerist' as he phrased it in his memoirs. The sport bequeathed its own nobility. 'In general,' wrote Azikiwe, 'politicians who have at some time participated in team sports like football tend in their political roles to be more fair and reasonable.' Azikiwe was born in northern Nigeria just after the turn of the 20th century, and had lived among the vast country's three largest groups, Hausas, Igbos and Yorubas by his early teens. He was enrolled at Lagos' Wesleyan Boys High School during the First World War, and spent much of his free time in 'open spaces, played football with mango seeds, limes or oranges or old tennis balls.' At 19 he joined Diamond Football Club, and won the Lagos league. Encouraged by his father, a civil servant, he went to university in the United States, travelled to Britain and then to Ghana to set up the first of his several West African newspapers, in whose columns subtle and not-so-subtle agendas would be shaped for a future beyond the rule of the British.

Returning to Nigeria shortly before the Second World War, Azikiwe, or 'Zik', became strongly persuaded of sport's capacity to bring together Nigerians. He recalls being turned down for membership of the Yoruba Tennis Club because he was Igbo. So he set up an alternative, Zik's Athletic Club, ZAC, funded by his newspaper group and by members' subscriptions. ZAC centres became hubs of sporting and social activity, soon had branches across Nigeria, and fielded strong football teams in the major cities, especially Lagos, where the league soon had to accommodate ZAC first and second XIs, or 'Bombers' and 'Spitfires' as they were known to their supporters, who watched them in their thousands. For the founder, the Bombers and Spitfires were there to be celebrated as teams who opened their doors to any player, no matter where he came from, but also as pathfinders for a sophisticated, captivating sort of football. 'When the ZAC machinery began to operate,' Azikiwe recorded with a flourish, 'spectators were treated to scientific soccer technique.' Opponents, he purred, 'could not resist the tactics of the ZAC.'

Where there was a crowd, there was a potential political audience. Azikiwe had known some confrontations with the British governors of Nigeria for his editorials and his speeches. They recognised a populist. So when he sought permission for a football tour of the nation by his crack ZAC Lagos team for the purpose of raising funds for the Allied war effort in 1941, they granted it, ensuring he would be under careful scrutiny. Azikiwe's motives were several. His ZAC footballers would gather Nigerians at matches in numbers in various cities. He would combine the event with a party or a dance and he would address those who were there. He would talk about the necessity of a European war – in which Nigerians were implicated as members of a British dominion and in tens of thousands of cases as soldiers – because of the evils and racism of Nazism. Soon enough, though, his lectures would slip gently into stressing the need for a people to enjoy freedom and sovereignty. They were essentially anti-colonial, under the mask of support for the Empire's most urgent challenge. And his speeches were studiously dotted with sporting metaphors, references to fair play. When ZAC played the Army team in Port Harcourt, he praised 'the spirit of inter-racial fellowship carried into the realm of sports.' The tour was inclusive, joyous, the matches events to be at. As for the parties afterwards, some 'featured a bevy of attractive ladies dressed in high Parisian fashion.' The enterprise also confirmed a developed football culture across the north, south, east and west in Nigeria. Not all listened with absolute attention when Azikiwe, the ringmaster, told them Nigeria should prepare for independence 'within 15 years', but many would applaud him, when after the British withdrew in 1960, Zik, the keen and talented former amateur footballer, became Nigeria's first president.

Most of West Africa gained its independence in the same year, preceded by Ghana in 1957; and by Guinea, whom the French granted its independence in 1958, two years before releasing their grip on Senegal, Ivory Coast, Mali, Upper Volta, Dahomey, Togo, Mauritania, Niger, Chad, Cameroon, Congo-Brazzaville and the Central African Republic. They enthusiastically took each other on at sport. Ghana played Nigeria for the Azikiwe trophy and by the mid-1960s, free Africa's leading clubs were competing in a continental competition for the Kwame Nkrumah trophy, named after Ghana's first head of state. In the 1970s, a new piece of silverware was being presented to its winner, this one bearing the name Ahmed Sekou Touré, president of Guinea. These were presidents who wanted their stamp on the continent's premier passion, some of the first to power of Africa's so-called Big Men, big on theory, big on national symbols, big on self-projection.

In football, a modern, progressive, stylish Africa could show itself off. Nkrumah thought so. He had studied at the same university in America as Nigeria's Azikiwe, had not been as much of an active sportsman, but on gaining the leadership of Ghana, quickly identified sport as a vehicle for uniting the disparate peoples of a country whose boundaries had been drawn up with little regard for ethnic and religious difference. In the old Gold Coast, as Ghana was known before independence, clubs had developed with a distinct, tribal or regional identity; Asante Kotoko among the Asante, Hearts of Oak in and around Accra, Mysterious Dwarves and Venomous Vipers at Cape Coast. In Nkrumah's Ghana, a new superclub would be established just after independence. They took the name Real Republicans, and set about collecting the best footballers from around the country, greatly to the resentment of Hearts, Kotoko and the others who found their resources plundered. Real Republicans would be a short-lived, artificial experiment – they won just one championship – but provided a prototype for what would become a dominant national team.

Nkrumah took a close personal interest in Ghana's Black Stars, as Dr William Narteh, a historian, explained to me one afternoon in his office in the University of Ghana in Legon. The Black Stars are his specialist subject, to which he brings an academic eye, and like many Ghanaians looking back over half a century of independence, an unashamed nostalgia for the country's first leader and a firm set of opinions. 'Nkrumah saw the game of football very early as one of the mediums through which to bring changes, whether it was in local politics or national politics,' Narteh says. 'He took very good care of the teams, the organisation, their wellbeing, regular income. If you were playing football you were attached to a particular company so that the players who were in the national team and may be away for months at a time had that support. Nkrumah would call the players to the seat of government before a major tournament and his message was about projecting values, humanity, and always that "You can do it." A lot of African countries were then still under colonial rule, he wanted to project the idea of black power, that "What they can do, we as blacks can also do". He wanted the players to have a feel about what was happening in other countries. He made sure they felt the presence of the head of state with them. Nkrumah was held in high regard but you can see in the photographs, he was also close to them, quite tactile, putting a hand on their shoulders.'

Narteh has collected hundreds of photographs from the years after independence. What makes him most wistful, leafing through the line-ups of the Ghana national XIs are not the quaint tweed caps worn by the charismatic goalkeeper, Robert Mensah, nor the density of the crowds packed into the stands with tops of acacia trees in the background, but the size of the logos on their breasts. The black star on the 1950s and 60s jerseys sometimes stretched halfway across a ribcage. 'You look there and you see how the black star is significant. I'm very disappointed that in the national team jersey we wore at the African Nations Cup in 2008 you don't find anything that says "Black Stars".' Where other national teams would call themselves after beasts, Ghana had seized on a most evocative name for West Africans. The Black Star recalls the shipping line formed by Marcus Garvey, the Jamaican father of Pan-Africanism to connect the Americas to Africa, symbolically to undo the wrongs of slavery. 'The Jewish nation has its Star of David, Islamic nations have the Crescent,' says Dr Narteh. 'In the Pan-Africanist struggle we have the Black Star. We believed in the star of Africa, part of the African family worldwide and we should not forget it. It is not propaganda. It is the means by which we keep our people abreast of issues. We rally around it. Our team should be a team with a deep philosophy behind it.'

Ghana wanted a team with dash and flair. They invited the most famous footballer in Britain, the first European Footballer of the Year, Stanley Matthews, to join the 1957 independence festivities, his duties to dress up in a robe of finest kente cloth and sit on a throne designed for his coronation as the 'Soccerthene', the monarch-in-chief of football. Ghana's players were told to learn from Matthews how to play a more 'scientific' football, the same phrase Azikiwe had used with such pride of his ZAC Bombers in Nigeria a decade and a half earlier. The sport would be a branch of learning, with a clear job to do in the advancing of free Africa, along with their centrally planned economies and the battle against tribalism.

Though the French and British influence remained strong, Africa would now look elsewhere for its models. Matthews, who began a long and affectionate relationship with Africa after his first visit to Ghana, might quietly have advised them to seek inspiration from places other than Britain for state-of-the-art football in the 1950s. They did. The Black Stars played tour matches against Real Madrid, the European champions, and went to Germany, home of the world champions. They so liked their trip to Hungary, a place then associated strongly with vanguard tactics, they invited a Hungarian, Josef Ember to take over as their guide. Their principal mission was to flex their muscles in Africa. A Gold Coast-Nigeria rivalry on the field had began to establish itself even before independence. In 1955, the smaller of the nations walloped the larger 7-0 and made enduring heroes of the Ghanaian strikers CK Gyamfi and Baba Yara. Nigeria and Ghana squared up in the qualifiers for the 1962 World Cup, Zik's new republic against Nkrumah's: forty thousand Ghanaians whooped over a 4-1 win in Accra. The duel took on a yin-and-yang quality: Ghana accumulated twice as many African Nations Cup triumphs as Nigeria before the turn of the millennium; yet Nigeria reached three World Cups before Ghana made it to their first. The enmity accumulated grudge and nuance. A full 50 years after Ghanaian independence, you could watch the Black Stars play the Super Eagles on a biting, cold night in Brentford, West London and hear Nigerians use cat-calls dating back to the 1970s at their fellow West African émigrés. 'Ghana, Go Home!' jeered Nigerian fans, remembering the aggressive slogans of an epoch when Ghanaian economic migrants flowed into oil-rich Nigeria.

■ ■ ■

When the African Cup of Nations took place in West Africa for the first time in 1963, the cogs behind the Black Stars' 'scientific' machine were engaging smoothly. Ghana hosted five other competitors in a tournament gradually reflecting the diversity of the continent. Savvy, experienced Egypt had won the first two Nations Cups. Ethiopia, featuring the Italian-Eritrean Vassalo brothers, arrived as defending champions. Nigeria sent a team, and Ghana, stronger and seemingly fitter, beat Sudan 3-0 in the final. Names were made, nicknames inscribed in the consciousness: Wilberforce 'Netbreaker' Mfum, the centre-forward with gelignite in his boots; his partner in attack, Edward 'Sputnik Shot' Acquah; Ofei Dodoo, aka 'Little Bird', provider of much of Mfum's ammunition from midfield; Edward Aggrey Fynn, the lean central defender, called 'The Professor', master of the geometric pass, graduate in the 'science' to which the Black Stars aspired. Their head coach was popular, too. CK Gyamfi, the goalscorer whose career had peaked at the time of independence and who had been taken on by the German club Fortuna Düsseldorf, proved an admired leader, and a keen student of strategies. Gyamfi led the Black Stars to the Tokyo Olympics in 1964, and after a trip to South America, decided that for Ghanaian football, Brazil should provide the template for African footballers who liked to improvise and dwell on the ball. The Black Stars, with a distinct 4-2-4 formation defended their continental title the next year in Tunisia, champions defeating hosts in the final.

Club football, and the Nkrumah trophy, would give French-speaking Africa its first chance to shine, post-independence. Ghana hosted the semi-finals and final of the opening, 1965 Champions Cup and discovered that home advantage could take you so far but was no guarantee of the right result. Nkrumah's project, the Real Republicans, were knocked out by the eventual winners, Cameroon's Oryx Douala. A Malian club, featuring a teenaged Salif Keita, star of the future, reached the final. Keita played for Real Bamako in the next final, too, before absconding to Europe in secret because the Mali authorities took a dim view of a national sporting treasure serving an audience other than his compatriots. Other states would ban footballers from playing professionally in Europe: like Zaïre, where Africa's most notorious 'Big Man' president, Mobutu Sese Seko even discouraged European Christian names in line with his programme of 'authenticity', and at the same time altered the national XI's nickname from Lions to Leopards. By the early 1970s, with the best footballers corralled at home, the Zaïrois clubs had become true heavyweights: Tout-Puissant Engelbert, of Lubumbashi, won the Champions Cup in successive years, 1969 and 1970; AS Vita Club, of Kinshasa, seized the same prize in December 1973.

They growled at visitors. Zaïre became a genuinely threatening place for away sides. Ghanaian teams – national and club sides – shared some epic confrontations with Zaïrois XIs in the late 1960s and early 1970s. A young Brazilian, Carlos Alberto Parreira, had been hired as coach of Asante Kotoko and the Black Stars at the time, and recalls how the Zaïrois president made his own martial presence felt. 'We would go in to the stadium in Kinshasa and it would have been packed with what seemed liked 90,000 or 100,000 people for hours before the start,' recalls Parreira, 'and then armoured cars would roll in and circle around the athletics track outside the pitch, with Mobutu in the central one, waving to the crowd, with the guards pointing guns. It was scary, especially when they seemed to all start shouting "Mercenary! Mercenary!" at me, who stood out as a foreigner.'

■ ■ ■

One very special foreigner was much taken with Zaïre during one of his frequent trips to Africa. Muhammad Ali, the charismatic heavyweight boxer, had been passing through Cairo during the 1974 African Cup of Nations and as he watched the winning team, The Leopards, he had the idea put to him by an enterprising journalist that he might come to fight in the land of these football champions. At least that's one version of how the year's most hyped sporting event, The Rumble in the Jungle, Ali versus George Foreman, in Kinshasa in October, came about: that it was inspired by the Leopards of Zaïre.

President Mobutu would shower attention on Ali and the big boxing match later in the year. First, he was keen to get involved in what would become a landmark episode in Africa's World Cup odyssey. Mobutu, a former sports journalist before his rise through the military to the nation's leadership, via a coup, made quite a fuss of the African champions. The players attended a solemn state function to receive medals annointing them Chanceliers de l'Ordre National. Adelard Mayanga, the skilful striker from that side, keeps a photograph of the ceremony, showing the player wearing a pair of outsized, modish sunglasses as a General Lundula pins a medal to his lapel. Meanwhile, the tailors were getting to work on what would be a fetching set of jerseys for their World Cup adventure that June. Zaïre would not wear their crests modestly in a corner of their chests. Emblazoned across the fronts of their yellow or bright green shirts would be printed a life-size face of a leopard, the word 'Leopards' in a crescent above it, and the name of the country bold and in capitals below. Just as their president was creating his own iconic look, with his leopard-skin hat and his ornate sceptre, there would be no mistaking where this team came from.

Mobutu's pleasure at overseeing the departure of the first black African squad to a World Cup would be abundantly clear to all the players. On the eve of the last decisive qualifier, against Morocco, the squad received an invitation to meet Mobutu aboard the president's spectacularly ostentatious steamer on the Zaïre River. 'We spent the whole evening with him,' recalls Mayanga, 'and it was so he could give us personal motivation to win the game. He promised each of us a villa, a car, and a trip for our whole families to anywhere in the world. And some of it he did, when we had won. I still have the house, not a huge one, up in the hills. And we got the car. But the trip abroad never happened. It seems the money for that disappeared.' Mayanga raises his eyebrows: 'I should say, it disappeared, as usual.' Mobutu's patronage had a price. For some time, Zaïre's best footballer had been forbidden by the state to play professionally overseas. 'We were amateurs,' recalls Mayanga, 'but we had been given this mentality that we should play for the love of the country. We did feel that. When we lost, I saw players in tears because they had let down the people, or disappointed our bosses. It was Mobutu who put that mentality into us.'

Muhammad Ali had applauded Zaïre at the Nations Cup, and, in spite of some controversial refereeing decisions in their favour, The Leopards had qualified for the World Cup in West Germany thanks to some strong individual talents. Mayanga was a slick enough dribbler and distributor of the ball to be nicknamed 'The Brazilian'; he had what he describes as an 'all-terrain stamina'. That got him another term of popular endearment: 'Goodyear', after the tyres. Up front with him would be an excellent finisher. Mulamba Ndaye had set a longstanding record in Cairo for the Nations Cup, scoring nine goals in the tournament.

Compromising the commitment to 'authenticity', Zaïre had taken on an outsider as head coach, Blagoje Vidinić, the Yugoslav who was already an old Africa hand. In the months ahead of the expedition to West Germany, Vidinić detected flaws, particularly in their defence: at the Nations Cup, they conceded goals in every game except the replay of the final. Drawn in a group for the World Cup finals with Scotland, Vidinić's native Yugoslavia and the world champions Brazil, Zaïre would be tested. The Scotland manager Willie Ormond declared after seeing Zaïre in Egypt that he would expect his team to defeat the Leopards 'by five goals'.

While insisting they took up no offers to play professionally for clubs abroad, the Zaïrois authorities had worked on making the Leopards more worldly. There had been a tour to Brazil. Friendlies against European club sides had been organised in the weeks ahead of the World Cup. Before that, they retreated into the wilds to begin preparations, to the hauntingly beautiful Lake Kivu national park, with its views of the Virunga mountains. Established as an exclusive resort under the Belgians, to view rare wildlife, the park was an idyll. For the footballing Leopards, it would be a place to bond. 'There was a competitive element between us,' recalls Mayanga, 'between those from Lubumbashi and from Kinshasa, who had a real rivalry through their clubs, Tout-Puissant and AS club. But as a national team we'd mostly been together since the beginning of about 1971. One of Vidinić's great strengths was that he had been able to make us a like a big family over those four years. Mostly, that's how we were…until the problems started in Germany.' Zaïre played warm-up matches in Italy and in Switzerland. 'Some went quite well,' says Mayanga, 'but we found the training very hard, very intense. There had been some fatigue after the Nations Cup and now we were training three times a day.' In interviews with European newspapers already intrigued by the most exotic World Cup ever – 1974 had Zaïre, it also had Haiti – Vidinić began to talk about the naivety of his players. He retained their confidence, as far as Mayanga was concerned – 'he made me the player I was and we looked up to him' – and Vidinić sensed the pressure building upon them from the powers-that-be. Zaïre's delegation to Germany would be famously numerous, the state heavily represented among them. Vidinić found he needed to forbid Mobutu's Sports Minister and his entourage from entering the dressing-rooms. Alas, it was beyond his authority to prevent some members of the delegation helping themselves to money set aside for the players, an issue that would cloud the lead-up to the second, disastrous match against Yugoslavia.

Zaïre scored no goals at their first and only World Cup. They conceded 14 in their three games. They had their most effective centre-forward, Ndaye, banned for more than half the tournament. They would commit one of the most notorious infringements of the rules in the World Cup's history. Yet, for all that, they actually began the adventure quite promisingly. At the end of the 2-0 defeat to Scotland in Dortmund, Ormond, the victorious Scotland manager, acknowledged it had been harder than he expected. *The Times'* Geoffrey Green gushed: 'Zaïre were an eye-opener. Their movements are snaky, they have a low centre of gravity, and their control is on the ground, with the accent always on attack, as fresh as a summer breeze on a lovely summer night.' A warm evening it was, and an unexpectedly dark one for the five second-half minutes when the floodlights in the Westfalenstadion failed. By then Scotland were tiring, Ormond thought, while Zaïre's stamina surprised him. Mayanga recalls a penalty appeal to which 'the referee closed his eyes' and a chance 'Goodyear' himself had allowed Scotland's goalkeeper David Harvey to retrieve. The Scots scored their goals either side of the half-hour, through a Peter Lorimer shot and a header from Joe Jordan. 'We were weak in aerial duels and that, basically, was the difference,' believes Mayanga.

Back at the hotel in the village of Ascheberg, the players learned the cost of defeat. Mayanga: 'Now we were straight into the administrative problems. Before the Scotland game, the authorities told us, "Go out and play and, even if you lose, and lose honourably, we'll give you your bonuses." We never saw them. We were disappointed with the score but everybody was saying we gave a good account of ourselves. I think the arguments were behind the loss of motivation for the next game.' Indeed, there had been talk of a players' strike, which would have been foolhardy.

Where to start with the Yugoslavia debacle? Not with Mayanga. He had been dropped. 'Goodyear' felt utterly flattened, dismayed. But after watching from the substitutes' bench, he was entitled to think, after 23 minutes, his exclusion was an act of mercy. Yugoslavia had scored four times. Worse, Ndaye had been sent off, in a case of mistaken identity, punished for the defender Mwepu Ilunga's aggressive berating of referee Omar Delgado. Worse still, Vidinić was by then running out of attacking alternatives, having substituted goalkeeper Mwamba Kazadi, picked out as 'excellent' by Ormond in the previous match and hard to blame for either of the first three Yugoslav goals. His replacement, Dimbi Tubilandu, had barely entered the field when Zaïre let in their fourth.

In the press and radio booths in Gelsenkirchen's Parkstadion, and via radio trottoir in the cities of central Africa, conspiracy theories sprang up: that Vidinić, by dropping Mayanga and replacing him with a midfielder still bandaged from a previous injury, had purposefully weakened the team because he wanted his native Yugoslavia to win and boost their goal-difference; that Vidinić had bowed to pressure from a senior, pushy Mobutu crony who had a preference for Tubilandu, the goalkeeper from AS Vita Club of Kinshasa, over Kazadi, from Lubumbashi's Tout-Puissant. A reputed seer, one Mama Tuseya, had ahead of the match forecast a 'small accident, which will be the sacrifice the gods of victory need for Zaïre to win'. This was no accident, it was catastrophic. A dark theory gained currency: that the players had stopped trying because they felt ripped-off by their bosses.

By the time Vidinić told Mayanga to join in the action at the interval, the score stood at 6-0. 'I'm not a psychologist,' says Mayanga, 'but at half-time I thought the coach was a bit distracted. He had changed the line up and it was turning into our worst game. He had taken off Kazadi, who was a good goalkeeper, and put in Tubilandu, who was 5ft 4in tall against these six-foot-plus Yugoslav forwards. The poor goalkeeper! We were static on the field, the defenders were nervous, our marking wasn't up to standard, our clearances were poor, we hadn't had any clear chances. We had really shown our amateurism. But you also have to remember Yugoslavia were one of the best teams of the era.' By the end the consolation was only that the Africans avoided double-figures. Final score: Yugoslavia 9, Zaïre 0.

Could the World Cup turn any more humiliating? For one man, it would. The moment that would forever be taken as the epitome of a clumsy, jarring, unworldy debut of sub-Saharan Africa at the great festival of football was still to come, the incident that would seem to spell out the Leopards' lack of stealth. Its perpetrator, Mwepu Ilunga ought never to have been on the field in the final match against Brazil, Ndaye having received the card against Yugoslavia that should have been Ilunga's. Ilunga knew better, too, than to respond to what he saw as Brazilian procrastination over the taking of a late free-kick a little way outside the Leopards' penalty area by advancing from the six-man defensive wall and whacking the dead ball as a bemused Jairzinho and Roberto Rivelino prepared to address it. He had broken the rules embarrassingly. Brazil led 3-0 by then, and the South Americans were awarded a free-kick and the chance to make it four. Ilunga lurched from the wall in the 85th minute, belting the ball from its designated spot. He collected a caution. But, he felt and would later explain, he had wasted some valuable seconds. Why? Because it had been made clear, from the very, very top, to the players that a greater margin than three goals would be deemed unacceptable back home. Mayanga describes the pressure brought to bear on the Zaïre players even when they knew their tournament was over after two defeats from two matches. 'They said to us the Brazil match was about honour. We had to come out with honour: three goals or less. Vidinić told us to go and enjoy it, that it would be his last game with us, and that Brazil played the same style as we did so we had a chance to show something. We didn't play badly, actually. Better, I think, than we had against Scotland.'

The homecoming would feel eerie, set next to the lavish send-off a few weeks earlier. 'There certainly wasn't such a big crowd at Kinshasa airport,' reflects Mayanga. 'People had believed that as the best team in Africa we would be one of the best in the world. People just looked at us sadly. They asked: "How did it happen? How come we lost?". We had to give answers to reporters and their questions were severe. We had to explain that up against high-level professionals, we couldn't, unfortunately, match them.' Then the summons arrived, not so much an invitation as a rounding-up. Across the airwaves it was announced that the 22 squad members were required to appear at a specified time before President Mobutu Sese Seko Nkuku Ngbendu wa za Banga. The call-up came publicly so that all Zaïrois knew the defeated Leopards would have to answer, in person, before – to translate Mobutu's full title – 'The Warrior Who Knows No Setback Because of his Enduring, Inflexible Will and Whose Power Spreads Fire as he Conquers All'. 'All the players heard about it on the radio, or via television,' recalls Mayanga. 'It was the day after we got back. The instruction was that we had to meet at his private office. He didn't shout, but he was absolutely firm. He told us: "I gather that certain players, rather than wanting to honour the pride of the nation, are thinking about transfers abroad. I can tell you all now that you are *not* going to be like the Senegalese, the Ivorians, the Cameroonians who go and play overseas!" We understood because, standing there in front of us, he was really furious. Of course we didn't talk about the bonuses. To this day, they still have not been paid. We were frightened. Personally, I felt threatened.'

Over time, it was as if the World Cup story of the 1974 Leopards was to be gradually erased, purged from Zaïre's history. The country never made it to another World Cup, would not even win another Nations Cup. With Mobutu's flight, overthrown in 1997, the country renamed itself the Democratic Republic of Congo. Many of its former football stars had long since left, part of a massive diaspora. In common with many exiles of a certain age, Adelard Mayanga has had a home in Belgium for some 25 years, his memories kept sharp by the company of Congolese contemporaries who have turned a district of Brussels, known as the Matonge, into a Kinshasa-in-exile. There you easily find a nostalgia for the 1970s, hear Zaïrois music from the era, and on the walls of a photocopy shop, see posters of the 1973 AS Vita Club team, the 1974 Leopards. There in his canary-yellow shirt, with the green Leopard's face, is pictured Mwepu Ilunga, he of the infamous dash from the defensive wall. Ilunga, who knew the rules better than most people imagined, has held various coaching posts in the Congolese Football Federation.

Others have had extraordinary escapades. Mayanga's Vita colleague Mafuila 'Ricky' Mavuba would live through fraught years and leave an unusual legacy to football. Married to an Angolan, Mavuba and his pregnant wife fled the war in Angola in the 1980s by boat. Their son, Rio, was born at sea. They found their way to France, for whom Rio became an international footballer in his late teens. As for Mulamba Ndaye, the record-breaking goalscorer, it was announced by the Confederation of African Football in 1998 that he had died. The news reached a surprised Ndaye in South Africa. He had *nearly* died, he explained, pointing to bullet wounds in his leg when robbers attacked him in Kinshasa stealing commemorative medals among other valuables. He fled all the way to Cape Town, where he was scraping a living ushering shoppers into car parking places, for a few rands in tips.

■ ■ ■

Besides Mobutu, others from Africa's cast of 'Big Men' leaders flirted with football. Uganda's brutal Idi Amin had a preference for boxing – he had been the country's light-heavyweight champion during British rule – but actively pushed the national XI to what would be its highest peak in an otherwise undistinguished record: Uganda narrowly lost the 1978 Nations Cup final to Ghana. But no one talked a better game, at greater length and in such detail, as the Guinea head of state, Sekou Touré. By the mid-1970s, the personality cult created around Guinea's Supreme Leader of the Revolution extended to celebrating his poetry, his invincibility and his peerless expertise in football strategy.

Just as his friend and ally Nkrumah had done with the Real Republicans club in Ghana, Sekou Touré supervised the creation of a national superclub, Hafia. In his one-party state, football provided a corollary: a league where only one team was likely ever to win. All the best Guinean players were corralled at Hafia. Guinea and Hafia played some enchanting football, according to the press reports of the time and not just those in the loyalist newspaper *Horoya*. They passed the ball neatly and quickly and looked for finesse from a trio of swift attacking talents: Maxime Camara, 'Petit' Sory, and Alioune Keita. Their main asset, though, was the creative intelligence of Cherif Souleymane, whose instinctive reading of the game and excellent peripheral vision marked him out. When Guinea qualified for the Mexico Olympics in 1968, the Spanish-language media hailed Souleymane: 'El Crack de los Juegos', the Hotshot of the Games. Driven by their commitment to attacking football, Guinea could also be loose and inconsistent. 'Our defence is not as good as our attack,' the striker Sory reflected at the All Africa Games of 1973, where they lost the final to Nigeria, a match conspicuous for the zip of the Guinean forwards and the hardness of their backs: two Nigerians had retired injured before half-time. So when a different type of defender like Djibril Diarra emerged on the Guinean scene, with a confident touch allied to his muscular physique, he drew special admiration. He was nicknamed 'Beckenbauer.' The forward Maxime Camara would be otherwise honoured. He entered Sekou Touré's cabinet after retiring as a player. The Guinean president had become his father-in-law.

Wise move. It was clear that, if you were a Guinean footballer, pleasing the father of the nation was a sensible idea. Hafia did so spectacularly in 1972, 1975 and 1977, winning the Champions Cup. As for the national XI, Guinea distinguished themselves under the beating sun at the 1976 Nations Cup in Ethiopia, though an experimental format for that year's competition would work against them. Instead of a final, the medals were decided by a round-robin system, and a draw between a more conservative Morocco and the flamboyant Guinea meant gold for the North Africans and silver for the Guineans. Sekou Touré praised the squad nonetheless on their return to Conakry: 'You have shown a character that everybody else admires and respects,' he told the players. By the year's end his tune had changed. When Hafia lost the Champions Cup final to Mouloudia of Algeria on penalties, the homecoming would be terrifying. The defeated players were incarcerated for several days in one of Guinea's grim, torture-house prisons and roughed up.

Africa is more democratic now than it was in the 1970s. But there are places you still find the Big Man's props, portraits of the head-of-state hung in the foyer of government buildings, major boulevards bearing his name, and you can still roll-call many of the first fathers of the nation in the names of countries' principal football stadiums. Ivory Coast play home games in Abidjan at the Félix Houphouët-Boigny arena, Senegal in the Léopold Senghor; in Yaoundé, Cameroon use the Ahmadou Ahidjo. And in Liberia, they have the Samuel K Doe stadium in Monrovia. There, one man would show off not only some of the greatest skills ever to emerge in Africa, but the sort of leadership and independence that made him a compelling candidate for the job of head of state.

■ ■ ■

Of the hundreds of goals scored by George Oppong Manneh Weah in his 20-year career, one above all defines a spirit of independence. It was scored in September 1996, the opening weekend of Italy's Serie A season, for the champions of the most glamorous league in the world, Milan. They held a 2-1 lead, nervously going into the last five minutes of the 90. Verona, their visitors, had been awarded a corner just in front of the noisiest sector of milanisti. The ball slung into the Milan penalty area a little heavily, reaching well beyond the far post, dropping just beyond the angle of the six-yard box. There, Weah tamed it in an instant, cushioning the falling ball with the outside of his right foot. He barely looked up. Weah was ready to embark on his mission. A quarter of a minute later, he had scored just about the best goal anybody at San Siro that day had ever seen; he had scored perhaps the greatest goal in elite football for 10 years up to that afternoon and in the decade since; he had scored almost as perfect a virtuoso, one-man goal as could be imagined.

At this stage in his life, Weah was anointed for moments like this. He owned the title World Footballer of the Year, an award made by Fifa and voted by coaches of national teams across the world. He had tenancy of the Ballon D'Or, a prize dating from the 1950s and given to the European Footballer of the Year, except that the definition had just been changed to accommodate players like Weah from outside Europe: to exclude him would have ridiculed the prize. Weah had arrived at Milan, the pre-eminent club in the world, to play at centre-forward. He had contributed substantially to their winning the league in May. He became a darling of the Milan president, Silvio Berlusconi, the prime minister of Italy. He was the most celebrated African footballer of his generation.

The journey from one goalmouth to the other took 14 seconds.

After four, five, six, seven gentle prods, player and ball had reached the halfway line. The clock on the big scoreboard had turned towards five o'clock and the shade cast by the unusual girders that form the tubular stadium's roof had created a vivid chiaroscuro on the grass, so that a shard of sunlight, about three metres wide, stretched from the Verona goal to the centre circle. As Weah burst into it, the black and red of his shirt suddenly brilliant, the white of his shorts, socks and sweatband bright against his skin, three Veronese players regrouped enough to attempt the first intervention. A pair of them prepared a joint ambush. Weah rode both challenges simultaneously with a pirouette through 180 degrees, let the ball run its own course before retrieving it again as if he was picking up a briefcase he had dropped off in a cloakroom. Some 45 metres from the opposite goal, Weah lengthened his stride. His movements until now had been subtle, balletic. Now there was power. He slipped the ball to the left of a defender and, accelerating suddenly, recovered it after passing the Verona man on his right. Arriving at the edge of the Verona penalty area, Weah had left all opponents but the goalkeeper in his wake. He chose to shoot from there, some 18 metres from goal, from an angle made sharper by the advance of the goalkeeper. Weah directed his shot with the instep of his right foot, still accelerating and leaning to his right to gain just enough backlift to arrow it precisely into the bottom corner of the net: 3-1. Over the 85 metres of his safari, no other Milan player had been involved in the move; one Veronese had had slight contact with the ball in an unsuccessful tackle. Weah, in his then hesitant Italian, told reporters the goal had been 'for Italy, for Africa and for Milan.' Eagerly, witnesses ascribed its daring, its absolute individualism as the part that belonged to Africa.

Satellite television beamed the Goal of the Decade to many corners of the earth but, alas, to few Liberians. In Weah's country, the national electricity grid had ceased functioning some years earlier. Nor was the Liberia Telecommunications Corporation, where the 21-year-old Weah had once been employed in a menial job, to be relied on when the Milan superstar sought to share his achievement with family and friends in Monrovia, the capital. Besides, some of his family were dispersed elsewhere. A few months before his wondergoal, Weah had moved several relatives out of the country, following an arson attack on his villa there. The vandals, almost certainly supporters of the warlord president Charles Taylor, had struck just after Weah called for the United Nations to send a force to Liberia to control a slaughter that had claimed 200,000 lives, displaced a million Liberians, turned children, boys and girls, into soldiers and made it one of the most wretched zones of Africa.

Weah was barely in a position to take the vandals on, though his had become a powerful voice in Liberia. No citizen of that country had wider global recognition. Hardly any footballers from Liberia before him had even found work elsewhere. As a very young man Weah left behind Monrovia clubs with warrior names like Young Survivors and Invincible XI to sign a contract in Cameroon, with Tonnerre Yaoundé. He felt homesick at first, isolated, an English speaker bewildered in French-speaking Africa. But of course he scored goals, and, Cameroonian football being one of the leading exporters of players to Europe in the 1980s, was soon recommended to a French coach named Arsène Wenger. Wenger took him to Monaco in the French league on a hunch, though he detected no absolute guarantees in this footballer. He was struck by Weah's athleticism, and a close control honed by a childhood spent anticipating the irregular bounce of worn-out balls on patchy surfaces but was initially concerned by the inconsistency of Weah's shooting. Wenger backed the young West African to work on and improve that part of his game. He also recognised a certain presence. His Monaco colleagues felt it on the morning Weah first walked into the changing rooms, tall, stern, in a long white robe, anything but incognito.

He was unique, too, for being a highly exportable Liberian footballer. Liberia has a very different colonial hinterland from all its neighbours. Alone in sub-Saharan Africa, Liberia had not been colonised by a European state. Nestling on the chin of West Africa's bulging jaw, it stood apart from the French and English territories all around it. Modern Liberia's ties reached across the Atlantic. Some of the clapboard buildings in Monrovia less damaged by the conflict of the 1990s evoke the plantation mansions of the southern states of America. Its patois owes heavily to American English. Its flag is borrowed from the USA, the same stripes, and a single white star on its upper blue quarter, all the legacy of a 19th century experiment that sent freed slaves from America back to this portion of West Africa to govern, to create their own black overclass that would dominate indigenous Liberians for the best part of a century. Still, Liberia could boast of being black Africa's first independent state long before the Europeans withdrew from the continent, though one with little inclination to join in with the hobby that united those vanguard states on the playing field. Young Liberians were more encouraged to take to basketball than football while the Americo-Liberians, the so-called 'Congos', the 20 per cent of the population whose antecedents voyaged from America, held most of the power.

The nation's priorities changed overnight in 1980. George Weah was 14 when his country woke up to learn that president William Tolbert had been murdered in his presidential palace and that the leadership had been seized by Samuel K Doe, a 28-year-old army sergeant. Weah remembers the fall of the regime being welcomed, and that he, a few months earlier, had joined a protest march through the capital over the rising price of rice. 'For the poor, people like us, the coup meant we could live like proper citizens at last,' recalls Weah. 'Before that there were two classes: the privileged and us others. Now we "Natives" could flirt with "Congo" girls without getting in trouble. We could have passports. I remember people dancing in the street.' His own special gift would gradually earn him greater respect than it might have done in previous epochs. Weah had had his wayward years as teenager in an edgy city where marijuana was cheap and days long and underemployed. His football got him noticed, suddenly carried prospects. 'Most Liberians thought of footballers as illiterates with no education,' says Weah. 'When Samuel K Doe came to power, football developed there to turn into a passion. He wanted football to be the popular sport.' The worldly, sage George Weah of his 40s is anxious to stress that he can only look back on the reign of Doe as 'despotic', but that the new president had 'contributed to the democratisation of the sport'. Under Doe, Liberia entered a World Cup qualifying tournament for the first time in 1980. He later financed a training expedition for The Lone Stars, for two months in Brazil, a young Weah, already starring for the Invincible XI, included in the squad.

Weah's rise as an exceptional footballer in the company of Europeans was rapid. He thrived at Monaco, moved to Paris Saint-Germain and then, as the first African since Eusébio to be lauded as the best player on the planet, to Milan. Weah the West African superhero emerged at the same time. The Liberian national team regarded him as their Pied Piper, their guide. En masse, before international fixtures the squad would often visit the home of Emma Klon Jlaleh, the grandmother who had brought up young George, and join her in prayer. In Monaco, Weah persuaded

Wenger to take on half a dozen younger Liberian footballers, some as triallists, some on contracts, some apparently there as much as anything to keep Big George company and support Weah's vocational drive to uplift the standards of 11 Liberians enough to make something of the national side.

Before Weah, Liberia had been a backwater in African football; after Weah, it had a profile. If ever a team revolved around an individual, it was Liberia under Weah. The Lone Stars, as Liberia are known, became an XI of one lone star and 10 satellites revolving around it. If Weah had produced the epitome of a one-man goal for Milan that afternoon against Verona, he was acting the part of soloist with each outing under the flag of his country. Weah was not simply Liberia's captain, but, once earning his high salaries in France and in Italy, he was their patron. Weah would fund the team's travel costs, their kits, their training camps. When Liberia, with a population of just over three million outpaced Ghana (more than 20 million) and came within a point of Nigeria (140 million) in the race to qualify for the 2002 World Cup, Weah provided from his own pocket six-figure bonuses to push the rest of the team towards that fairytale target. Naturally, he scored regularly; but his understanding of the captain's responsibility would sometimes lead him to play in defence, figuring that he, the gifted striker, might do the job better than the mortals assigned at centre-back. Weah had already carried Liberia further than they had ever been. In the year of his Milan wondergoal, 1996, they reached the African Cup of Nations finals for the first time. By the time he neared retirement, after boarding the lucrative circuit of short spells at Chelsea, Manchester City and in the United Arab Emirates, his patronage sometimes seemed to be the only thread keeping the Lone Stars in existence. As civil war engulfed wider and wider areas of the country, Weah could be found desperately trying to charter airlines to fly Liberians to Ghana for a qualifying match they were obliged, because of fighting in Monrovia, to play abroad. In the event, the Lone Stars had to make up numbers by fielding Liberians who lived in refugee camps in Accra.

By then, persuasive voices had begun to convince Weah that the Pied Piper of Liberia could become a leader not just of teams and fans but of a people. The villainous Charles Taylor's regime fell in 2003, its leader eventually brought to account at a UN War Crimes tribunal in The Hague. Liberia prepared for democratic elections. A movement called the Congress for Democratic Change promoted an end to corruption, violence and elitism. They announced their presidential candidate: George Oppong Manneh Weah, the 39-year-old former footballer and millionaire. After a first round of polling, 29 per cent of Liberians chose Weah ahead of 21 other candidates. A Harvard-educated economist 28 years Weah's senior, Ellen Johnson-Sirleaf came second, with 19 per cent of the vote. That pair would go into a fresh play-off to decide the identity of Liberia's head of state.

An obvious question to put to any candidate for the leadership of Liberia is: why take the risk? It is a dangerous job. One day in 1990, Doe was seized by guerrillas loyal to a warlord named Prince Johnson, and tortured to death. He became the most public victim of Liberia's violence largely because his suffering – he had an ear severed off – was filmed, and bootleg copies of the video circulated for many years, retailed in large numbers around Monrovia. Why would a wealthy ex-footballer want a post with a fatal history? 'It is an obligation,' Weah told me after his first shot at the presidential elections. 'It is something the people asked me to do. I have a responsibility to my people. They have confidence in me. They want to see me, they want me to be their leader.'

After the first results, and his 29 per cent share, Weah stood favourite to win the 2005 elections. He had campaigned hard and took the same vim into the run-off between the two best placed candidates, between the ex-footballer and the economist, Ellen Johnson-Sirleaf. He travelled the treacherous roads of the Liberian interior, meeting, greeting, perspiring, and responding to the inevitable cattiness as the final day of polling approached. His past gave his party an easy slogan to rally voters: 'Just one more match to win!'. His wealth, earned from his sport, made him an attractive candidate because he came across as incorruptible, not in it for personal enrichment. But his background also gave him tricky questions to answer. Could he be trusted? Had he not changed religion as a young man from Muslim to Christian? Had he not taken up French citizenship for convenience's sake when he played in France? With such a scant formal education, what could he know about the mechanics of government? In his calm, bass voice, Weah responded: 'I'm only a soccer player but somebody who can strive for change. Nelson Mandela was an advocate and became one of the greatest presidents in the world. People look for good examples. I say: "If I can become the greatest player in the world, you people can do it too".'

He defined himself as the candidate of the common man and woman, the boy from the mangrove slum who made it all the way to Milan. 'You know when you look at the streets in Africa, we don't have much. And that's where we start from. So you have to go back to the streets and try to help people there. We become somebody because somebody helps us. If I hadn't had a contract to go to Cameroon I wouldn't have become the world's greatest player. Football gave me hope and an avenue to speak to people.'

In end, he spoke to too few. In the run-off, Weah polled just over 40 per cent of the vote. His Congress for Democratic Change protested against irregularities and, briefly, some angry Weah supporters took to the streets in Monrovia. He then accepted the result, a historic one for the continent because it put a woman, Johnson-Sirleaf, in power for the first time via a democratic election. In what would be presented as a magnanimous gesture by the reluctant losers, Weah, the incorruptible, offered support for the new government. 'We're a very peaceful party,' he said. 'We had a peaceful election and even though the result of that election could have started another war the people believe it is time for change and the change is peace. We're hoping it will always be like that. The most important thing is that there is no war, that people are happy. Liberia has always been a good place but it has been tarnished with the image of war.'

Would he stand again? 'I hope that at the next party convention I will be the one the people choose,' Weah told me two years later. 'I want to serve Liberia. And I have contributed as much as anybody in Liberia to the people of Liberia. There's no question about that.'

CHAPTER FIVE

DESERT
FOXES

In the garden of Mohammed Maouche's whitewashed home in the suburb of Ben Aknoun, perched up on the hills over the port of Algiers, there sits an old car. A bleached canvas sheet protects it against the city's chill winters and its searing Mediterranean summers. Maouche reckons that with one of two of the parts, spark plugs and distributors he finds harder and harder to come by, his vintage MG could still be taken out through the narrow streets that snake down into the city to meet the wide boulevards of the sea front. The last time he gave it a spin, it turned heads, as it would, its roof open, its driver a professorial looking man with swept-back grey hair and scholarly white beard. Maouche tends this car like others in retirement potter about their allotments. It is his museum, an aide-memoire for an extraordinary episode in the history of his country and the sport that made his living and helped shape modern Algeria. The worn cogs of its milometer record intrepid journeys. It is a vehicle as significant as a tank or a warplane.

Maouche opens up one of the valances of the bonnet to fiddle with a valve and brushes away some soot to reveal the manufacturer's plate: MG, Abingdon. He recalls the day in 1960 when he walked into a dealership named JP Richard in the 16th arrondisement in Paris and purchased the glamorous green automobile. At the time he was a successful young footballer buying a flashy sports car: nothing unusual in that. Except that Maouche did so with funds provided by an organisation, the Front de Libération National (FLN) of Algeria, outlawed for terrorism by the French government. Barely a year earlier Maouche had been released from imprisonment near the French-Swiss border. With Maouche at the wheel, his new wife in the passenger seat, the green MGTF was about to begin an exhausting dash around Europe, asking well-paid and admired professionals to give up their salaries, their jobs and sometimes to divide their families in the cause of African nationalism, to join the FLN Team.

It was a matter of principle, and the principle was simple. By the mid 1950s, the FLN had begun a war with France over its colonial hold on Algeria; some of the most conspicuous Algerians in France were sportsmen. Indeed, Algeria had by then become the African continent's principal exporter of football talent to Europe, almost exclusively to France, from where the Mediterranean was regarded simply as the line that marked the difference between la France metropole and la France outre-mer, though its grip on North Africa was loosening. Self-determination would shortly be granted to Tunisia and Morocco, the neighbouring French colonies of the Maghreb. Algeria presented a different case. It had oil and a million French settlers, the so-called *pieds-noirs*, on its vast territory, and they remained in control of the economy, a privilege they felt ready to hold with violence if necessary. For Algeria to achieve its independence would require eight years of fighting and some notoriously bloody episodes. There would be a propaganda war, too, and few could promote the idea of a free, proud and successful Algeria as powerfully as the country's finest footballers.

Within Algeria, organised football had the same complex genealogy as elsewhere in colonial Africa: white played against brown, sometimes with a camaraderie that escaped social divisions, sometimes in an atmosphere that emphasised them. 'Football was an area where Muslims and the *pieds-noirs* could meet as equals, at least over 90 minutes,' recalls Maouche, a rising star in the Algerian league in the early 1950s, 'although of course the wealthier European clubs always had the means to recruit the best players.' Standards were high, and conditions tough, as one of colonial Algeria's most celebrated chroniclers would vividly record. 'On hot afternoons, the tongues would hang out like those kabyle dogs you see at two in the afternoon in Tizi-Ouzou. In Oran the pitch was bumpier than the shin of an opposing centre-forward,' wrote Albert Camus, the novelist and goalkeeper for the Algiers university side. 'There was a striker nicknamed "The Watermelon" for his corpulent physique. He was, quite simply, a nightmare: he'd come down on you with all his weight, into the kidneys, massage your shins with his boots, sandwich you against the post. And each time, Watermelon would smile a Franciscan smile, and say "Sorry old son".' Evidently, Algerians competed hard. So did the crowds. As tensions between the Arab-Muslim majority and the settler com - munity grew after the Second World War, trouble at stadiums increased. Just after the French Cup final in 1957, a pro-France member of the Algerian assembly, Ali Chekkal, would be assassinated on leaving the arena at Colombes. In Algeria, where half a million French troops had been dispatched, the FLN had declared *pieds-noirs* civilians and collaborators legitimate targets and placed the sport firmly on its agenda, pressuring Muslims to boycott the local league. One effect was to drive more of the best players to seek positions in mainland France. By 1958, some 53 Algerians had contracts with French first and second division clubs.

Mohammed Maouche was among them, one of the first to be approached with the idea that they should give up their livelihoods in the name of the revolution. He became a ringleader whose own tale in the history of the FLN Team has perhaps the most twists, turns and detours than any others. Maouche was only 20 when he knew his career as a footballer had really taken off. Spotted playing as a skilful inside forward in Bologhine, he joined France's Stade de Reims, who within months of his arrival had reached the very first final of the European Cup, against Real Madrid. Maouche watched his new team-mates sharing a field with Alfredo Di Stéfano and Ferenc Puskás. By the end of his first full season in France he had been selected for the French military team, one upside of the stipulation that all Algerian men on the French mainland do French national service. Maouche won the world military championship with France, along with his compatriot and contemporary, the dazzling number 10 Rachid Mekhloufi, a star of the French champions, Saint-Étienne. In early 1958, the pair of them would be among four Algerians short-listed for France's squad to go to the World Cup in Sweden. The centre-half Mustapha Zitouni, of Monaco, would be a certain starter in the XI, Mekhloufi an outstanding candidate for the attack. On the one hand, they felt flattered; on the other, they could not live entirely divorced from their experiences as immigrants whose families lived an edgy, dangerous day-to-day existence in North Africa, where torture had become routine. 'You sometimes did not know who your enemies were,' Maouche says of the culture of suspicion, in which informants, *pieds-noirs* militias, French soldiers, FLN activists all struggled for control of individual districts and of a country. 'It was a horrible time in Algeria. We were all oppressed by it.'

Football liberated them from time to time, let them imagine flying a flag that was not the French tricolore. Maouche cites the 1954 match between a North African XI and France in Paris, arranged to raise funds for the victims of an earthquake in Orleansville, Algeria. In front of a lively crowd, the hosts lost. The imposing Zitouni set up the veteran Moroccan Larbi Ben Barek, the celebrated 'Black Pearl' of Marseille, for the first goal, and the North African XI finished the evening 3-2 winners. Whistles accompanied the French from the field and a hushed, ironic debate could be heard in the bars around the Parc des Princes and across the water in Algiers and Oran about whether the logical next step for the French head coach was to pick an entirely North African team when France took on the then world champions, West Germany, a few days later. 'That match, and the fact that some of us went to play as an Algerian XI in the World Friendship games in Moscow in 1957 gave us the germ of the idea of having our own team,' recalls Maouche. 'We certainly had enough good players. You could compare the Algerian influence then to the overall African influence in the French leagues now. We made up an important part of it, and I think we brought our own style. We were good "instinct" players but with a belief in the collective. Mekhloufi and I liked to play number 10, like Lakhdar Belloumi, who we called The Wizard of the Maghreb in the 1980s, or Zinedine Zidane, whose parents came to France in the 1950s. We were the types who would take as much pleasure from providing the decisive pass for a goal as for scoring it.'

The new question these artists had to ask themselves would be harder: would they take as much pleasure from leading a rebellion as winning championships and going to a World Cup?

Mohammed Maouche first had the idea put to him at the end of 1957. A man he looked up to and had got to know when he

Larbi Ben Barek, Africa's first global superstar, strikes at goal for Olympique Marseille against Sedan in 1954, leaving defender Albert Eloy off balance. The Moroccan brought dazzling technique to the French and Spanish leagues and was selected by the France national team for 16 years after he first crossed the Mediterranean in 1938.

Fans gather to watch the Nigerian team during their historic 1949 visit to England. The tourists, most of whom played barefoot, recorded several victories over English amateur and semi-professional sides. Some of their players were later asked to play at English professional clubs.

Eusébio, in the colours of Benfica during the European Cup final against Milan in 1963. The so-called Black Panther, from Mozambique, then a Portuguese colony, played in five European Cup finals, scored 473 goals in 440 matches for Benfica and registered 40 more for Portugal.

Salif Keita, African Footballer of the Year in 1970, in action for Saint-Étienne in the French championnat. Keita had to flee incognito from Mali to start his professional career in France. He later played in the Spanish and Portuguese leagues and served the Mali national team with distinction.

Algeria's best footballers gather in Tunisia for their first team photo after leaving their clubs in France, in secret, in April 1958. They had answered a call from the National Liberation Front of Algeria to join the struggle for independence. Organiser Mohammed Boumezrag is standing, far left. Star striker Rachid Mekhloufi is crouching, second from left.

The FLN team's Kaddour Bekhloufi, Abdelaziz Bentifour, Amar Rouai, Abderrahmane Boubekeur and Mustapha Zitouni listen to the broadcast of France versus Switzerland in the lead up to the 1958 World Cup. Zitouni had been selected for the game by France, but instead stole away to North Africa.

FLN team players, led by Abdelaziz Bentifour, inspect their rough-and-ready training facilities soon after arriving in Tunis. They had given up well-paid careers in the French championnat to join the Algerian nationalist movement as sporting freedom fighters.

Zaïre, African champions in 1974, show off their bold 'Leopards, Zaïre' shirts ahead of travelling, as the first World Cup finalists from sub-Saharan Africa, to West Germany. There, the Leopards lost all their three matches, conceded 14 goals and were summoned to explain themselves to president Mobutu Sese Seko on their return.

An Algerian fan waves banknotes at the players of West Germany and Austria as they pass the ball around without ambition during the last group match at the 1982 World Cup. After Algeria's shock victory over West Germany, the North Africans were denied progress only by a tepid 1-0 German defeat of Austria, a result that suited both European sides.

Diego Maradona, Argentina's captain, catches up with his old friend, Thomas Nkono, the Cameroon goalkeeper, at half-time during their encounter at the 1990 World Cup. Cameroon would go on not only to beat Maradona's world champions 1-0 on the tournament's opening night, but to progress to within eight minutes of a place in the semi-final.

Cameroon's Roger Milla, 38, performs his trademark jive after scoring at the 1990 World Cup against Colombia. 'Not quite a samba' as novelist Eugène Ébodé described it, 'but an erotic dance in front of the flag, just to show the virile way that the defence had been pierced.'

Kalusha Bwalya, the captain of the Zambian national side, pays his respects at the graves of his former colleagues. Most of the Zambian team had been killed when the aircraft transporting them to a World Cup qualifying match against Senegal in 1993 plunged into the Atlantic, off the coast of Gabon.

George Weah, World Footballer of the Year in 1995, in the jersey of his national team, Liberia. Weah single-handedly raised the profile and status of football in the small, war-torn West African country while emerging as a global superstar for clubs like Milan, Paris Saint-Germain, Monaco and Chelsea.

On the campaign trail. After his retirement as a player, Weah took to politics, running a close second in the presidential elections that brought democracy and peace to Liberia in 2005: 'I want to serve Liberia," he said, "and I have contributed as much as anybody in Liberia to the people of Liberia."

Nigeria celebrate their gold medal at the 1996 Olympic football tournament in Athens, Georgia, USA. They had just beaten Argentina 3-2 to claim Africa's first senior world championship in the sport. Sunday Oliseh is standing, first from the left on the back row, Nwankwo Kanu is second from left, seated, on the ground.

South African president Nelson Mandela, dressed in his national team jersey, joins the players celebrating their 2-0 victory over Tunisia in the final of the 1996 African Cup of Nations at Soccer City in Soweto. To Mandela's right, seated, is his predecessor, the last head-of-state of the apartheid era, FW de Klerk.

managed the Algerian side at the Friendship games in Moscow, Mohammed Boumezrag, called on him at Reims and let the notion slip into conversation. Boumezrag, a broad, round-faced man with a neat moustache, had enjoyed a decent career as a footballer and coach in mainland France and came from a background of political feistiness, his father an imam, his grandfather a famous 19th century revolutionary. Mohammed Boumezrag was a persuasive talker too, mixing zeal and authority in the proposal he discussed with the best Algerian players of the time.

'I remember he came to see me just before Christmas,' says Maouche. 'At first, he said nothing about the scheme, we just chatted a bit, just so he could get an impression of how I might react.' After further meetings, Boumezrag hinted at how sweeping and dramatic the plan would be: that a team of Algerian professionals would exit France over a weekend, gather at the FLN's headquarters in Tunisia and launch an illegal national team as part of Algeria's nation-in-waiting, in exile. Boumezrag made his list of candidates and one by one put the question firmly to enough players to form a decent squad: 'Are you in. Or are you out?'

Boumezrag knew the answer he would get from Maouche, studious, bright and a young man who had already lost relatives to the violence in Algeria. Others had been touched as directly by the conflict. The Monaco player Hacene Chabri had a developed political conscience, so much so he had been identified by French authorities as sympathetic to the FLN. But there was much to give up. Freedom, for a start: those, like Maouche, who were still doing their compulsory French military service, albeit as sportsmen, faced charges of desertion, and arrest. Wealth, for another thing: Mustapha Zitouni, the France international, earned a handsome salary at Monaco, had been praised by Di Stéfano and had been the subject of a lavish bid by Real Madrid. Zitouni's first question on hearing Boumezrag's proposition would be: 'Could we do it after the World Cup?' The reply was simple: No. To do so then would defeat the object, which was to celebrate Algeria, to show high-profile support for independence and to hurt France. Zitouni gave his okay.

After Zitouni had agreed, Meklhoufi, the star from Saint-Étienne, would then be approached. 'I didn't hesitate,' Meklhoufi insists. 'Okay, I would have to give up my club. And yes, I was thinking about the World Cup, but what did that count for in comparison with my country's independence? The aim was to make a statement because at the time the French propaganda had the FLN as a band of terrorists. But then we left, and that was a revelation to some French people that all the Algerians felt united in this.' In several cases, that point had to be put to wives and partners. 'Some of the players had married French women,' Maouche remembers, 'and I saw marriages broken up by what was to happen. Of course, there were some players, Algerians who appreciated their lives in France, who said they did not want to join. We had to be discreet with them, so they could stay, say no and not be a security risk with the information they had heard.' Who were they? Maouche smiles at the question. 'That is their business.' Half a century on, he keeps as his secret and theirs the names of those who chose the comforts of their lives on the mainland ahead of joining a perilous sporting coup.

Boumezrag and his chosen allies selected the weekend of 13–14 April for the grand exodus. France were due to play a friendly against Switzerland a few days later and Zitouni, committed to turning his back on Les Bleus, was inked in for the first XI. His absence when the French squad gathered would be conspicuous and guarantee immediate impact and resonance. The fixture list for the championnat that Saturday and Sunday also offered some favourable combinations of where the Algerians preparing for their secret exits would be designated to play. Monaco, where three Algerians played, were at home to Angers, who included one Amar Rouai, successfully enlisted for the coup, in their midfield. That meant a quartet of rebels close to the Italian border at Menton. Mekhloufi's Saint-Étienne, not so far from the Swiss frontier, had a home game. Transport arrangements were made for small cadres of players to cross out of France at various points, meeting points assigned. They would regroup in numbers only once outside France and join up as a squad in Tunis.

As the weekend approached, the adrenalin pumped. For Mohammed Maouche, life had changed from imagining himself up against Di Stéfano in European Cup finals to taking a lead role in something dreamed up by Le Carré. He was no longer an elegant inside-forward but an eager insurgent. 'It was very, very serious in the planning. Every detail was studied. We didn't have big meetings about it, talks were almost always individual-to-individual. Of course there was a list, but hardly anybody knew all the other names that might be on it. It was all very secret. By the time I became very involved in the recruiting of players I would never meet them in hotels, or cafes or public places and we would not talk for long, just a few words and a handshake. We had to reduce all the possible risks, but as Boumezrag would always tell us: "There is no zero-risk in any of this". Of course, he was right.'

The first of the defectors slipped out of the country on the Friday night. Abdelaziz Bentifour, a veteran of the North Africa XI match, told his coach at Monaco he felt unwell, too sick to play the match against Angers. His excuse accepted, he slipped across the French frontier into Italy, to await his co-conspirators in San Remo. After the Monaco-Angers game was over, Chabri shuttled Zitouni the same way and returned to pick up Rouai and his wife.

But then, on the way back for a third time, Chabri found himself stopped by customs officers, who asked 'Why all the coming-and-going?' Fatefully, they then demanded his papers.

There was no zero risk. Up in Saint-Étienne, plans were also going awry. Amid all the intrigue and plot, football itself turned rebel. Saint-Étienne surprisingly lost at home to struggling Béziers, a setback not helped by an alarming injury to their most creative player. Mekhloufi, giving away no clues that his mind might be on the long sabbatical away from his flourishing club career, had scored his side's one goal in the 2-1 loss. Shortly afterwards he challenged for a ball with such force that his collision with his own team-mate, the Cameroonian Eugène Njo Léa, left him in need of hospital examination for concussion. The Great Escape appeared badly off track. Hamid Kermali, a Lyon player, had cried off sick from his club's away trip to Nîmes so he could depart with Mekhloufi soon after the Saint-Étienne match. His compatriot instead left the stadium accompanied by medical staff, bound for the infirmary. Kermali turned up in his ward hoping to find Mekhloufi alone and in a condition to travel; he found a man dressed as a mummy, Mekhloufi's neat moustache and a pair of bleary eyes poking out beneath a bandaged head. Under the watch of doctors, in his pyjamas, Mekhloufi was not about to be sprung. So, Kermali travelled home to Lyon to rethink.

At half past seven the next morning, Mekhloufi did make his escape, still in bandages, escorted briskly from the hospital by Kermali, without the medical all-clear and still with his head strapped. They stopped by the Saint-Étienne offices to retrieve Mekhloufi's kit bag and, crucially, his passport, concerned at the delay to their journey but reassured that on the airwaves and in the newspapers, they had heard no hint of alarm about the great defection. Still, they were on edge when another escapee,

Abdelhamed Bouchouk, joining their little cadre from Toulouse, arrived late, explaining his wife had got cold feet. He had had to agree that she could join him later in Tunisia, where nine of the eleven fugitives were due to have gathered by the middle of the next week. Just as Mekhloufi's group made it across the Swiss border, more than a day behind schedule, the first news broadcasts began to suggest France had wind of the disappearing footballers. The French national squad had been ordered to gather in Paris that Monday: Les Bleus were puzzled because there was no sign of Zitouni.

Meanwhile, Chabri, who had shuttled the Monaco group and Raoui into Italy from Menton, was still being held by police. French intelligence records, it emerged, had him listed not just as a footballer: he was also under suspicion for smuggling arms and money for the FLN. Interrogated in Nice and then in Marseille, he held out for the two days he thought would assure the passage of his colleagues across the Mediterranean before admitting his part in the plot.

As for Maouche, already one of the scheme's architects and, in time, one of the principal movers in sustaining the FLN Team, his adventure was just beginning. He remembers the details with clarity, and a remarkable benevolence, given what happened to him on the weekend of 13–14 April 1958. Maouche, off duty from Reims that Saturday, had been due to rendezvous with the Mekhloufi group in Lausanne, Switzerland early on the Monday. Tall, upright, his dark hair brushed back, he entered the first class waiting room at Lausanne station at 7am, looking every bit the privileged student or young professional. And he waited. And waited. His accomplices never showed. Maouche knew nothing of the injury sustained by Mekhloufi in the match against Béziers, nor the overnight hospital stay. Nor of Bouchouk's delayed arrival. Concerned and cut off, Maouche decided to return to Paris, where he could contact some of the organisers to find out what had happened.

Barely had he disembarked the train in the French capital than he knew his own participation was now in serious jeopardy. 'When I got to the station at Paris, that's when I saw the newspaper front pages,' recalls Maouche. '*L'Équipe* had a huge headline saying that nine Algerian players had disappeared, and that Maouche of Reims was missing. They knew a lot. Their sources said that I had crossed the border into Switzerland and then returned the same day to the station at Saint-Louis, on the frontier, to come back.' He barely had time to reach the editorial page in which France's sports newspaper mused on the longer-term possibility that from here on, 'the France team remains, but the word "France" will have a narrower meaning,' or to read *Le Monde* putting the flight of the footballers into the context of a spiralling collapse of the republic's government. On the one hand, much of mainland France had become disgusted by the atrocities committed in its name against Algerians across the Mediterranean, and viewed the war as futile. On the other, the *pieds-noirs* community were a noisy, forceful lobby. The crisis had led to a clamour for General Charles De Gaulle to return to politics. Maouche glimpsed all this on the station's news-stands, while looking desperately for the next train to the Swiss border. He might be lucky, he reasoned, and slip again, incognito, out of the country and join up with the rest in Rome, or in Tunis. 'Besides,' he smiles, 'I had no choice. There was no zero risk, Boumezrag always said. Unfortunately when my train drew into Saint-Louis on the frontier again, there were the *flics*. A police border guard got on the train. Then another stepped in at the other end of my carriage. I was blocked in. It crossed my mind to jump from the window, but by then I was bound to be arrested and charged as a deserter.' Maouche would much later discover that the group of comrades – Kermali, Mekhloufi and company – he had been due to meet in Lausanne had proceeded instead to another city, Montreux, thanks to the delays and confusion in that phase of the plan.

Maouche seems remarkably philosophical about their laxness given what happened to him next. The local police took him in. And then? 'Well, the first three days in the cell were hard. There was an especially vicious gendarme involved, very racist towards Algerians. I was badly beaten. Then I was sent to the military prison in Versailles, put in a tiny cell, given just bread to eat and they asked me, threatening, if I had relatives in France, as part of the interrogation, and they started to ask about what I was trying to do and about other players.' Maouche would not break.

■ ■ ■

The majority did make it, and though the debut matches of the newly assembled, richly-talented 'Algeria' side, the FLN Team, were some days away, a keen contest would quickly be fought through the media. The first nine players made their way to Tunis, where they settled into the Hotel Majestic, to take instruction from the government-in-exile of the FLN, and await reinforcements to make up a squad, find willing opposition and draw up a fixture-list. A statement was issued from the FLN in Tunis announcing the arrival of the first footballers and declaring they had 'answered the call to arms. As long as France wages a merciless war against their people and their nation, they now refuse to contribute their important and appreciated work to French sport. Like all Algerians, they have to suffer in the rapidly developing racist, anti-African and anti-Muslim climate.'

French conservatives took a different view. *Paris-Match*, the society magazine gave over four pages of its late April edition to 'The Stars of French Football Turned Fellaghas, or Terrorists', a spicy enough story for them to cut back even on that edition's coverage of Belgian King Baudoin's spring ball. They pictured Zitouni, the would be World Cup star, strolling through a Tunis casbah with four other footballers, all snappily attired while a woman dressed entirely in hijab, just to their left, tip-toed along the pavement. *Paris-Match* then turned to the altered circumstances of the players' wives: 'Now they are in the teetotal land of veiled women!' Quelle horreur! To make the point they unearthed a photo of Abdelaziz Bentifour pouring drinks at a bar he co-owned in Nice; of the goalkeeper Abderahmane Boubekeur, his wife and French friends with a bottle of champagne at his former home in the Côte d'Azur. They noted that Madame Zitouni, an attractive Parisienne, had taken the precaution of having her fridge and washing machine relocated to North Africa.

The sense of sacrifice would be felt quickly, and not just because of a perceived lack of domestic appliances. Lives had been turned upside down, the exiles realised when they learned Maouche and Chabri had been detained in France. There was also the small issue of the team being one short of an XI, although the FLN had an active amateur squad of guerrillas training and practicing in Tunisia so there were some ringers available to supplement the professionals. Working for a paramilitary organisation would be a challenge for the stars of le championnat. The defectors had all had their club contracts in France cancelled by the Thursday after they left, and the FLN agreed on a monthly stipend of FF50,000, less than 30 per cent of what Boubekeur and Zitouni had been paid at Monaco, but, as their new bosses pointed out, considerably more than the maximum earned by the top brass in the paramilitary high command.

In their new posts, in Africa, the training regime was hard, four-hour sessions six days a week, plus lengthy briefings from the theorists and generals of the revolution. For practice they would accept what sites were available on the FLN camps or what their Tunisian hosts could provide. A photo taken soon after the landing of the first batch of exiles shows Bentifour, who had played international football for France only months earlier, looking bewildered at the state of a sandy training pitch dotted with pebbles. Another shows he and Zitouni listening to France-Switzerland, the match where Zitouni would have played at centre-half, on the radio. Wistful? They were obliged to say not, and never, ever would.

Nor would they ever call themselves 'fellaghas', a derogatory term. But freedom fighters, yes. 'Going along the Tunisia border, you would see the refugees from the violence in Algeria and that would hit hard,' remembers Maouche, whose adventure had more chicanes to run through but who would eventually join the group. 'They soon learned, as we all would, that they were not just flag-bearers but also combatants now and would live by those rules. Oh yes, there was discipline. What do you expect? We were working in the paramilitary structures of the FLN. If you made mistakes, you could spend time in the FLN prison. You couldn't drink or say anything risky or anything like that. It could be severe discipline but with time we got used to it. And it was the same discipline for everybody. There were no stars in the group.' In truth, there hardly needed to be. The hastily arranged debut matches for the 'national' team of Algeria turned into walkovers. The FLN Team walloped Union Sportive Tunisienne 8-0 in their first outing; they then took on a Tunisian national XI twice, scoring 15 goals over 180 minutes and conceding just once.

To fulfil the FLN's manifesto, that the team should 'represent

Algeria with dignity, high profile and with flair', the players needed to spread their wings. A tournament was arranged, where the Algerians immediately established themselves at the top of the regional, Maghreb triangle: Tunisia were beaten again, Morocco invited over to Tunis and defeated 3-1. They took to the desert road between Tunis and Benghazi, crammed into small buses, to play Libyan sides, where they again won with ease, gathering more patriotic pride than professional challenge. And pride they felt. They played in jerseys with the star and crescent embroidered on their chests, the Algeria flag hung over the venues they performed at, and they stood in line to the stirring sound of the Qassaman, a national-anthem-in-waiting. The FLN Team were bringing good gate receipts in for the cause, too, because folk wanted to watch the likes of Mekhloufi and Zitouni.

In the winter of 1958, they undertook a six-match tour of Morocco: Played 6, Won 6, Goals For: 25, Goals Against: 3. They sought fixtures in Egypt but found the regime there, headed by the Arab nationalist General Gamal Abdel Nasser, a friend of the FLN, curiously reluctant to engage them on the football field, at least against elite Egyptian teams. Several factors were at play: Fifa, obliged to condemn the FLN Team as an illegitimate 'national' squad representing a nation that did not officially exist, not only refused to recognise the Algerians, but threatened to ban those of its members who shared a pitch with them. Morocco and Tunisia were prepared to suffer for that, but Egypt was a founding father of Caf, the African Confederation aligned to Fifa, and had a developed national side, a good one. Hence the suspicion that the Egyptians, winners of the inaugural African Cup of Nations in 1957, did not wish their status as champions dented by taking on a set of footballers with some of the best CVs in Africa.

How strong were the FLN Team? By the time of the next wave

of recruitment, powerful enough, reckons Maouche 'to have done something special at the World Cup.' He, like Mekhloufi and Bentifour and certainly Zitouni, might have been at the 1958 tournament in Sweden in the colours of France. They monitored events there with interest. They learned of the goalscoring exploits of Just Fontaine, who set a World Cup record with his 13 goals during the finals. Fontaine, a French-Moroccan, had been a team-mate of Maouche at Stade de Reims, and a good friend to whom Maouche provided passes from inside-forward and with whom he would banter in Arabic. And Fontaine would be one of several who welcomed Maouche back to the training headquarters at Stade de Reims one day in 1959, saying how they missed him, and cautiously asking for details of his unique story in the gathering odyssey of the FLN Team.

The details of his story were these: after his roughing up in Saint-Louis, Maouche, mercifully, came upon a more benign streak of French justice. He was charged with desertion. Presiding at his army tribunal would be a General Loth. Here at last, a stroke of luck. Loth was a passionate football fan, and, serendipitously, an honorary president of none other than Stade de Reims, European Cup finalists of 1956, and one-time employers of Mohammed Maouche. Loth might have sentenced his young-striker-turned-revolutionary to eight years in a French jail. Instead he banished him for one year to the Alps, to serve the army patrols there under a sort of house arrest, isolated, remote and anonymous. And, as it turned out, rather useful for the strong athlete that Maouche was. He learned to ski with such accomplishment that he struck up a long friendship with two future French Olympic downhill champions. 'It was imprisonment but in a gilded cell,' reflects the prisoner.

For all that, patrolling Mont Blanc was neither Maouche's

metier nor his calling, and when he came down from the mountains, he found a changed France, and heard encouraging reports that the FLN Team was not only very much alive but had grown to such an effect there was a voracious hunger for more good footballers and sophisticated organisers. The struggle in Algeria had become ever more violent, with gangs of *pieds-noirs* ultras acting independently of security forces against the Muslim population. That, in turn had hardened opinion in mainland France. 'I would say by then 90 per cent of French people in France wanted an end to the war and to let Algeria go,' says Maouche, 'and when I returned to Reims, and then moved from there to Racing Club in Paris, nobody said a word against what I had done, the cause I had committed to. On the contrary, I was treated with respect and warmth.'

His close circle, though, were no longer his football colleagues, but revolutionaries. The push for Algerian independence had turned urgent, the role of the FLN Team having acquired a high profile. Maouche met and fell in love with Khadidja, the secretary of a radical lawyer and FLN activist in Paris. Within weeks, they were the movement's Bonnie and Clyde. Given a case full of francs, Maouche was instructed to get himself a good fast car, and told that he and Khadidja should use their cover as a honeymooning couple to work through a list of the remaining Algerians playing in the French championnat and gather as many as he could. The FLN Team, he was told, would be busier than ever and it needed numbers. And it needed Maouche in charge. The revolution, he sensed, was approaching its endgame.

So Mohammed and Khadidja purchased from JP Richard in the 16th arrondisement their green MGTF, the car preserved so lovingly in Maouche's garden in Ben Aknoun, Algiers. Whatever ostentation the good-looking young footballer and his new wife projected as they sped between cities in their sports car had been deliberate. Their wish was to look as unlike insurgents as possible. When police regarded with suspicion a hectic itinerary, they would pass it off as the whim of eager young sightseers, embarking on the highway of married life. What the young husband was really doing was risking a return to prison as he retook the road of recruitment. They zoomed from Paris to Le Havre, Rennes to Bordeaux, Nîmes to Troyes, Reims to Paris and back again, meeting for short exchanges with Algerian players to boost the FLN Team's squad numbers into the 30s for the demands now being scheduled for these Maghrebi Globetrotters. They slipped back and forth across borders to hold meetings with FLN exiles in Belgium and Switzerland, to establish sites for the eventual rendezvous. Remembering Boumezrag's 'There is no zero-risk' warnings, they established tighter guarantees than the fateful plans of 1958 that had cost Maouche his freedom.

Though news of the FLN Team's exploits was effectively censored within France, the Algerian football community had heard enough to respond in large part with enthusiasm to the cause. In 1960, Maouche led and arranged the biggest single defection of footballers. He recounts his major part in the enterprise without boasts, without personal rancour for the indignities of his detention, but sometimes with a wide-eyed relish for the moments of daring and espionage. Nor can his retelling disguise his admiration for the sangfroid shown by his new wife. He recalls a cadre of recruits, himself included, coming under suspicion in a Berne hotel from Swiss police, themselves under pressure from the French gendarmerie. Passports for the individuals inside were demanded, so Khadidja Maouche slipped out of the kitchen exit of the hotel restaurant with an empty shopping basket. She returned an hour or so later, an FLN operative having discreetly and silently slipped a set of Tunisian travel documents into her bag as they passed one another in a grocer's store.

On reaching North Africa, by boat via Sicily, Maouche and his new brigade were greeted with relief by the original team members, many of whom the adventure had fatigued. The number of professionals stood at too few to be taking on a fixture list of the size lined up for the FLN Team. This new wave of recruits, gathered and guided by Maouche, would bring the number of players who represented the FLN to 32. No longer were they spreading their message and entertaining crowds simply in North Africa, but had travelled to an enthusiastic Middle East. In Baghdad, they were serenaded by the Iraqi public with chants of 'Vive Algeria, down with De Gaulle!' An invitation to tour the Far East would be eagerly accepted by the FLN. In Vietnam, Ho Chi Minh made a point of comparing the colonial experience there with the French grip on North Africa. One of his army chiefs would be more direct in the banquet after the FLN Team had thrashed a Vietnamese side. 'We beat the French,' declared General Giap, a veteran of the Franco-Vietnamese war, 'and you've just beaten us. Now you must go and defeat France!'

Their hosts seemed fascinated by their exotic guests. 'We were the true ambassadors of Algerian independence,' reflects Maouche. 'Certainly, I was one of the more politicised members of the group, but we all had a sense we were carrying the flag for our country and our continent. On our travels, the public in the Far East would ask us: "Where is Algeria? In Africa? Why aren't you very black?" I would sit across the table with people and talk about the amalgam of people that make up Africa, and sometimes have to explain that we did not come from a continent of savages.'

They provided a sporting master-class, too. In Mao's China, the FLN Team gave coaching clinics to mass audiences, although there, they would be briefly surprised on the field by the standard of the opposition: they suffered two losses. Mostly they continued to outclass the teams lined up against them. If, at the state receptions laid on for the players and in the approving cheers and songs in the grandstands, they had a clear sense of their impact as revolutionary pathfinders, for Arab unity, and Africa's firm stride towards sovereignty, what they barely experienced was a good, hard, close game of football. In Europe, they found it. Fifa's threat to any country entertaining the FLN Team met resistance from the Communist Block then forming in Eastern Europe. While national teams ran a risk if they took on 'Algeria', club and representative sides received the go-ahead from their political leaders behind the Iron Curtain. The Algerians approached tours to Russia, Yugoslavia, Czechoslovakia, Bulgaria, Romania with relish. There would also be a chance to play in Hungary, a land that had achieved a football pre-eminence in the mid-1950s.

There would be two tours to Eastern Europe. Between the first and the second, they had improved markedly, benefited from having had their core individuals hot-housed together for months on end, their numbers swelled with each new wave of recruits from France. In Bulgaria in 1959, they had played five, won one, drawn one and lost twice. In Bulgaria in 1961, they won three out of five. On their first trip to Romania they beat Rapid Bucharest but lost their other two fixtures; when they returned there 24 months later, they went four games undefeated. Their Russian expedition in the summer of 1959 had been successful – four wins out of six, one loss – and they would triumph in all four matches in Czechoslovakia. But going back east, opponents noted how the battle for places had intensified and so did new members of the squad. The striker Ahmed Oudjani, a prolific scorer in the French league, would, among others, complain about his lack of starts.

The arrival of Oudjani and Maouche as attacking options in turn seemed to rouse the genius in Mekhloufi. The final tour, to five Eastern European countries and a last foray to loyal Libya would stimulate the FLN Team's best football. Mekhloufi was by now 25 years old, and if his career as a professional had taken a spectacular detour since he abandoned the French champions, here was opportunity to show what he could do. In Yugoslavia, the FLN Team gained the sobriquet 'Brown Diamonds', and though they lost in Zagreb, a handsome win in Rijeka and a 9-0 extravaganza in Tuzla whetted the Balkan appetite for the final tour match in Belgrade. The FLN Team took on the Yugoslav Olympic side, essentially the country's national team. Eighty thousand watched Mekhloufi lead a dazzling 6-1 deconstruction of the opposition. An imaginative provider and increasingly a superb finisher, Mekhloufi scored four times that night. He took his form with him to Bulgaria, where he contributed a hat-trick to a 7-0 win in Târgovişte. He would be man of the match again against the Hungarian national XI in Budapest, where the heirs-apparent of a nascent, independent Algeria had overwhelmed the successors of the Mighty Magyars 5-2.

During that stopover, indeed, the players believed for a moment that the nascent independent Algeria had already come into being. News of a coup in Algiers had reached the Hungarian politburo. What they communicated to the touring sportsmen, however, was a muddled Chinese whisper. Yes, there had been an attempted putsch against the government of De Gaulle, but it was led by generals loyal to the idea of French Algeria and concerned that the government of Paris was inexorably moving down the path of full self-determination for its colony. The coup failed.

Within a year, De Gaulle had signalled the French retreat from North Africa. Algeria celebrated its independence on 5 July 1962 after a final, grotesque episode of bloodletting and scorched-earth sabotage led by *pieds-noirs* ultras. Almost a million people fled across the Mediterranean in the months around the official transfer of power while those who had fought for sovereignty for the FLN abandoned their fatigues to return to civilian life. That included the 30-odd footballers – 'the precursors of our independence', Mohammed Maouche calls them – for whom the future suddenly appeared a little confusing. They were gratified by the personal reassurance from the new head-of-state, Ahmed Ben Bella, that he as a football man – he had once played for Olympique Marseille – would be the last to forget their contribution to the nation's freedom. 'We can't complain,' says Maouche, with a sweep of his hand across the small cottage and ramshackle garden that is his home in Ben Aknoun. 'They have always made sure we are housed. Those of us who needed it, and are still on this earth, have our government pension for what we did. I think we are still respected here.'

And in France? How did the defection sit with the football community they had so dramatically abandoned? 'For me, I cannot say I ever had a problem,' says Maouche. 'The others? Maybe isolated individuals would bear them a grudge for what happened, but remember by the end of the conflict, 90 per cent of people in France were sympathetic to the cause of Algerian independence.' Witness the experience of the winger Saïd Amara, who received a death threat by post when he returned to Bordeaux, whom he had left to join the FLN in 1960. The mayor of Bordeaux answered back by publicly stating that, he, the citizens and the club were delighted to count Amara again as one of them. As for Mekhloufi, whose brilliant career in club football had been interrupted for the best part of four seasons in the cause, he asked Ben Bella for permission to resume a career in France. With Mekhloufi back in their forward line, Saint-Étienne won the French championship again in 1964. He became the club captain and in 1968 signed off his career in French football with victory in the Cup final. Presenting the trophy that day at the Colombes stadium would be General De Gaulle, whom legend has it congratulated the Saint-Étienne star and former figurehead of the FLN Team with the words 'La France, c'est vous.' It's a nice tale, though not one told regularly by Mekhloufi.

Maouche had given up more than anybody in the FLN Team: he had lost his freedom for over a year. He had already made his peace with Stade de Reims after serving his sentence in the Alps, although they had thought it politic to loan him out to Red Star of Paris for a period, lest there be rancour among their supporters. When he then defected a second time, he still retained the goodwill of ex-employers and colleagues. He would return to football in Europe, but in Switzerland, the country whose frontiers he had become so familiar with, from his bizarre eyrie on Mont Blanc, or from his furtive crossings by rail or at the wheel of his beloved MG. In retirement, he and the car returned to Algiers, where he coached and managed the national team in its greatest era, the 1980s. Or, at least in its greatest era after independence. The FLN Team, the renegade enterprise that forced the world to take notice of a country, may be the best national XI Algeria ever had. Just look at the figures: Played 91, won 65, drawn 13, lost 13. Goals For: 385. Goals Against: 127. That's some record for a team who never played a match at home.

CHAPTER SIX

CARAVAN FROM THE SAHARA

León felt like an oven. Temperatures in central Mexico in June 1970 crept towards the mid-30s, and the players felt heavy-legged, sapped of energy. Perhaps that was why Sigi Held, the West German striker, had not gathered his wits enough to take advantage of the bizarre situation suddenly confronting him in the opposition defence. Referee Van Ravens had blown the whistle to begin the second half of the opening match in Group Four of the ninth World Cup finals, and Held need only have slung an accurate drive towards the goal and he would have scored. The goal was utterly unguarded, the goalkeeper still trotting out from the dressing-room when the half-time interval had been officially brought to an end.

Allal Ben Kassou, hurriedly strapping his gloves, got away with his tardiness. A moment of possible farce had passed. But before any assumptions start forming about Africa's first match at a World Cup finals for nearly four decades turning into a display of naivety, with players too slow out of the locker-rooms to be ready for the second half, just pause to consider the scoreboard: at halfway through West Germany versus Morocco, it read 1-0. West

Germany, runners-up in the tournament four years earlier, were losing against the debutants.

Up in the press box, the *Süddeutsche Zeitung*'s correspondent, searched for precedents for the scale of the upset currently facing the team of Franz Beckenbauer and Gerd Muller, of Sepp Maier and Uwe Seeler. 'Morocco beating a top-favourite German team is like little North Korea overcoming the mighty Italy four years ago,' wrote Hans Schiefele. Seizing on an error by defender Horst Höttges, Jarir Hoummane had slipped the ball past Maier for the game's opening goal and Morocco, in their fetching vermillion strip, gained confidence. They played with a lightness of touch and a zip that suggested they could only grow stronger under the sort of sweltering sky more familiar in Fez than Frankfurt. The Germans were under par. Gerd Muller, 'Der Bomber', had even squandered a chance for a quick equaliser just before the half hour.

Africa had waited 36 years for this day, 3 June 1970, its first match at football's major showpiece since an Egyptian squad boarded a ship called the *Helwan* and travelled from Alexandria to Naples in Mussolini's Italy, lost 4-2 against Hungary and returned home again. Since then, World Cups had found colour television, most of Africa had fought successfully for independence and rather less effectively for its right to be recognised as an important part of Fifa. Africa's World Cup saga would be a slow-burner. The continent had boycotted the 1966 tournament in England in protest at the organisers' refusal to grant Africa a single, automatic place among the 16 finalists. In 1962, Morocco had finished highest at the end of a long set of qualifiers but had to play off against Spain to make it to the finals in Chile. They lost. So 1970 was a watershed. To get to Mexico, the Moroccans had emerged through a marathon of hurdles – including replays, and even the toss of a coin to eliminate Tunisia – to assume the pathfinder role for the continent. Little could they have suspected that battles with West Germany would define Africa's World Cup expeditions for much of the next 16 years.

The Lions of the Atlas had set off for Mexico with the blessing of the king, and, as important, the backing of the army, whose club, FAR Rabat, provided a basis of professionalism for key players in the national squad, like goalkeeper Allal, the man late out of the León dressing-room, and the industrious midfielder Dris Bamous. The national team were coached by a Yugoslav, Blagoje Vidinić and though he looked over his resources and saw no Larbi Ben Barek, the 'Perle Noir' of the 1940s and 50s, to call on, nor a finisher like Just Fontaine, the forward from Marrakesh who scored 13 goals for France in the 1958 World Cup, he had in Hoummane an excellent striker of the ball, particularly on the volley, and in Ahmed Faras, a young forward who later became African Footballer of the Year. Vidinić would sometimes chide Faras and others for too much flourish and across the Moroccan squad there was a suppressed flashiness. Defender Kacem Slimani practised hard at his scissor-kicks and was wont to clear the ball with both legs off the ground if he could, a trick guaranteed, if it comes off, to please audiences across Africa. But steadied by Boujemaa Benkrif, Morocco were usually solid at the back.

They stayed that way into the second half against West Germany. Some Germans wilted, notably Helmut Halle, blond, blue-eyed and pink-faced by the time he was withdrawn by Germany coach Helmut Schön. Höttges, at fault for Moummane's goal, would also be substituted. Maier in the German goal would be tested once or twice, but just as a major shock began to look probable, Uwe Seeler equalised, set up by Muller. Muller then headed home to make it 2-1. 'German XI in luck again,' ran the *Süddeutsche*'s headline. Morocco's dream debut had fizzled.

They lost their next match, against Peru, 3-0, but just before they left Mexico, Morocco put down a marker. A goal down at half-time to Bulgaria, the Atlas Lions' Maouhoub Ghazouani scored on the hour. It finished 1-1. Africa had claimed its first point from a World Cup. It was something to take home, along with a large number of souvenir sombreros, of maximum diameter, very visible in the photographs of the team's return to Casablanca airport.

■ ■ ■

Africa's first progressive steps as a World Cup power would almost all be made by Maghrebi teams. By the end of the 1970s, North Africa had begun to wrest the leadership of club and national football from the west of the continent. Sixteen of the Champions Cups between 1980 and 2000 were won by clubs from Algeria, Morocco, Tunisia or Egypt. Eight of a total of 15 places granted to Africa at World Cup final tournaments between 1978 and 1998 would be taken by Mediterranean countries. In part, it happened because Egypt and the Maghreb had ceased to be distracted by the alternative engagements that connected them with the Middle East rather than their own continent. Their leagues would in time also maintain higher competitive standards than most of sub-Saharan Africa. In Cairo, the peppery rivalry between Al Ahly and Zamalek had grown up since the 1920s and in the 1980s it spilled over into a bullish continental joust. Algerian clubs with strong nationalist backgrounds, like Mouloudia of Algiers, and JS Kabylie, from Berber territory, began to exert themselves in the Champions Cup. And Tunisia, the slim land sandwiched between vast nations, happened on some lucky breaks, some exceptional talents like Tarek Dhiab, the two-footed African Footballer of the Year in 1977, and a degree of feistiness.

Tunisia would be Africa's representatives at the World Cup in

Argentina in 1978. Months before they flew to Buenos Aires, they lost their collective rag. In the third place play-off at the Nations Cup in Ghana, they conceded a 42nd minute equaliser to Nigeria, protested long and loud to the Togolese referee who had awarded it and, led by their captain and goalkeeper Sadok Sassi Attouga, walked off the field in Accra, never to return. Tunisia were promptly banned from African competitions for two years, Attouga suspended for three. It was not an ideal build-up. In Argentina, they had been drawn against Poland, third-placed at the previous tournament, Mexico, and world champions West Germany. In the tournament's opening match, the Poles and Germans drew 0-0, a dull contest. The following night, World Cup 78 took off. The hosts won amid ticker-tape and fireworks in the capital and up in Rosario, Argentina's *La Nación* proclaimed: 'One of the most unexpected results in the history of the World Cup': Tunisia had beaten Mexico 3-1. Africa had its first ever win at a finals. Dhiab had a splendid game, Naili, the stand-in goalkeeper for the banned Attouga, impressed and the Tunisians, unlike in Accra, had responded coolly to falling a goal down to a penalty just on half-time. Second-half goals from Ali Kaabi, Nejib Gommidh and Mokhtar Douib had put Tunisia top of Group B.

The appeal of the underdog attracted the support of neutrals, so did the precision of their football, and the urbane charm of their head coach, Abdelmajid Chetali. The German press, now aware that Tunisia-West Germany, the final group match, would probably have a strong bearing on qualifying for the next round, warmed to Chetali, who was married to a German and had taken some coaching courses there. They liked his team's 'Tactik und Technik' football too. 'They have technique and strength,' warned one German report, 'and they close up together in defence like an accordion, and quickly spring from there into attack.'

Against Poland, their second match, the Tunisians emphatic-
ally won around the neutrals in Rosario, firecrackers launched from
the stands to celebrate their forays, hostile whistles directed against
Poland as the European team came under increasing pressure at
the end of the game. Tunisia had begun with great purpose, Khalid
Gasmi dispossessing Kazimierz Deyna, the Poland captain,
Temime Lahzami and Tarak Dhiab whipping past challenges. In
between, an error by Ali Kaabi at left-back would be punished by
Grezgorz Lato, just before the interval. Kaabi wept after the final
whistle. Dhiab had hit the crossbar, but Lato's would be the only
goal of a very close game.

West Germany had in the mean time put six goals past Mexico.
So Tunisia would need to beat the Germans to go through to the
last eight. Cordoba's Carerras stadium reached close to capacity at
the prospect either of another German goal-fest or a dramatic
overthrow. When West Germany's Manfred Kaltz tripped
Mohammed Ben Rahaiem in the 18-yard area, they anticipated the
latter. Referee Augusto Orosco gave no penalty. Ben Rahaiem then
drew a desperate save from Sepp Maier. It finished goalless, Poland
duly defeated the meek Mexicans and progress to the second group
phase was in European hands.

Chetali wondered at what might have been. He suspected the
schedule had favoured the big two, a draw a cosy cushion of
advantage. 'If Poland and West Germany had not played the
opening game, one of them would have finished third in this
group,' he argued, perhaps clutching at straws. And as the rest of
the tournament rolled out a red carpet for his team, Chetali chided
them for their lack of urgency in the closing stages of the draw with
Germany. 'I don't know what came over my players. I wanted
them to attack, to turn 0-0 into 1-0, but they started going
backwards in the last five minutes and they seemed happy to have

achieved a draw against the world champions.' In time, Tunisia would be back at a World Cup, then another, then a third and a fourth, but never with the panache, nor a win like the cherished victory they had conjured up on their 1978 debut.

■ ■ ■

The legacy for Africa was immediate. By 1982, and the next World Cup in Spain, Fifa had expanded the tournament to 24 finalists and Africa's allocation of places had doubled: to two. Both were World Cup novices, Cameroon and Algeria.

The Algerians had formed a dashing team, their 2-0 win over Nigeria at the hostile Surulere stadium in the away leg of the final qualifying tie a resonant result because of Nigeria's feared reputation in Lagos. Proximity to Spain meant 3,000 fans could plan to travel, many of them by ferry from Oran and Algiers, though the draw had put the Algerian fixtures almost as far across the Spanish mainland as possible. They would play their matches in Gijón and Oviedo. On arriving there, they found themselves billeted in some style, in the handsome Asturian finca of a well-heeled Spanish eye surgeon. 'The thing I remember most is all the animal heads on the walls, lions, gazelles. We felt quite at home there,' recalls Salah Assad, the squad's inventive left-winger. 'I think the owner was quite a hunter.' Impressed by the local taxidermy, Assad noted that, as the day of their World Cup debut neared, most people assumed the Algerians were about to be stuffed.

For their opening match, the Desert Foxes faced . . . well, the same lot that had stood in the way of Morocco in 1970 and Tunisia in 1978. It was West Germany versus the Maghreb yet again. World champions twice already, European champions from two summers earlier, the Germans had a strut about them, as they enjoyed themselves in front of the cameras on the beaches of north-west Spain in their tight shorts and longer hairstyles. Harald Schumacher, their goalkeeper, predicted in front of microphones that his team would score between four and eight times against the Algerians. Assad found himself trailed by a German reporter persistently asking how he, at outside-left, regarded his confrontation with Germany's Manfred Kaltz, supposedly the finest right full-back in the game. 'This guy got on my nerves,' recalls Assad, 'so I told him to come back and ask me after the game.' Kaltz had been quoted as saying he knew little about Algeria. The German players did not, as their coach Jupp Derwell later revealed, watch the videos of Algeria he had prepared for them, because, said Derwell, his players would have laughed at the suggestion. Up in the Finca El Campuluto, Germany's opponents found it helpful to cultivate the feeling they had been underestimated.

And Les Fennecs, the Desert Foxes, needed a cause like that to unite them. Reshuffles among the coaching staff over the previous six months had unsettled their lead-in and there were tensions between the players employed by clubs in Europe on the one hand and those who had spent their entire careers in Algeria. The World Cup had perhaps come two or three years too late for the most celebrated member of the squad, Mustapha Dahleb, a deity in the French championnat, an idol to fans of Paris Saint-Germain, but, at 30, playing at a lesser pace than some of the bright talents around him, such as Lakhdar Belloumi, soon to be justifying his nickname as The Wizard of the Maghreb; or Rabah Madjer, who would go on to great heights and score one of the more impudent goals, a back-heel for Porto, in the history of European Cup finals; or the skilful, sometimes wilful Assad. This trio, as with others in their early 20s, took itchy feet to the World Cup and some frustration that their national football association had outlawed any of them from moving to European clubs before they were 28. They had effectively been nationalised, although they were minded to protest about that restriction on their freedoms, not least the determined young Assad.

Despite these issues, their preparation games had gone well. A tour of Switzerland had sharpened their quick counter-attacking game and they had troubled strong opposition – Real Madrid and Peru – in the build-up with their width. Assad recalls: 'We wanted to show ourselves off in these games and we were determined to be in the line-up. Players would say they were fully fit when they had little injuries. We knew we had good players who would not necessarily be in the side, even Dahleb. We knew we had footballers who were strong on the ball, great dribblers. And we knew we'd have a lot of applause. Algerians had come to support us, we had Africa and the Arab world behind us. A lot of the Maghrebians who lived in Spain came to our games and as soon as the first game started we realised the Spaniards were with us, too.'

By the time the opening game was drawing to a close, there was little doubt about the majority support. All around the Molinón Stadium, a continuous shriek willed on the final whistle. The underdogs held a 2-1 lead, Algeria were beating West Germany, and a World Cup of some surprising early results now anticipated a sensation. Africa was about to record a victory at a World Cup finals for only the second time and against the favourites to win the tournament. Deservedly losing, Germany pushed and pushed for a second equaliser, and as the nervous shrill surrounded them from the terraces, Algeria produced a cameo moment of haughtiness that turned the nervous whistles to applause. Deep in his own half, Assad, under pressure, lobbed a West German marker, instead of hoiking the ball clear. He found Dahleb, who promptly nodded the ball over another opponent's head to collect it on the bounce behind his marker's back. The pair of them had taken control of the left flank throughout. This was their final, swaggering stamp of authority.

West Germany, by contrast, had looked careless in possession time and again. A feature of the game had been the interceptions and rapid safaris upfield of Chaabane Merzekane from right-back for Algeria. The decisive interventions would be those of Djamel Zidane, carrying the ball from midfield, at pace, unshakeable in possession. Zidane's pass to Belloumi set up the opening goal, Schumacher parrying Belloumi's shot, Madjer prodding in the loose ball nine minutes into the second half. Another forceful run from Zidane invited Assad to extend the lead shortly afterwards. Algeria's fans, bouncing up and down, had turned their section of the stadium to a hum of jubilant green-and-white. Germany were rattled, their hulk of a centre-forward, Horst Hrubesch, booked after a frustrating hour where he had been beaten to almost every header by the giant centre-half Noureddine Kourichi. When West Germany did score, through their captain Karl-Heinz Rummenigge, Algeria answered almost immediately: Dahleb to Assad again and a whippy low cross turned in by Belloumi. Hrubesch flashed a couple of efforts off target, but the coup held. 'It felt,' wrote the *Süddeutsche Zeitung*, 'like the sinking of the *Titanic*.'

Next up for Algeria: Austria in Oviedo. The Algerian presence in the stands had swelled, although, alas, a familiar visitor to African World Cup campaigns had also announced itself in the team's camp: trouble over bonuses. The players sensed earlier financial promises had already been broken, and several felt more and more uncomfortable about the ban on their accepting offers to play for European clubs in the light of the rave reviews given to Madjer, Belloumi and Assad after the West Germany game. 'I felt,' recalls Assad, 'that we were having our dreams taken away. Some of us did feel very angry, and I think if these things had been sorted out, we would have played better against Austria.' Algeria lost 2-0, to leave the group in a state of delicate poise, Austria on four points, West Germany and Algeria on two each, with Chile bottom of the table, having lost twice. The West Germans held a superior goal difference. Then there was the ominous scheduling: on Thursday 24 June, Algeria were to play Chile in Oviedo. Austria-Germany had been timetabled for the following afternoon in Gijón. In other words, the two European teams would know what maths would guarantee their progress while Algeria and indeed Chile, who had a remote chance of going through if they won by a large score in their final game, could only throw down a gauntlet.

In Oviedo, Assad took it on himself to do so. In the absence, injured, of Belloumi, he wanted to take a position closer to goal, no longer confined to the left flank. Within half an hour Assad had scored twice and within 34 minutes, Algeria were 3-0 up against the South Americans. An alarming loss of authority in the second half would reduce their advantage. The 3-2 victory left them with a goal difference overall of zero, one worse than Austria.

What happened on the Friday reeked. Africa's World Cup hopes were plain hijacked in Gijón. West Germany needed to beat Austria to go through; Austria could afford to lose by up to two goals and still join the Germans there at Algeria's expense. Hrubesch scored after 10 minutes. From that point, all pace and urgency would be sucked from the contest as if by a giant syringe. As the contest became more and more torpid, the crowd turned agitated. Algerians there waved peseta banknotes at the players. When referee Robert Valentine refused an Austrian penalty, they bellowed in anger. Even German television called it 'the most shameful day in the history of our Football Federation.' Others struck on another way of describing how Austria and Germany had come to a mutually agreeable result by the time Valentine blew his whistle. They called it The Anschluss.

The Algerian Federation lodged a complaint with Fifa, in vain. Curiously, those who took the blow with most stoicism were the Algerian players. Some had gone to Gijón to watch the staged stalemate between Austria and West Germany; others had felt they would rather not. 'Some were out shopping already,' recalls Assad. 'Frankly we knew we were going home. We assumed Austria and West Germany would do what suited them both. They're neighbours. We all knew we should have made it harder for them anyway by playing better against Austria and beating Chile by more goals.' By then, shrugs Assad, the disputes with the Federation over money and over the futures of those with ambitions to move abroad had also created resentment: 'We were youngsters. Some of us wanted to be out of there, quite honestly.' West Germany, who had sneaked through at Algeria's expense, finished second in the tournament, and managed to turn themselves even less popular by then because of a grisly challenge by goalkeeper Schumacher which hospitalised a French player, Patrick Battiston, in the semi-final. Fifa changed the rules for future tournaments as a result of the flaccid German-Austrian ceasefire. Matches that decided final league positions would from then on take place simultaneously.

■ ■ ■

If the Spain World Cup said a sad, sympathetic farewell to Algeria, outraged on their behalf, Africa acknowledged them as the new flag-bearers for its football. The Desert Foxes and the rest of the continent's north happily accepted that role. In the final rounds of qualifying for the next World Cup in Mexico, in 1986, the region achieved as close as could be imagined to a clean sweep, Algeria and Morocco taking the two African places with victories over Tunisia and Libya, Egypt having been eliminated a round earlier. As the rivalries across the Mediterranean lands sharpened, statesmen promoted the game aggressively. Between 1982 and 1994, each of the five countries of the north built and spruced up stadiums to host an African Nations Cup. Muammar Gaddafi responded to US sanctions on the import of Libyan oil by putting on a show at the 1982 Nations Cup, his Libyan team reaching the final. Hosni Mubarak's Egypt invited the continent there for the 1986 version; King Hassan's Morocco hoped their hosting of the event two years later could be a convincing blueprint for staging a World Cup and Algeria became African champions for the first time in front of their own supporters in 1990.

Some charismatic fans Algeria had too, among them a figure who would beguile visitors from abroad with his knockabout and circus during matches of the Desert Foxes. He was known simply as 'Yamaha', a cheerleader almost as widely recognised as the great players of the time; and his was a time of some of the country's genuine greats, footballers like Madjer and Belloumi. He was a clown whose pre-match variety show could draw more applause than the hour and a half that followed, his stunts and his mischief providing as much theatre as the match. Agile at climbing whatever barricades separated fans from players, or the mass of supporters from VIPs, his catch-me-if-you-can chases with the police along the running-track at the huge July 5th stadium became part of what Arabic calls the 'houl', the whipping up of an atmosphere. His antics would turn suddenly to a double-act when his younger brother, who had the same, urchin features, joined in. Yamaha was said to have changed the way football was watched in Algeria from the 1980s onwards, to have come up with the idea of bringing a saxophonist in to accompany the percussion of darbouka drums. He was an iconoclast, who, with the approval of the crowd around him, would shout cheeky, witty put-downs at the men in suits in the directors' box. He was liked by the players, travelled abroad with the national team as if a mascot, chanting, jiving, a frenetic court jester, with a mobile face and a mouth so wide he could apparently hide his whole fist in it.

His real name was Hocine Dihimi, though everybody knew him as 'Yamaha,' a moniker explained in various ways: that the flat in the poor, densely populated area he grew up near the Avenue Belouizdad in Algiers stood next door to a moped repair shop; or that he buzzed around like a scooter weaving through the traffic, charting his own course, with a haphazard independence of spirit and imagination. *El Watan* newspaper called Yamaha 'a national figure, famous for the joy he mobilised in big crowds and around football.' The Yamaha show would draw even those uninterested in the sport to their windows in the whitewashed apartment blocks that overlook the quaint, ageing August 20th stadium where Chabab Rhiadi Belcourt, CRB, his local and favourite club, play. 'A symbol without knowing it,' *El Watan* added of him, 'a symbol of a youth that wants to enjoy life, a vivaciousness that has grown in Algiers, thanks to football.' If that sounds a little solemn, it's because Algerian society was entering a period at odds with itself, rising Islamism answered by iron government, leaving a shrinking space for vivaciousness.

A restlessness had also developed among the gifted generation of Algerian footballers. After the adventures in Spain, Madjer and Assad, among others, won their battles with the Federation to be allowed to launch careers with leading clubs in Europe. Madjer joined Porto, Assad moved to Paris Saint-Germain. Their trips home to represent the Desert Foxes in qualifying matches for the

1986 World Cup confirmed in their own minds that European club football had improved them as footballers and that the national team had grown in strength in the four years since Spain. 'We were an even better team than in 1982,' claims Assad. 'We ought to have waltzed into the second round with cigars in our hands.'

But Algeria, grouped with Brazil, Spain and Northern Ireland, had not been long in Mexico when the irritations of their previous expedition resurfaced, an edgy schism between some of the footballers who earned their living in Europe and those based in Algeria; rows about money with the Federation. Their opening match, against the Irish, soured the mood further, a contest easily caricatured as the nimble versus the niggardly. Madjer withdrew in the first half after a clash of heads with the Irish defender Mal Donaghy, an incident put down to more than simply chance as Donaghy had clattered into the same player moments earlier. The Irish played 'scandalous anti-football' fumed *El Moujahid*'s reporter. The game finished 1-1, Djamel Zidane equalising an early goal from Norman Whiteside.

After the Northern Ireland match, the Algerians withdrew to their hotel and to a stand-off with their paymasters over the difference between promised bonus agreements and what they were now being presented with. A distraction ahead of the collision with Brazil? Apparently not, when just after the hour, Algeria created chances for both Assad and Belloumi to put them 1-0 up. They wasted them. A defensive error soon afterwards allowed Brazil's Careca to score the game's only goal. With one match left, Algeria required victory against Spain to go through. Mexican television, apparently trying to celebrate the gaiety of nations that is the World Cup, broadcast the chilling Gillo Pontecorvo film *The Battle of Algiers* the evening before the Desert Foxes took on the Spaniards.

The next afternoon's entertainment would scarcely be more uplifting. Beaten 3-0, Algeria finished bottom of the group.

There was some Maghrebi might still in the tournament, though. Morocco, a happier group with fewer expatriate players among their number, were to make history in Africa's World Cup odyssey, but their campaign took time to gain momentum. They were based in Monterrey, where the phenomenon of the Mexican Wave would be introduced to football. Soon we knew why: Group F would give its crowds long periods where they needed something to lift them off their seats. The first four matches involving the Atlas Lions, Poland, Portugal and England produced a mere two goals. Morocco scored neither of them. A pair of goalless draws left the African team, the outsiders, second with a match to play. There, Morocco would show they had more to offer, that they were merely being discreet about it and had constructed their World Cup campaign in the right order. It did not, like Tunisia's 1978 expedition or Algeria's 1982 blitz, begin with a bang to fade quickly to whimper. This one had legs.

Morocco had goals in them. Abdelkrim 'Krimau' Merry, a striker with a broad chest on which he could stun a ball capably, was a strong leader of a forward line where he would initially be partnered by his younger brother, Mustapha. Behind them lurked Aziz Bouderbala, elegant and inclined to guard the ball at his feet as long as he could. He and Abdelhamid Dolmy would keep opposing midfields chasing and hunting the ball. The jewels, though, were goalkeeper and captain Badou Zaki and the number 10, Mohammed Timoumi, African Footballer of the Year in 1985, a proper trickster, who had been illuminating the African Champions Cup for his club FAR Rabat: one mesmerising episode of Timoumi's keepy-uppy skills at the humiliating expense of some Egyptian defenders would be replayed for many years on Moroccan television. Timoumi was quick, too, though sometimes not quite speedy enough for his own protection. A nasty injury had kept him out for a long period in the year ahead of the tournament.

Morocco had qualified for Mexico '86 having conceded a single goal in eight matches. Zaki took credit for much of that, as for an alert save, tipping over a dipping shot in the opening fixture against Poland. After that draw, the Moroccans were struck by how early the Poles showed symptoms of fatigue. But they hardly capitalised. Asked about his team's caution, Morocco's head coach José Faria turned belligerent with the media. 'We'd like to play beautiful football, but you can't always do that, especially coming into a big tournament. You have to protect yourselves a bit. You want spectacular? Go and watch Hungary.' Hungary had been walloped 6-0 by the USSR a day earlier.

Down in the lower reaches of the group table, England had offered neither spectacle nor protection. Beaten 1-0 by Portugal, they needed a pick-me-up in the group's second match, against Morocco. The England manager Bobby Robson thought muscle and height would be the key. He identified the big centre-forward, Mark Hateley – known as 'Attila' while he played for Italy's Milan – as Morocco's likely nemesis. 'We'll lean heavily on them and they won't like to see Hateley up there,' predicted Robson, 'they'll be terrified of him.' Wisely, someone relayed these comments to Morocco's players, probably Faria, a cunning sort, a Brazilian who had converted to Islam since moving to North Africa and combined the job of national coach with guiding FAR, the army club. He showed them Robson's quotes and some choice cuttings from British tabloids. Bingo. 'The English were clearly insinuating we didn't count for very much in international football,' recalls Krimau, the striker. 'Frankly, they'd have been better off keeping quiet. After the game I said "We just played against a team from the Middle Ages." I'd still say so. England showed very little except their own nervousness and their frustrations at their own limitations.' Morocco-England was a poor game. Krimau might have inflicted more than a post-match barb had he not miscued a first-half effort. Bouderbala troubled England with his changes of pace and his control and Morocco went into the interval at a distinct advantage. England's captain Bryan Robson had left the field having aggravated a shoulder injury and the midfielder Ray Wilkins had been sent off. Booked for fouling the slippery Timoumi, Wilkins then threw the ball petulantly at the referee when another decision went Morocco's way.

Back in Morocco, the Atlas Lions were deemed to have let England off the hook, drawing 0-0. 'An unfinished symphony,' *L'Opinion* newspaper called it. They criticised the coach's conservative streak: 'Faria's demons overcame him.' There was a gleeful reminder of Robson's unfulfilled game plan: 'Mustapha Biaz in the defence made Hateley look ridiculous.' But *L'Opinion* still had to speak for a nation on tenterhooks. Two draws from two matches was respectable, but Morocco still needed to win their final game against Portugal to make history and be the first African country to go beyond the group phase. Krimau remembers it as if hesitancy had all been part of the plan. 'Against Poland and England, we played a tactical game. We held back on our attacking instincts and closed up the game a bit. We wanted to keep our hopes alive. But for the Portugal game it was different. We put our foot on the gas and we sparked right from the start.'

Against Portugal the approach would be strikingly different. A lightness of spirit seemed to infect the party, recalls Krimau, as they changed cities and arrived in Guadalajara, where Brazil were billeted along with hundreds of Brazilian fans. They mixed with the Brazil squad. Krimau has a jersey the player Socrates gave him the day before the Portugal game. There, Morocco's performance once again made Brazil and Africa football soul-mates, Faria transformed from roundhead to samba-man. Timoumi found his platform. His fine weighted passes would start the move that put Morocco one goal ahead and set up Krimau to shoot for 3-0. Goal number two, the second from the winger Abderrazzak Kaïri, had been a beauty, a volley struck on the run that crashed past the goalkeeper like a bolt of lightning. Kaïri credited his well-timed arrival in the penalty box to meet a low cross to repeated practice, a move perfected in training. It stunned Portugal. A score of 3-1 left Morocco top of their group, a point clear of Poland and England. Africa had broken its World Cup glass ceiling, made the second round. The country assessed the size of the hurdle they had crossed, a first not only for Africa but for . . . well, *L'Opinion* spelled it out: 'The exploits of the heroes of Mexico honours our land and should make proud the whole Maghreb, Africa, the Arab Nation and the Islamic world.'

So to the knockout rounds, and West Germany against Morocco. Again. Sixteen years after Morocco had become the first team from Africa to reach a World Cup finals via a qualifying tournament, and made their striking first impression by taking the lead against West Germany, here they were again in Mexico, up against the same opponents. Now Monterrey, not León, felt like an oven. Thermometers measured 35 degrees in the shade, and the Germans looked heavy-legged, sapped of energy. Déjà vu. The team wearing white seemed static, their players pausing for longer and longer on the touchline to slurp from water bottles, apply ice to the backs of their necks. The team in red moved more freely, if cautiously. Only this time, the score stood at 0-0. And that was how it stayed for 117 minutes.

Morocco-West Germany turned out a poor sequel to the 1970 version. It was a grind. Germany laboured. Morocco retreated. The most breathtaking piece of football in the first 110 minutes had come from a goalkeeper, Zaki's stunning parry when Karl-Heinz Rummenigge met a low, hard Felix Magath cross. Franz Beckenbauer, the German head coach called the opportunity 'a thousand per cent chance of a goal'. Neutrals called the contest the least entertaining match of the tournament. Extra-time dragged, beckoning the players towards penalties. 'The German players were shattered,' remembers Krimau, 'the extra time was killing them.' Nor had the performance of Morocco's goalkeeper made West Germany optimistic about a shoot-out. Zaki had made other good saves and his personal World Cup record now stood at one goal conceded in nearly four and a half hours.

When West Germany earned a free-kick two and half minutes before the end of extra-time, it looked the last throw of the dice. It was a long way from Zaki's goal, more than 30 metres. To the surprise of the German captain Rummenigge, who had imagined he might strike the free-kick, Lothar Matthäus seized the ball and lined it up. He opted not for height but a shot that fizzed just above the grass, curved around the defensive wall and, for just about the first time, rendered Zaki helpless. The shot crept inside his left-hand post. Game over. If Morocco had overachieved by arriving within three minutes of a shoot-out for a place in the quarter-finals, they felt suddenly cursed. An extraordinary sequence had been concluded. Four times in five World Cups, North Africa had taken on West Germany. In the course of 387 minutes of football, the Germans had led those contests for a mere 12 minutes, the Maghrebis for more than four times as long. And West Germany always progressed.

CHAPTER SEVEN

THE TORTOISE AND THE HIPPO

Thanks to the Saharans, chiefly to Algeria and Morocco, Africa had a World Cup presence, a respect, by the late 1980s. Thanks to Cameroon, black Africa had also redeemed its international reputation after the misadventures of Zaïre in West Germany in 1974. Cameroon had travelled to the 1982 tournament in Spain with Algeria, made almost as good an impression as the Maghrebis and returned home bearing almost as big a grudge about the manner of their departure. The Indomitable Lions drew all three group matches, and between their lively centre-forward Roger Milla hitting a Peru post after seven minutes of their opening game and Tommy Nkono, their acrobatic goalkeeper, making a rare error to permit Italy a lead in their third, they had done little wrong and, to their minds, been regularly wronged by match officials. To this day, Milla gets worked up about why a 'goal' he scored against the Peruvians in the 0-0 draw was ruled offside; or about the penalty not awarded when he was fouled in the Polish penalty area.

Cameroon left Spain unbeaten. Their long World Cup saga

was just beginning. By the end of the next decade they had set new milestones for the continent, and Milla had become as famous a figurehead for its football as the great Eusébio.

The big question, the enigma with Cameroon, endures: How on earth this small country arrived so quickly at the vanguard, and so steadily maintained that status. Between the Cameroonian club, Oryx Douala, winning the very first African Champions Cup in 1965 and the city of Douala proudly producing a footballer like Samuel Eto'o Fils, perhaps the best centre-forward in the world in the first decade of the 21st century, stretches more than 40 years of extraordinary milestones. Cameroon have made more appearances at World Cup final tournaments than any other country in Africa; Cameroon were the first African team to reach a quarter-finals at a World Cup in 1990. Cameroon can boast four African Nations Cup triumphs, and that for a country who only joined the biennial event in 1970, when it had been up and running for 13 years. They became Olympic football champions at the Sydney Games in 2000, Eto'o starring, Brazil knocked out on the way. The most powerful man in the running of the continent's football, the head of the Confederation of African Football since the late 1980s, Issa Hayatou, is a Cameroonian. Eleven times in its first 35 years, the African Footballer of the Year award has gone to a Cameroonian. It's not as if this is a status they have acquired by dint of sheer numbers: Cameroon, with less than 20 million people, barely gets into the top 15 in Africa's population hierarchy. There are at least seven Nigerians for every Cameroonian; yet Cameroon have been champions of the continent at its favoured sport twice as many times as Nigeria. Nor is this a bought success. Cameroon is poor. It usually sneaks into the International Monetary Fund GDP league table between 90th and 100th in the world. Cameroon is also notoriously inefficient, and, bluntly, rather crooked. It typically comes at around 140th out of 180 countries in Transparency International's global Corruption Index.

So why has Cameroon been Africa's trailblazer at football? Eto'o gives an articulate discourse in answer to that question, all about spirit, endeavour and the pride of the so-called Indomitable Lions, the sobriquet the national team assumed in the early 1970s. He will also refer you to a Cameroonian folk-tale that he finds useful. He tells it like this:

Once upon a time there was a tortoise, eating little onions on the banks of a lake, when suddenly he was surprised by an enormous hippopotamus emerging out of the water.

'What are doing on my patch?' roared the hippo. 'Don't let me catch you here again, or I'll squash you.'

The tortoise, a proud and clever creature, answered: 'You come back here tomorrow, at noon, and we'll see who's the strongest.'

'Are you mad?' exclaimed the hippo. 'I can't think of any animal in the jungle stronger than me.'

'I'll beat you, you'll see,' smiled the tortoise, slipping back into the forest as the hippo eased himself back into the water.

A little later, the tortoise spotted the huge form of an elephant approaching him, coming so close he almost trod on his shell.

'Look out,' cried the tortoise.

'What are doing in my forest?' boomed the elephant. 'If you don't shift now, I'll squash you.'

An idea came to the tortoise. 'Look,' he said to the elephant, 'I'm told you are the strongest of all animals. But I'd like you to prove it. At midday tomorrow, I'll meet you here. You'll find the end of a rope and when it goes taut, start pulling it. I'll be at the other end.

'I certainly shall', *trumpeted the proud elephant.*

At noon the next day, the rope went taut, the elephant seized his end and tugged with all his might from the forest. On the banks of the river, gripping the other end the hippo, instructed to do likewise, pulled and pulled. They exhausted themselves, watched from the bushes by the hiding tortoise.

The elephant gave up, and as the tortoise emerged, he asked him: 'How did you do that?'

'I just dug my claws into the ground.'

'From now on, you can walk here whenever you like. We are allies,' declared the elephant.

A little later, the tortoise found the exhausted hippo. 'How did you do that?' wheezed the hippo. He got the same explanation as the elephant.

'I admire you,' said the hippo, 'you're welcome on my river-bank.'

Cameroon, explains Eto'o, are the tortoise in the fable, tough and cunning through practice. 'We have a survival spirit,' he adds, embarking on a brief history lesson. 'We were explored by the Portuguese, then colonised by the Germans, the French and the English, and in Cameroon there are 230 ethnic groups, there are mountains and deserts and jungles. We are strong survivors.' Look on the jigsaw that is the map of Africa, and Cameroon is one of the oddest shaped pieces, tapering up at its northernmost point to Lake Chad, broadening out to border Gabon, Equatorial Guinea and Congo-Brazzaville along the south. Its long jagged western edge fences off Nigeria, with whom territories have from time to time been disputed. In the east, its concave frontier pushes up against the Central African Republic. There the Baka people mostly live, or what in colonial times were called the pygmies. At one corner of Cameroon, it is hot and almost desert-like; at another it steams and sweats. It has jungles, and it has a volcanic mountain. Not for nothing is it called all-Africa in miniature.

■　■　■

Eto'o's brief resume of Cameroon's history is sound. The Portuguese found the Atlantic inlet at Douala an accommodating port in the 15th century. The Germans had found it useful 400 years later and they were in turn displaced by France and Britain after the First World War. Those two influences made modern Cameroon a mélange not only of its wide mix of African languages but Anglophone and Francophone parts, the latter the majority. All this made for potential schisms, rifts. Add to that the tendency of the French colonisers to give preferred employment status to immigrants from elsewhere in Africa – Gabonese, Sierra Leoneans, Senegalese – and, clearly, Cameroon has had to live through several tiers of complexity.

Under the French and British, football gained its popularity. Kept at arms' length from the matches played by the European settlers for the first half of the 20th century, Cameroonians defined their own form of the game and had to tolerate some petty tyrannies from their rulers. When a group of supporters and players registered the named of their club in the then capital as Olympic Douala, mimicking Olympique Marseille, the French authorities forbade it. So Oryx Douala, named after an antelope, was born, one of a number of clubs with names that celebrated the creatures of central Africa's savannahs, rivers and forests. There was Caïman de Douala, Léopard de Douala, L'Aigle de N'kongsamba (Eagle of N'kongsamba, inland of Douala). In Yaoundé, now the official capital, they favoured titles that made a big noise: Tonnerre Yaoundé (Earthquake),

Canon Yaoundé (Cannon). Of these, Africa would in time hear plenty.

Oryx Douala made the first big impression after independence in 1960. Serial domestic champions, they were invited to the inaugural Pan-African club championship in Ghana. They won it. Oryx wore all yellow with a wide, black stripe across the midriff of their shirts and were admired a good deal more for the verve of their attacking than the solidity of their defence. Oryx were a caution-to-the-wind team: in the mid-1960s they were said sometimes to field six forwards in the XI. It gave them a startlingly inconsistent record in domestic football but their triumphs of the first part of the decade made icons of several footballers. An inside-forward Jean-Pierre Tokoto would be an enduring star of Cameroonian football all the way to the early 1980s. A teenager from the Champions Cup line-up, Emmanuel Koum, was fished out by scouts from Monaco in France. Striker Mbappe Leppe had the widest fan club and is usually remembered for the surprising balance he maintained between power – he was six foot four – and the delicacy of his touch.

In France, meanwhile, Cameroonian footballers had already made a lasting impression on the game. A defender named Zacharie Noah played for Sedan when they won the French Cup at the end of the 1950s and left on world sport a specific genetic privilege: his son Yannick won the French Open at tennis in 1983 and his grandson, Joakim, became a basketball star in America's NBA. A centre-forward named Eugène Njo Léa had moved to Europe in the early 1950s to study law, but played so well that by the middle of the decade he was one of the French championnat's best, his goals propelling Saint-Étienne to the 1957 league title. He became a significant figure in the history of European and African football for two reasons. He was one of the first black players from sub-

Saharan Africa to turn professional in Europe, and one of the finest. Above all, he shaped the way the game worked. Qualified in law, he was the principal mover behind the French Footballers Union, the UNFP, and led a challenge against contract regulations that tied players to a club until they were 35 unless the club agreed to let them go elsewhere. Njo Léa was, in his way, to the 1950s what Jean-Marc Bosman, the Belgian who challenged European football's transfer system, would be to the 1990s. For that, he was the first in a very, very long line of Cameroonian footballers not afraid to speak up for themselves.

For his impact as a successful black African abroad, Njo Léa became a role model, but if you were a young boy growing up in Douala, scoring goals on soggy patches of ground in the wet season, on baked earth in the dry, chances are you wanted to be like Mbappe 'Marshall' Leppe. That's how a young Roger Milla imagined himself, as he collected photographs of Pelé to put up on his bedroom wall. Milla's father, who worked for the national railway network, was a football fan, involved in the running of Caïman de Douala. The Milla family had moved there when Roger was 11, which meant a change from his rural pleasures, firing at birds from his homemade catapult when he was not dribbling an orange or a ball made of rolled up newspaper and twine with his feet. In Douala, Milla became the talk of his quartier for the way he could dribble and it earned him pocket-money, as local sides hired him game-per-game. Milla was light on his feet, but he had strong, powerful thighs. At 17 he became the Cameroon schools' high-jump champion. Two years earlier he had made his debut as a forward for L'Éclair de Douala in the second division. His terrain would be grassless pitches, although Cameroonian football was about to get a face-lift. Just as Milla was making a name for himself, having moved up a rung in the ladder to Léopard de Douala, the country had a chance to host the growing attraction that was the African Nations Cup.

The year was 1972. Cameroon was exciting. They made great music there, and the lord of it, the saxophonist extraordinaire, Manu Dibango had just released his 'Soul Makossa', to success on both sides of the Atlantic. Dibango composed the official hymn for the Nations Cup. Two new stadiums were erected, the 100,000-capacity Omnisports in Yaoundé and the Reunification in Douala. Cameroon rolled out its red carpet for the cream of the continent's national teams at the same time as it announced the political unification of the Anglophone and Francophone parts of the country. Football had a grounding in both parts, although clubs from what used to be the English-speaking parts would for the next 30-odd years nurse a feeling they had fewer opportunities than the others.

The diversity Eto'o would still be talking about a generation later has long been part of Cameroon's football fabric. At the period of unification, tribal distinctions had become an issue in the national sport, an issue heated enough to involve the president of the Republic of Cameroon. In the late 1960s, the Minister for Youth and Sports, a Michel Njiensi, formulated a bill to de-tribalise the main clubs of the Cameroon league. He observed that the older sporting institutions of Douala and Yaoundé had taken on an identity that went beyond their locale, and some of the football clubs were associated with the majority language-group, or tribe, in their areas. To Njiensi, like many of Africa's young politicians in the post-colonial honeymoon, national unity was a dogma worth chasing and cultivating. Njiensi wanted to change the names of the teams, but his suggestions about how a reformed, de-tribalised, league might read seemed terribly dull. Instead of Union, Dynamo, Leopard, Oryx or Caïman, he proposed Douala I, Douala II or

Douala III. Instead of Canon or Tonnerre, he suggested Yaoundé I or II. The rationale was noble enough: cronyism that discriminated against, say, Cameroon's Bassa people or favoured its Bamileke community had been recognised as a social tinder-box. Minister Njiensi had seen it expressed in the chants and hostilities at football stadiums.

But his plan fell flat, just as an imposition altering the identities of Celtic and Rangers in Glasgow, or suggesting a Basque clear-out at Athletic Bilbao would if it came from the parliaments of London or Madrid. In Cameroon, supporters marched against Njiensi's bill, and, as if to demonstrate the rationale behind the proposal, muttered that the Minister was only acting that way because he was a Bamileke, an ethnic group caricatured as pushy and ambitious. Returning from an extensive overseas trip, the then head of state, Ahmadou Ahidjo, abandoned his Sports Minister's initiative, and promptly enough removed Njiensi from his cabinet. 'We found out then,' concludes André Ntonfo, author of *Football et Politique du Football au Cameroun*, 'that the regime liked our football the way it was, which is deeply tribal. We realised football was a powerful factor in affirming ethnicity, and that a majority of Cameroonians were not ready to give that up. And we also found out that our leading sport was highly politicised.'

A German coach, Peter Schnittger, came to similar conclusions soon after he arrived in Cameroon to take charge of the national team ahead of the 1972 Nations Cup. Schnittger had some experience in Africa when he accepted the post. This, he soon saw, was both the most brilliant task he had been assigned and the most complex. 'At that time, the national team was mainly made up of players from around Yaoundé,' recalls Schnittger. 'That was inevitable as the Yaoundé clubs were the best teams at the time. Once we had done very well in the Nations Cup tournament and had reached the semi-finals, the new Minister came up to me and said: "Peter, Cameroon have played really well, but remember you also have some Bamileke players you could use." It was indirect pressure on me to change the team but it had been put in such a way, that it made sure it looked like these would be *my* choices, if I obeyed him.' Schnittger adds: 'I'm afraid in my experience the interference of politicians in the job of the coach is typically African. But I kept the same team, no changes, which would actually end up causing problems. It meant they could turn to me and say: "Ah, you should have changed the line-up here and there."'

Perhaps Schnittger ought to have. Cameroon lost the semi-final of the Nations Cup they hosted, beaten by the eventual champions, Congo-Brazzaville. The margin of defeat was narrow, and agonizing. The attempted comeback from an early 1-0 deficit featured a mesmeric run from deep in defence by the team's libero, Paul Nlend, who swept aside challenge after challenge, and as the spectators rose to their feet, skimmed his shot against a post. Up in the gantry, as the hollow anti-climax of a 1-0 loss became a probability, one of the two commentators for state radio was overcome with emotion. Abel Mbengue had been providing his excitable narrative in French, and in the spirit of union, was accompanied by the voice in English, of Peter Essoka. Mbengue, distraught at events on the field, turned silent for the final quarter-hour, apparently in tears. The Francophones were stuck listening to English. 'The minutes are dying away,' whispered Essoka, 'Cameroon is going out of the tournament.' Post-mortems on the team would soon be overshadowed by a massive corruption scandal, not the last in Cameroonian football, but the most spectacular. A huge portion of the revenues from the 1972 Nations Cup had, it emerged, been siphoned off by some of the senior administrators of the event. The scammers would spend the next five years in N'kondegui prison.

At this point, the Cameroon national team was given its new name. The Indomitable Lions would gradually wear their title with growing distinction, while Cameroon's clubs roared their way to further titles. Canon Yaoundé won the Champions Cup three times between 1971 and 1980. Tonnerre won the inaugural African Cup-Winners Cup in 1975, and were runners-up a year later. Canon won the same competition in 1979, as did Union Douala in 1981. 'There was a snowball effect,' recalls Schnittger, 'kids identified with the players who were becoming successful and wanted to play football. At that time, the football being played there was, if you like, natural, spontaneous. It also had a status because even then you had footballers, like Jean-Pierre Tokoto, a very good midfielder, who had made names for themselves, were known abroad, but the national team was still mainly made up of local footballers. They hardly had access to grass pitches; it was a wild football in a way.' It was also a rugged, all-weather game, adds Schnittger. 'It is very hot most of the day. You had to get up very early to train properly if you weren't going to be totally fatigued. When I got there, I liked to work from half past six to eight in the morning.'

He particularly liked working with Milla, the electric young goalscorer from Léopard de Douala, one of the clubs Schnittger coached in addition to his national team tasks. 'I remember the moment when Roger Milla first came to the attention of the rest of Africa,' says Schnittger. 'He was very young still, and thin, not an ounce of fat on him. His legs were like chopsticks. He weighed maybe 60 kilos, but he was so fast. He had great belief in himself even then. We had a quarter-final in the Champions Cup against Hafia, from Guinea, who were very strong then and had to go away to Conkary for the first leg. There was an African Union summit going on there at the time, so in the stadium were all these heads of state, and Fidel Castro, too. At half-time, Hafia were 2-0 up. In the second half we scored four. When Milla scored his first goal, he just exploded into life. He was like a gazelle, bounding around. He scored a hat-trick in the end. The next day, the team went on an official visit to the Guinea leader, Sekou Touré and all his guests from the summit. Sekou Touré made a speech, saying "This was not a victory just for Cameroon, nor the Leopards, it was a triumph for all the youth of Africa." People were just bowled over by Milla.' Fully 17 years later, at the 1990 World Cup, a large portion of the planet would be seduced by the same man, 38 years old, legs a little broader than chopsticks, but still bounding around like an antelope on the sierra.

Milla's successes in Africa were achieved mostly with Tonnerre Yaoundé, whom he joined from Léopard. Tonnerre prided themselves on the sophistication of their football. So learned was their style, they liked to imagine, that fans called them Tonnerre 'Kalala', the Ewondo word for 'book'. They were about textbook technique, epitomised in the tricky feet of Bonaventura Djonkep, the elegant passing of Paul Nlend, the vision of midfielder Paul Gaston 'Monsieur Football' Ndongo. And galvanised by Milla, who fascinated almost every coach who came across him. 'To have Roger Milla in your team was to have a diamond,' says Claude Le Roy, the Frenchman who took over the national team in the early 1980s. 'You could spend a week training with him and he would not make a single technical mistake. Remember, he spent much of his life practising in bad conditions. Then he spent a long time in France and if you look at the clubs – Saint-Étienne, Bastia, Montpellier, Monaco – they may not always have the very top clubs there, but when he was with them, they usually won something, a trophy or promotion: *because* they had Milla in the team. In terms of pure quality, Roger Milla really belongs among the greatest players. If he had been playing in his era for Brazil, that fact would be properly recognised. This is a man who had an international career for 20 years. He is a force of a nature.' Le Roy pauses, before adding: 'You could sometimes see it was not a rational force. He often just could not understand why other players could not do the things he found so easy. That was also a part of his character.' Le Roy here is being generous and polite. Milla was brilliant. He was also bolshy. Some of his colleagues among the Indomitable Lions had a nickname for him, derived from his sometimes volcanic temper. They called him 'Gaddafi', after the firebrand Libyan dictator.

There had been glimpses of Milla's exasperation when Cameroon went to the 1982 World Cup, and came home unbeaten after three group-stage draws. Milla and the rest of the Lions bemoaned refereeing decisions, notably one that ruled out a Milla 'goal' as offside. It had also been a frustrating fortnight for the centre-forward because of the conservative line-ups chosen by the short-lived French coach of Cameroon, Jean Vincent. Milla was often left alone up front. But the fact of Cameroon reaching that tournament accelerated the snowball effect, the success-breeds-success impetus that Schnittger had identified. Cameroon had already put a marker down in African club football in the 1970s. The Indomitable Lions would take up that baton for the next decade.

Oryx, Union, Canon, Tonnerre, capricious weather and at least 50,000 spectators ensured Cameroon became a notoriously hard place to visit. Bruce Grobbelaar, the Zimbabwe goalkeeper, recalls the unusual conditions and fevered atmosphere at a qualifier for the Spain World Cup between his team and the Lions in Douala: 'There was the fiercest tropical rainstorm I have ever seen,' recalls

Grobbelaar, 'but almost as soon as it stopped the pitch dried out to be sandy and dusty again.' There was something odd about the frames of the goals that day, too: close scrutiny revealed the crossbars were insufficiently high to meet Fifa regulations. They had to be changed. Zimbabwe held out valiantly until late, when Jean Manga Onguene, soon to be named African Footballer of the Year, put the first of two Cameroon goals past Grobbelaar. 'That goal produced one of the strangest experiences of my career,' recalls the Zimbabwean. 'At first, the crowd started whistling. Then the noise became just unbelievable. It was like a swarm of angry bees. It went on and on, ringing in my ears until I thought it was going to drive me crazy. It seemed to affect our entire defence. We lost concentration.'

After their trip to Spain, Cameroon won the Nations Cup for the first time, in Ivory Coast, in 1984. Two years later, under Le Roy, they lost out only on penalties in the final against an Egypt led by the outstanding Mohammed El-Khatib, in Cairo. They then regained the continent's premier trophy in 1988. Le Roy, who had taken over amid scepticism, made himself a popular figure with that triumph and for the enthusiasm with which he had scoured the country for talent. Le Roy's trips up-country, round the mountains, into the forests left him awestruck by the excellence of Cameroon's athletes.

Le Roy was especially taken by specific qualities that players from a certain background, the Bassa, seemed to share: a particular strength in jumping and apparently hanging in the air for extra fractions of a second. 'I had a curiosity about this,' remembers Le Roy, 'and one day I went to the village of François Omam Biyick, who was one of my best young centre-forwards, near a place called Pouma. I had noticed the balance and co-ordination of many of the players from that region and I thought: "Hey, it wasn't coaching that gave them that." When I went to the village I found people were playing a special game. It uses a small ball, and it is a bit like head tennis, and the court was the space between two houses: If I head the ball and it hits your house, I win. If I save the ball that you have headed, I win. And so on. And I was told they start doing this from very, very young. That's why you get so many players with such great co-ordination especially from the Bassa regions, and you get this fantastic jumping quality.' The proof? Exhibit one: the goal Omam Biyick scored with his head in Cameroon's 1-0 defeat of Argentina in the opening match of the 1990 World Cup finals. He was not well marked, but his spring heels propel him to an impressive height, and he does seem to linger long enough to direct his header. 'It's not just Omam Biyick,' adds Le Roy. 'There's also all the goalkeepers from there.'

Indeed, the goalscoring forwards are only part of the Lions' growing indomitability. Goalkeepers have kept Cameroon near the top of Africa for just as long. They too were an enigma at first, and then role-models for a snowball of talented successors. There were good reasons, growing up and aspiring to play football in Cameroon, to choose something other than goalkeeping. You just need to look at the ground on which they were obliged to practise diving and dropping full-length. 'It was simply far harder for them to train,' says Le Roy. 'With all the stones, or the bottle-tops lying around on the pitches they use, of course people found it unbelievable that Africa could create goalkeepers. There weren't the conditions for it.'

Two men, contemporaries, would not be put off by rough landings. Joseph-Antoine 'Jo Jo' Bell grew up not too far from Pouma, site of gravity-defying junior pastimes. Bell was a rapid mover, with sharp reactions and a very sharp mind. Thomas 'Black Cat' Nkono, two years younger than Bell, was a quieter sort, but no less determined. Once he set his mind on football, he would rise at five o'clock in the morning, undertake to hitch or if necessary to walk the 15 mile round trip from his home near Edea, itself not too far from Pouma along the creviced mire that passes for the Douala-Yaoundé highway, to learn the trade and to practise. Nkono recalls his first coach, François Bayoubekiou, instilling a culture of hard work from his loudhailer as he trailed his group of youth-players on his moped as they ran their circuits.

Bell and Nkono both gravitated first to Douala, and spent time, as Milla had, at L'Éclair de Douala. They both shone, showed contrasting skills. Nkono was the taller man; Bell made up his inches with his forceful presence. Nkono had a mighty throw with which to launch counter-attacks, a device that would connect him with uncanny precision to Milla when they established their relationship for the national team. Bell was much better with his feet than Nkono – Bell took penalties as well as saved them – which is an asset even Nkono concedes to his rival, while insisting that he, Nkono, was 'the more natural, instinctive goalkeeper'.

'The potential in the two of them was just fantastic,' recalls Le Roy. 'But in a totally different way. Tommy had his sobriety, and then you had the showmanship of Bell. That reflected their characters too.' Both men are engaging characters, good storytellers, generous interviewees, holders of firm opinions. And they are chalk and cheese. At various points of their long careers, they would both curse the bizarre coincidence that made their peak years coincide almost exactly. Had they been centre-forwards, they might have dovetailed nicely. Had they been centre-halves, theirs could have been a formidable yin-and-yang of a partnership. But Bell and Nkono, Jo Jo and Tommy, were instead obliged for the best part of 20 years to compete for a single job as goalkeeper of the Indomitable Lions. The rivalry became one of Cameroon's most compelling soap operas. Nkono the calm; Bell the ostentatious, with his quotable phrases. Sport enjoys these sorts of duels between opposites. British athletics had it when the urbane Sebastian Coe and the rough-edged Steve Ovett were the best middle-distance runners in the world; German tennis had it when the blond, excitable Boris Becker challenged for world number one with the darker, colder Michael Stich. Cameroon had in Bell a polemicist, a loudmouth, outspoken on almost every issue. It saw in Nkono his alter-ego, a measured figure, who spoke in a baritone, chose his words carefully. Even in their mid-50s, it remains clear from both men there was never much love lost between them. Neither Jo Jo nor Tommy could ever settle for being told they were second-best. As the edge between Tommy and Jo Jo developed, Cameroon started going to major tournaments not with two outstanding goalkeepers but with a first-choice goalkeeper and a first-class grumbler in reserve. The roles alternated. When Nkono went to the 1982 World Cup as number one, Bell seethed. At the triumphant Nations Cup in 1984, Bell had the job, and did it more than capably. In 1986, defending their Nations Cup crown, Nkono was back in the saddle. Le Roy took Jo Jo rather than Tommy to the next, victorious Nations Cup in Morocco in 1988.

Nkono, African Footballer of the Year in 1979, joined Espanyol of the Spanish first division after the 1982 World Cup, a significant challenge to a widely held prejudice in European football about not only African goalkeepers but black ones. Bell also outgrew Cameroon. After winning the Champions Cup with Union Douala, he moved to Africa Sports in the Ivory Coast, from there to Arab Contractors, of Egypt, and on to Olympique Marseille, where he would become captain of France's most-supported club. The rivalry, as Nkono recalls, sharpened their skills even if it did nothing for their mutual bonhomie. 'The competition was so strong,' remembers Nkono, 'that we both worked and worked to try and stay ahead of the other.' The rivalry, as Bell recalls it, was 'strong but in the end it was badly used.' How so? 'Africans don't like democracy,' explains Bell, who could give you a political argument if you asked him what the weather was like. 'Democracy means you have to accept there are two parties. You have to accept the other party also has a role to play. But in Cameroon, he who has power is worth everything; the other guy is worth nothing. They only know totalitarianism. Instead of being pleased to have two good goalkeepers, they wanted to have one, all on his own.'

By the time Cameroonian football reached its zenith, the World Cup of 1990, the Tommy-and-Jo-Jo show had been running for well over 15 years. Their soap opera was ready for its car-crash moment, Roger Milla for his finest hour.

■ ■ ■

La Réunion is almost as east as you can go in Africa. It is a small island almost 500 miles beyond Madagascar. Fly another 120 north-west and you'll see Mauritius. Réunion is remote in longitude, latitude and in time. It is a throwback, a colonial outpost in that it still belongs to France. French people take beach holidays there. Some Francophone footballers wind down their careers in its local league.

Roger Milla, twice African Footballer of the Year in the 1970s, was doing just that after he left behind his good, solid, much-travelled, 13-year sojourn in the French first division and his distinguished reputation as one of the finest centre-forwards to impact on the African Cup of Nations. He was in his late 30s, had been around the block. 'To finish my career that way seemed idyllic,' recalls Milla, 'because the football there was African, technical, just like I play.' The level of competition? 'I believe the top clubs would do okay in the third division in France.' In between trotting around for JS Saint-Pierroise and playing a spot of social tennis in the middle of the Indian Ocean, Milla planned a trip home to Cameroon just before Christmas 1989, to guest as the star attraction in a testimonial match for his old colleague Theophile 'Doctor' Abega. In Douala, a sizeable crowd turned out to watch the old masters. Milla felt sharp, too, and scored a pair of handsome goals. The next morning, newspapers wondered in print if Cameroon's greatest player, or rather their greatest former player might not do worse than some of the fringe men that Cameroon may be taking the following summer to the World Cup finals, for which the Indomitable Lions had qualified, impressively. The Milla recall made for an entertaining diversion, a curio of a talking point over the New Year holidays.

Three months later, Cameroon travelled to Algeria for the African Nations Cup. The Indomitable Lions were dreadful, losing their first two group games and beating only a lightweight Kenya once they had already been eliminated. They were also a shambles. In goal, Nkono had a poor tournament; so Jo Jo Bell regained the number one jersey. The Lions had new head coach, a Russian, Valeri Nepomniachi who seemed, distant, cold and flummoxed. It was hard even for him to explain why. He spoke no French, and very few words of English.

As the World Cup finals approached, it became clear these factors need be no obstacle to Nepomniachi. There were plenty of loudmouths in the Cameroon party ready to talk instead of him, and people high up in the game's busy hierarchy willing to take decisions in his place. The state president was one. Soon after the return from Algeria, His Excellency Paul Biya, Cameroon's leader, demanded Milla go to Italy as part of the Cameroon 22. Biya's commandment was non-negotiable. 'He signed a decree,' recalls Milla, 'which was brave of the president but a risk. If I was not up to standard, he would take some of the blame.'

The recall of Milla, three years after he had retired from international football would be badly received by the other players. Bell said it would be like France recalling Michel Platini, then the French manager, who retired from playing three years earlier. He might have made even more surreal comparisons. In terms of Milla's age, it was like England calling Kevin Keegan, twice the European Footballer of the Year in the mid-1970s, out of retirement to play alongside Paul Gascoigne and Gary Lineker at Italia 90. So Milla joined up with a scowling, sceptical pride of Lions and made a poor first impression. Jules Nyongha, Nepomniachi's assistant remembers clearly: 'You have to say that Roger was not in very good shape.' The lean, slippery sprinter of his peak, predatory era had acquired excess pounds in his Réunion semi-retirement. Nyongha and the coaching staff put him through a gruelling training regime, explaining that it was in his interests to bear it in order to regain the respect of the other players. None doubted Milla had been the finest player of his generation. To a man, they all doubted the value of a whim that President Biya shared with a large portion of the Cameroon public.

The squad camped in Yugoslavia. There they played badly. Nepomniachi, deemed lucky to have stayed in the job after the Algeria debacle, fiddled with formations and line-ups. Planning seemed haphazard to the senior men like goalkeeper Nkono, who, knowing he was going to sit on the bench at best, was tempted to quit. A Cameroon XI met Hadjuk Split in a friendly and trailed 3-0 when Nepomniachi asked Milla to show what he had left. The old lion scored twice. 'It was then,' recalls Nkono, 'that we started to realise that maybe, even at 38, Roger could give us an extra dynamic. I talked to him. He needed to be persuaded that he couldn't start matches in the shape he was in but coming on later in a game, fresher, he could do damage. He and I have a long friendship, and I saw the hunger in him. When you know someone well, you can see these things. His eyes were shining with it. He was determined. He knew people said he was going to fail.'

Everybody assumed Cameroon would fail in their first fixture of the World Cup, that their initial task would be merely to act as the welcome mat on opening night for the world champions, Argentina, and for the Argentinian captain Diego Maradona. Their odds for the tournament had been set at 500-1, and that was by bookmakers unaware of events unfolding up near Lake Como, where the Indomitable Lions were billeted. The immediate pre-match trouble surrounded not Milla's awkward presence but Bell's big mouth. The goalkeeper had given an interview to a French newspaper heavily critical of the squad's preparations. His punishment would be banishment. Quite who made the decision to drop him from the XI – 'it was political,' grumbled Bell – to face Argentina is disputed, but it was only a matter of hours before kick-off that Nkono, who had expected to sit in the stands at San Siro as third choice behind both Bell and the younger Jacques Songo'o, was told he would start. It was such short notice that Nkono's wife, in Milan, had already set off on a shopping expedition in the city before her husband could tell her she should, after all, come and watch. It was such a surprise that a curious Maradona, whom Nkono knew from when they lived in the same city in Spain, asked the goalkeeper as the teams left the field at half-time: 'What are you doing here? I thought Bell was the man?'

The score at 45 minutes stood 0-0 and as Maradona chatted to Nkono, he already wore several bruises. The mammoth centre-half Benjamin Massing had been booked after 10 minutes for fouling

Maradona, Victor Ndip cautioned for targeting the same man midway through the half. Geed up after singing their martial pre-match songs, doing their best to ignore the simmering volcanoes – Bell and Milla – on the sidelines, Cameroon had roughed up the champions, Nkono barking at his defenders to press up the field, 'break their rhythm'. Anybody seeking an exposition of flow and fantasy from the Indomitable Lions needed to cling to brief cameos. What Cameroon did show was that, when they attacked, they possessed width with which to stretch Argentina, particularly through the dreadlocked Cyrille Makanaky. He had a first half effort cleared almost from the goal-line and a foul on Makanaky would give Cameroon the free-kick from which the game's only goal was scored. Makanaky flicked it on, Omam Biyick hung high and long in the air to power a header that Nery Pumpido, the unfortunate Argentinian goalkeeper, let wriggle from his grasp and over the line.

Could Cameroon hold their astonishing lead? They had been reduced to 10 men barely a minute earlier, Omam Biyick's brother, André Kana Biyick dismissed for pushing and tripping the substitute Claudio Caniggia. Poor Cannigia would attract almost as many fouls in the second half as Maradona had in the first. The most spectacular, a lunge by Massing after Caniggia had slipped past two other attempted muggings had such force behind it that the collision separated the massive Massing from his own footwear. As Caniggia writhed on the ground, Massing's boot lay several yards away, like debris from a motorway accident. Argentina's Jorge Burruchaga gave Massing a retaliatory push, to which the defender swiped out with his right foot, apparently forgetting it was a weakened weapon, dressed only in a long yellow sock. Massing then walked, one shoe off, one shoe on, red-carded. With a minute or so to go, Cameroon were down to nine men; or eight plus a pensioner. Milla had come on as a late substitute and, as if to show he could muck in with the rest of them, he made a robust tackle on Maradona.

If the 1-0 win represented as sensational a start as any World Cup had known, the two red cards also told of a brutal approach. At the sports desk of the British newspaper, *The Sun*, a sharp sub-editor sought to capture both aspects of the game: 'Loony Roons Bargy Argies,' read their headline. Other press reaction was more predictable. The hero of the victory, Omam Biyick, noticed that, as he gave a series of interviews to interested reporters from outside Africa, he was sooner or later asked: 'Do you have a witchdoctor?', or 'Is it true you eat monkeys?'. Elsewhere, Cameroon's victory, bruising though some of their football had been, set off some rose-tinted Afromanticism in the international press.

For Cameroon, it was to be Milla time from now on. Over the next fortnight, a worldwide audience of fathers watching with their children would learn to plan their afternoons and evenings around the second-half moment when a man with a trim moustache, a gap between his front teeth who was almost as old as they were would enter as a substitute to light up the sport's greatest event. After 60 minutes of Cameroon's second match, against Romania, Milla had his cue. Quarter of an hour later, shoulder to shoulder with his marker and apparently nudged off balance, he arrowed a stunning left-footed drive past Silviu Lung in the Romanian goal. Ten more minutes, and Milla had propelled a shot of still more impressive power past Lung, this time with his right foot. Milla 2, Romania 0. Time to rewrite the records: no man more advanced in years had ever scored in a World Cup.

It meant Cameroon were through to the next round with a game to spare, and so eased off. They rested some first XI players against Russia, and lost heavily, 4-0. They still finished top of the group, their reward a meeting with Colombia in Naples. Milla time arrived at 0-0 with 10 minutes gone in the second half. The Milla magic came not as immediately as against Romania, the teams maintaining their stalemate into the second half of extra-time. Receiving a long ball from deep, as he had for his first goal of the tournament, Milla snaked his way past the challenge of Andrés Escobar, the ball sent to Escobar's left, the veteran trickster slipping to the defender's right, and then angling his shot with the inside of his left boot beyond René Higuita.

Higuita had not seen the last of Milla. This was the same Higuita who had already put his copyright on the 'El Loco' sobriquet that World Cups like to attribute to a South American goalkeeper, largely because of his dashes from the penalty area, his swaggering certainty that he could play the keeper-cum-sweeper. Facing the emergency of a 1-0 Colombian deficit with 11 minutes to go, Higuita waved his colleagues up the field and advanced to a position close to the halfway line. He received a pass there; Milla hounded him. Higuita tried to manoeuvre his way, with the ball at his feet, out of danger; Milla pursued him and, stealthy as a pickpocket, whipped the ball away from the goalkeeper and, a few leisurely strides later, planted it in an open goal. Cameroon had become the first African team in the last eight of a World Cup. Milla's celebration would be the emblem of it: he approached the corner flag as if it were a dancing partner, wriggling his hips, undulating his shoulders. 'Everyone called it my Makossa dance, but it was totally improvised,' he remembers. 'I just wanted something to celebrate the fact of scoring in a World Cup.' He now had four goals to his name out of Cameroon's five; by the end of the afternoon, he was the tournament's leading scorer. He had been on the field just over 100 minutes in total.

Against England in the quarter-final, Milla came on earlier

than usual and took a decisive part again. Cameroon played some of their best, most fluent football, much of it involving Milla, but, well before he joined an engrossing contest, the Lions had been the more impressive, the cleverer of the two contestants. Jean-Claude Pagal's dummy, for instance: Pagal made a run to meet a Louis-Paul Mfede cross, drew his marker and then feinted to meet the pass, let it elude him and so invited the freed Omam Biyick to shoot. Omam Biyick fired directly at Peter Shilton. At the back, Cameroon were not so sophisticated, exposed by a straightforward cross-and-header routine from which David Platt gave England the lead. When England left similar gaps for Thomas Libiih, twice, to burst from midfield through the England back five, Libiih finished inadequately.

When Milla came on, he gave Cameroon sudden, surprising changes of pace and direction. As he eased himself space to tee up a shot from similar distance and angle as his second against Romania, Paul Gascoigne impeded him. Cameroon had a penalty, and Milla gave a forlorn Gascoigne a gentle, consoling pat on the stomach. The spot-kick, struck with authority by Manu Kundé meant 1-1. Thanks to Milla again, Cameroon then took the lead. The 38-year-old, with his back to goal, nudged the ball behind him with his heel, span round and completed a silky one-two with Eugène Ekéké. Milla's pass gave Ekéké time to measure Shilton's advance from his goal and chip the ball over the goalkeeper. At 2-1 up, Cameroon stood 25 minutes from a place in the semi-final.

They lost it through clumsiness. Massing, having served his suspension for the shuddering challenge on Caniggia more than three weeks earlier, stuck out a leg as Lineker sped goalwards and England had a penalty with 83 minutes on the San Paolo stadium clock. Lineker scored it. In extra time, Lineker found himself upended in a duel with Nkono – 'yes, it was a penalty,' admits the perpetrator – and Lineker again kept his sangfroid and converted. Eight minutes more and the bagatelle of a penalty shoot-out would have separated the sides. 'It was unjust that we were knocked out in that game because we had played better,' says Milla, who 14 years after his first African Footballer of the Year award, collected his second for what he achieved and showed over a period of three hours in Italy in 1990. Across the continent, Milla's distinctive post-goal routine, gyrating suggestively at the corner flag would inspire millions of imitators. 'Not quite a samba,' as the Cameroonian novelist Eugène Ébodé described it, 'but an erotic dance in front of the flag, finishing with the hand down by the groin, just to show the virile way that the defence had been pierced.'

■ ■ ■

When Cameroon went to a third World Cup in 1994, Roger 'Gaddafi' Milla had retired and unretired for a second time and, again, became the oldest man, at 42, to score in a finals. Bell was Cameroon's number one keeper, Nkono their third choice. The tournament went badly, Bell among the ringleaders as the players chased up broken promises from the Federation about money, and at the eye of another storm after a 2-2 draw against Sweden began their tournament. Accused of 'lack of patriotism' and at fault for the goals conceded, Bell offered to step down mid-tournament. His last match for Cameroon was a 3-0 defeat against Brazil.

After that Nkono and Bell both bade farewell to the Lions. So, finally, did Milla. They had been figures so dominant the subsequent generation of Cameroonian footballers would consciously have to carry their batons. Carlos Kameni, who as a teenager saved, parried, and pawed away shots and crosses all the way to Olympic gold in Sydney became Espanyol of Spain's iconic goalkeeper some 20 years after Nkono had been contracted in the same post. As for Milla, his heir declared himself early, symbolically: Samuel Eto'o likes to tell the story of being a spectator in the stands, a child being thrown Milla's shirt when the old Lion was coming to the end of his career. It may be apocryphal. What is not is the glee with which Eto'o remembers seeing Milla score for Cameroon at Italia 90. 'We were watching on the television, I was about 10 and when he scored the second goal against Romania, everyone just leaped up, running in every direction. It was mad singing, screaming and dancing. I'd never seen anything like it before.'

One afternoon at the 2006 African Cup of Nations, Eto'o told me several stories about his long, close relationship with Milla and he shared his theories on why Cameroon punch so powerfully above their weight. He lay under a duvet in his hotel room in Cairo, not wearing much, save around his left wrist a bracelet of tightly bound red, green, yellow and black beads. The lean, wiry, toned frame that has helped make him the most devastating goalscorer of his time, was perched up against the bedstead, his back resting on a pillow. He was relaxed, not bearing the exaggeratedly upright posture that marks him out when he moves on a football field, chest thrust forward, head held high.

Eto'o is a phenomenon, an indefatigable modern footballer, goalscorer and superb athlete. At Barcelona, the club Eto'o joined in 2003, the Eto'o physique became the subject of fascination to the medical staff there, particularly over the 18 months when he first joined the celebrated club, scored more than anyone else in the competitive Spanish league and helped make the team domestic and European champions between 2005 and 2006. Dr Gil Rodas, from Barcelona's sports science department, speaks of 'a privileged genetic inheritance,' and as he compiled his physical analyses for the club on players' fitness was struck by Eto'o's 'excellent oseo-muscular development, his wide, angular shoulders, robust upper body, tapered waist that makes his legs, strong though they are, look so graceful.' The Barcelona club doctor, Paco Seirullo, reckons Eto'o 'could have been a champion 400m runner had he put his mind to it'. In the city of Barcelona, they even admire Eto'o's teeth. The Catalan Orthodontic Association asked to use his profile, and indeed his brilliant smile, to front a health campaign aimed at encouraging children to brush, swill and floss more regularly.

Eto'o produced his smile readily enough, and around him in his hotel room were clues to another part of his constitution: a thin skin. Eto'o can turn super-sensitive if he feels undervalued. On the table beside his bed sat a substantial pile of faxes, sent from his native Cameroon, pages from the newspapers of Yaoundé and Douala. He was keen to know what was being written about him back home, and it can be imagined that if he were to take serious issue with any of it, he would say so. A claim for assault against Eto'o was once filed by a Cameroonian journalist with whom he had an altercation at a press conference. When he bares his teeth, Eto'o can be feisty. When he loosens his tongue, he is terrific company. We talked about some of his favourite goals. Many of them, with the Spanish league televised across the globe, are widely known; his long-distance shot against Liberia for Cameroon less so. We talked about the night in Zaragoza when, playing for Barcelona and having listened to a torrent of monkey-chants from a group of Spanish spectators whenever he had the ball, he made to leave the field with the match still going on. Eto'o has become a prominent figure in the fight against racism in his profession and he detailed some of the incidents of bigotry that used to punctuate his life when he first moved to Europe, to become a professional footballer. He was just 15 then, had been invited to join Real Madrid, who noticed all that oseo-muscular development, robust frame, graceful, sprinter's legs during a youth international in Ivory Coast and divined in the boy a sense of his firm ambition. The odds seemed set against him when he touched down at Barajas airport in a European winter dressed in shorts and found Madrid had forgotten to send anybody there to meet him. For years, Madrid hardly gave him a game. He eventually made his break-through after being lent to Real Mallorca. His excellence for Barcelona after that would become a weekly source of embarrass-ment for their rivals, the Madrid who found but then ignored him in the Spanish capital.

We talked about his passion for Congolese music, and especially the Kofi Olumide 'soukous' which jangled from his portable hi-fi. We talked about the crossroads at which the national team of Cameroon seemed to find itself in the first decade of the 21st century. For only the second time in 25 years, Cameroon did not go to a World Cup finals in 2006, failing to qualify because they missed a penalty in injury-time in their last qualifier, a penalty Eto'o, their best footballer and goalscorer, conspicuously did not take. Here, he turned the question around, and asks: 'Why should we automatically expect that Cameroon should always reach finals of everything? I expect it, I want the team to expect it, but we should be alert that other countries catch up. We're not a big country either. We have always had to make the best of what we have.'

Some of the older Lions tend to wonder out loud if Cameroon continue to make the best of what they have. The income from their serial World Cup performances is scarcely evident in improved facilities across the country. Ditto, the benefits the Indomitable Lions brand attracts from corporate sponsors, one of whom caused a major stir in 2002 not so much for the sums they brought into the country's football, but for the unorthodox garments they gave it. When Cameroon last won the Nations Cup, in Mali, they turned heads for what they were wearing. The manufacturer Puma, the suppliers of clothing and handsome funds to the Indomitable Lions had designed an unusual strip, about as unlike the loose-sleeved, brilliant green shirts with their 10-inch diameter yellow lion's head on the breast that Milla and company had worn in Italy as could be imagined. The jersey sported by Eto'o and his contemporaries as they prepared for a fifth World Cup finals in Japan and Korea was striking for its tightness and its minimalism. The shirts, a dark olive in tint, had no collars and absolutely no sleeves. Basically, they were vests. They were unorthodox. They drew some opprobrium.

The fashionistas at Puma naturally enjoyed the attention, purring to themselves over their radical design, boasting that they had found an ultra-modern solution to the problems of heat, a factor in Mali, a Sahel country, and an issue in the steamy Far East for the summer months of the forthcoming World Cup. What hardly needed saying was that this kit, on these players, could also intimidate an adversary with the force of a punch in the nose. The shirts had been tailored to reveal every centimetre of bicep, to advertise the contours of the torso, to hug the abdomen. Nobody needed Doctors Gilas and Seirullo from the Barcelona sports medicine department to point out that the men clad in these outfits were athletes of formidable physique. Puma had made outfits to put an extra shimmer into Eto'o's serpentine runs; on players like the muscle-bound Geremi Ndjitap or the ox of a centre-forward that was Patrick Mboma, these shirts were an invitation to opponents simply to raise a white flag. When Fifa raised an objection, Puma added a short, tight sleeve to the vests, but in the colour black, so it barely showed. Cameroon, feisty as ever, were defending their right to underdress. When Puma finessed their novelty clothing still further by inventing a one-piece kit – a leotard, in effect – Fifa banned it. They felt Cameroon were simply coming on too virile, too strong.

The tight new strip just advertised the fact that muscle had always been part of the Indomitable Lions' game. It reminded that Cameroon's most celebrated result, the 1-0 World Cup win over Argentina in Milan, had been made up of uncouth brutality as well as underdog bumptiousness. It featured a great header for the goal and it included two red cards and some thundering challenges on the most delicate-looking Argentinian player, Caniggia, and the best, Maradona. Cameroon have always had brawn.

The sharpest critic in Cameroonian football thinks they emphasise it too much. 'It comes from the market: exporting players to Europe is now the aim for everybody,' says Jo Jo Bell, severe as ever. 'They know Europe loves players who are strong physically, that the super-tough are the types of players from Africa who get promoted or sought after. And that causes African football generally not to progress so fast. The guys who get on are not necessarily the great African creators. There used to be a style that Cameroonian football had, and it was the style of the street. Everybody played in the streets. These boys got together and between them, they created the ways to succeed. Now I worry Cameroon football may be characterised not by a style, but by its absence of style.'

CHAPTER EIGHT

BURIAL OF THE SPRINGBOK

'We're back!' roared the back page headline of the Johannesburg *Sunday Times*. It was the second weekend of November 1991, and a little over 18 months since Nelson Mandela had walked free from Victor Verster prison to herald the end of apartheid. The country's major newspaper and a large minority of South Africans celebrated the sporting dividend of this new, liberated age. The national cricket team had arrived in Calcutta to play against India, their first official match for 21 years, international sanctions against the country's policies of racial segregation having been lifted.

A lesser, but determined argument persisted in the background about what to call these liberated cricketers. Mandela's African National Congress resisted labelling them The Springboks, a moniker created when only white athletes could represent the country on sports fields. Labels mattered, because much of the rest of everyday life had not changed with Mandela's release. South Africa remained a country where only white people could vote, live in the best areas, own the best land and govern. The cricketers in India found themselves cast not as the Boks of a bigoted history, but as pathfinders for a country with a fairer future, one the rest of the world no longer shunned and despised.

The nation's most popular game, meanwhile, quietly wondered what all the fuss was about. Football in South Africa had settled most of its arguments about racial segregation years earlier, but, in the early 1990s, it was still a strange creature, isolated because of sanctions, and, for that, a little unsure of itself. While the sports and the news pages were clearing space for cricket's momentous milestone, the Johannesburg *Sunday Times* sent me, a junior reporter, to cover a mid-table match in the National Soccer League, the NSL. My gig that day was QwaQwa Stars against Wits, a fixture with none of the stardust of a Kaizer Chiefs, Orlando Pirates or Mamelodi Sundowns game, but one that gathered up several of South African football's various different threads. Until the 1970s, Wits had played in a whites-only league; Stars had grown up in the lower reaches of the black league, and risen suddenly. Wits were from Johannesburg, the country's biggest city; Stars were provincial. Stick a pin in the middle of a map of South Africa, and you'd probably not be too far from QwaQwa. It lies to the west of the border with landlocked Lesotho, about 800 miles inland of Cape Town, 200 south of Bloemfontein and signposted in such a way that no one ever imagined it could ever merit a mention on the tourist route.

From Johannesburg, it takes about five hours to reach QwaQwa by car. Leaving the glass skyscrapers of the city centre, head out onto the Soweto Highway, the 'informal settlements' – squatter camps – and there's mile upon mile of maize fields. I knew I was in the Orange Free State when the radio mostly picked up stations in Afrikaans. I nearly missed the turn for Phuthatijaba, the capital of QwaQwa, but knew I was heading the right way when the roads became potholed, the children at the sides of them waved excitedly and there was seldom a traffic light at a crossroads. Technically, QwaQwa in the early 1990s was not really part of South Africa: it was one of the 11 'self-governing' territories formed under apartheid's grand plan to make South Africa a white state with pockets of land to which every black citizen would eventually belong. The plan would be as impractical as it was insulting, and hastened South Africa's vast economic disparities. QwaQwa suffered worse than most places. It used to finish bottom of most of the surveys on rural wealth, the majority of its resident men were unemployed; those who had jobs were working in mines up north around Johannesburg, or on farms in the Free State, leaving families in land that was agriculturally sparse, often housed in shacks. But Phuthatijaba had a football ground, a bowl to house about 30,000 if it wished, 25,000 sitting on concrete steps without cover from the fierce rain of the lowveld, or, more punishing, its beating sun. The Charles Mopeli stadium bore the name of the QwaQwa premier, and QwaQwa Stars were putting his dominion on the local football map. They stood third in the table the day they hosted Wits. Fans seemed buoyant. Though many more than 12,000 or so would have turned up for the visit of Chiefs or Pirates, they made an atmosphere, with the oboe sound of their vuvuzelas audible from distance. The vuvuzela is the instrument of South African football, the prototype made from the horn of a kudu, the new ones brightly coloured plastic.

Outside, a woman barbecued chops of mutton and sold them to fans. A child wielded a four-foot long transparent bag of bright orange corn puffs. The Wits team turned up in dribs and drabs. They had come not by bus but in various cars. Their manager, Terry Paine, emerged shaking his head at the length of the journey. Paine is a friendly, talkative type, who speaks with a Hampshire burr that half a lifetime spent living in South Africa has barely altered. He had been a well-known footballer in England in the 1960s and 70s, a winger talented enough to have made the victorious World Cup squad of 1966. Like dozens of English professionals, he came to South Africa towards the end of his career and stayed. He went into management, and would gain a high profile as a TV pundit. Some thought his Wits team rather too functional in style for South African tastes, all long balls hoisted up to corpulent centre-forwards. He in turn thought the typical South African game 'naïve'.

That day, Wits scored first in a 1-1 draw, and Stars played most of the pleasing football. As for the colour-count, it was pretty black and white: Wits had lined up with eight whites in their first XI; Stars had fielded 11 blacks. The crowd had been entirely black, as expected because you could count the white population of Phuthatijaba on one the fingers of one hand and the very few followers of Wits who travelled to away games tended to do so within their own metropolis.

After the match, Paine and his players complained about the referee, squeezed back into their Toyotas and Nissans and headed out of QwaQwa. I dictated my match report to my office in Johannesburg over a quaint public phone next to the Post Office that needed winding-up via a lever at the side of the instrument, as if ordered from Alexander Graham Bell's original catalogue. Back at the Charles Mopeli stadium, I talked to the Stars manager, another expatriate, like Paine and like several of the NSL coaches at the time. Augusto Palacios had come to South Africa at the end of his playing career and settled, despite some uncomfortable early collisions with the country's strange laws. Palacios, a Peruvian, is black. He could remember being told by a hotelier he was not allowed to check into the same room as his wife, who is white.

At Stars, Palacios was ably assisted by Jabu Khumalo, public relations officer for the club. Acting well beyond the call of duty, Khumalo invited me to a party to celebrate the christening of his daughter. A lamb would be skinned and cooked, Lion lager served in abundance, the music of Brenda Fassie, the pop singer, pumped from the stereo. No one discussed the Springbok cricketers' landmark date in Calcutta. I got to know some of the Stars players, like the NSL's leading scorer of the time, the late Roger Lupiya. Lupiya was from Zambia and had come south to play in the NSL for better wages than he could earn in Lusaka or for one of the Zambian Copperbelt clubs. In doing so, he paid a career price. Fifa sanctions meant anybody playing in pariah, apartheid South Africa at the time would be banned from then playing elsewhere, and certainly from representing their country. The NSL included many like Lupiya: Zambians, Mozambicans, Swazis, Zimbabweans, chasing rands and sending them home to their families. The league's best player was a Malawian called Ernest Chirwali, of Mamelodi Sundowns, who had briefly slipped past the Fifa ban by turning up in the Italian third division under a false name. A pair of Liberians, our newspaper would reveal, were playing in the NSL with forged South African identities and papers. There was more than a touch of the lawless Wild West about NSL football. It had flaws to iron out.

Fifa were vaguely aware of some of them, but the pace of political change in South Africa meant sanctions would soon be lifted. On the horizon, the country sensed, was the exciting prospect of a national team to be assembled. It was expected that clubs like Chiefs, Pirates, Swallows and Sundowns would supply a majority of the players. But in QwaQwa, I also met the man who would captain South Africa's first non-racial national team in their first competitive match some 10 months later. Steve Khompela played in defence for Stars, cool and composed, and he combined that with a job teaching economics to teenagers in Phuthatijaba. He later showed me the sparse facilities, the worn-out textbooks, at his school; told me about his battles to chase up truants and described the legacy of the hated Bantu Education Act, the syllabus set up for black education by the apartheid government in the 1950s, designed to prepare students for servility, not to stimulate them. Addressing his classroom, in his suit and tie, the idea of international football felt a long way away to Khompela.

It was not. Four weeks later, the president of Fifa, João Havelange arrived in Johannesburg for an inspection. Havelange was minded, he made clear, to welcome South Africa back into 'the football family'. He met Mandela, so the principal endorsement had been secured. Mandela reminded him that football was truly the national sport, that its hard road to unity had begun in the 1970s. When Havelange cast his eye over the NSL of 1991, he saw that, on the face of it, football was mixed, meritocratic, colour-blind. He also got a sense of its unique genealogy. The biggest two clubs, Kaizer Chiefs and Orlando Pirates, the so-called Soweto giants, had a fierce, noisy rivalry, the enduring rivalry of opposites. Pirates, The Buccaneers, wore a skull and crossbones on their breasts; Chiefs went by the slogan 'Love and Peace' to define themselves as distinct. To look further down the NSL table was to hop-scotch across the country's ethnic mosaic. There was Durban's biggest club, AmaZulu – the Zulus – and one of Cape Town's oldest, Hellenic, owned by a shipping magnate of Greek origin. A club called Lusitano – once very Portuguese – had just fallen out of the top division. Another, Dangerous Darkies, had recently joined it, their name designed to cock a snook at the establishment. Others had moved on. Witbank Black Aces had become plain Witbank Aces.

They all co-habited in a lively but isolated bubble. Fifa had thrown racist South Africa out in the 1960s, so its clubs had no experience of the Pan-African club competitions and those few South African players, black and white, who ventured abroad struggled through a mesh of red tape, visas and work permits. Most black footballers had supported the sports boycott, following the argument that even if football was a model of racial integration, no sector of the community should acquiesce until the nation had a fair democracy. The slogan of the epoch was 'No Normal Sport in an Abnormal Society'. Besides, several clubs had strong political roots. Kaizer Chiefs quietly raised funds for the banned African National Congress through exhibition matches in the 1980s. Activists on the wanted lists of security forces would sometimes move, incognito, from city to city disguised as members of teams. Football, the sport of the majority, assumed a prominent place in the timetable of prisoners of the notorious Robben Island, where Mandela had been held. Go back further, and the game had been fighting against racial barriers for a century. When Mohandas K Ghandi, the Indian civil rights leader who worked as a lawyer in South Africa, led a 1910 protest against discriminatory taxation, his demonstrators held a match to rally support in Johannesburg.

Football among the country's whites spent the best part of the next half-century trying to make itself as British as possible, with notable exceptions like the Portuguese of Lusitano and the Greeks of Hellenic. Soon after the National Party, apartheid's architects, gained power in the all-white elections of 1948, the whites-only league started to pay salaries to its players. In the white suburbs of the country's major cities, football attracted significant crowds and by the 1960s and early 70s, some very famous footballers. 'Just look at how many of the 1966 England squad ended up playing here,' Terry Paine points out. South Africa became an attractive place to go into a nicely-rewarded semi-retirement, or to play in lucrative exhibition games if you had a name in English football, you were white, and didn't mind listening to occasional arguments that by doing so you were endorsing the apartheid regime. The captain of England's World Cup side, Bobby Moore, turned out in what was known as the National Football League, NFL, for Hellenic; his team-mate Alan Ball had a stint there, so did Geoff Hurst, Bobby Charlton and Roger Hunt.

As for the other 85 per cent of the population, by the 1950s forced removals, and the restriction of access to public facilities would make organised sport in 'non-white' areas more and more difficult. While the white NFL became professional in the late 1950s the National African Soccer League, the most ambitious body for black players, raised money and standards as best it could, defying the weekly obstacles put in their way by municipalities here and there denying access to stadiums. It drew big crowds. Orlando Pirates gathered greater and greater support from Soweto and beyond for their stylish, flamboyant football. Papers like *The World* and *Drum* created pin-ups of footballers, like Eric 'Scara' Sono and Steve 'Kalamazoo' Mokone, whose move to play professionally in Europe made him an icon.

The game did its best to resist apartheid's mad science. While the law divided race groups into Indian, 'coloured,' black and white and ordered them to live, work and play apart, some sporting events could slip around the regulations via a loophole apartheid's statutes had created; they called matches 'international' fixtures, contests between the 'nations' of the discriminated. A body called the South African Soccer Federation united the disparate SA African Football Association, the SA Indian Football Association and the SA Coloured Football Association. They set up the Kajee Cup, a three-way tournament where a select Coloured XI played a

Black XI; the Black XI played an Indian XI and the Indians met the Coloureds. International careers, like Mokone's, were launched on the back of performances in the Kajee Cup. Leeds United of England spotted the wingers Gerald Francis and Albert Johanneson while they represented 'The Coloureds'. One Basil D'Oliveira featured on a Kajee Cup team-sheet in 1956, playing for The Coloureds. He too went to Britain, to become a cricketer and, on being chosen many years later for an England team to tour South Africa, a cause célèbre in the anti-apartheid struggle.

But the threshold most aggressively defended by Pretoria's government took longer to cross: the idea of putting black and white on the same pitch was forbidden, even in your spare time. In 1961, the state prosecuted two white men, five 'coloureds' and two Indians under Proclamation 255 of the Group Areas Act after they had been caught playing football together in a Durban park. The following February, Minister of the Interior Jan de Klerk reminded the nation 'no mixed team should take part in sports inside or outside this country.' So it stayed, rigid, for the next ten years.

■ ■ ■

One Wednesday night in November 1972, the South African police were tipped off about a suspicious event in Johannesburg. It had taken place at a Cup semi-final between two teams in the NFL, the white league. Berea Park had beaten Rangers 3-1, a victory inspired by a newcomer, a slippery trickster on the left wing. Arthur Williams, a short man, slightly bronzed, was 19 years old with jet-black hair. His display had been 'scintillating', wrote *The Pretoria News*, 'as he flashed down the left'. In the cliquey NFL, Rangers felt surprised they had never heard of this brilliant prodigy. He came from Pretoria, it was explained. Rangers became intrigued when, as

Williams dashed down the flank during the first half, spectators in the section nearest to the left wing as Berea Park attacked cheered him on with what seemed affectionate familiarity. 'Go, Smiley, Go!', they shouted. The cries came from a caged-off part of the Berea Park stadium which had a 'Non-Whites' notice above the gates. The spectators there recognised Arthur Williams as one of their own.

His real name was Essop Moosa. His fans all knew him as Smiley Moosa, and they knew how good he was because they watched him at weekends playing for Sundowns in a league where the grounds were shabbier, the football more flamboyant and the spectators very seldom white. After the Berea Park putsch, journalists tracked down Arthur Williams to his home in the Indian township of Laudium, outside Pretoria. The truth came out. His father answered the door, came clean: Arthur Williams was a cod name. The Special Branch called, gave Smiley a warning: 'Stay in the township. Don't try it again'. The NFL, somewhat to their credit, pointed out that nothing specifically in their statutes required all their players to be white. It was just that apartheid forbade black and white sharing sporting space, full stop. As controversy grew, the Berea Park manager, Mario Tuani, to whom 'Arthur Williams' had been recommended as a triallist, asked: 'What sort of a country are we living in?' Smiley Moosa knew the answer: he had been told firmly by the law that if he crossed the colour bar again, he'd be arrested.

Apartheid messed up Smiley Moosa's career. It messed up his life. When I last met up with him, in early 2007, he told me he had been admitted to a psychiatric hospital suffering depression. He had recovered, he said, but looking back over the period thought it likely his experiences during the 1960s and 1970s, pushing him this way and that because of bizarre laws as he tried to pursue to the full his talent as a footballer, had contributed to the illness. He said so without self-pity and, like many South Africans of his age, in their 50s, he joked about the surreal scenarios once imposed on the country by the weird workings of its racism. Apartheid messed up the lives of millions like Smiley Moosa. And people like Smiley Moosa also made a mess of apartheid's nonsensical logic. His skin was pale enough to pass off as a white man called Arthur Williams, but his ID book said he was 'Indian'. And under apartheid you had to be colour-classified because your classification controlled your rights, your place of residence, your education, your work, your choice of partner.

Yet Smiley Moosa's father, Issy, had somehow obtained a pass-book saying he was white. His mother found herself classified as Coloured. 'You know,' remembers Moosa, 'after the Group Areas Act, we would have to travel from the Indian township on one side of Pretoria to go and visit my mother's family on the other side, because they had to live in Eesterus because that was for "Coloureds". I was black because I was non-white, and people asked "How can you be called black?". I spoke Afrikaans in my family because my mother always had, but she had to be "re-classified" Indian because my father was. You know, this situation of ours was almost laughable.'

Born just as the National Party came into power, Moosa's child - hood was filled with petty indignities. To this day, he doesn't know how his father came by an ID book that said he was white. But it was useful. Issy Moosa liked to gamble, and as betting shops were open only to whites, his sons would wait outside while Issy, answering to the name of 'Johnny', placed his wagers on the horses. Win and there'd be a treat, maybe a movie. But family trips to the cinema also required stealth: 'When my father took us to the drive-in, we had to lie down at the back and put a blanket over us so that they couldn't see. Otherwise they might pick up that we were "non-white".'

The Moosa boys showed an early gift for football. Smiley's much younger brother Zane, would be one of the NSL's showmen – 'show-off' would be an equally fair description – in the early 1990s; luckier with his timing than Smiley, Zane would eventually play for the first true South African national team, in 1992. Smiley reckons he was better than Zane: 'I scored more goals, and my dribbling, which I was good at, was less for the gallery than his'. Smiley would be performing before the country's most demanding gallery by the time he was 16, representing Sundowns against Orlando Pirates in Soweto. In the mid-1970s he was invited to go to England for trials at Crystal Palace. There, he caught the eye of West Ham United. Their efforts to get him a work visa failed. Back in South Africa, Moosa would be voted the country's Footballer of the Year. Or at least, *part* of the country's Footballer of the Year. He was the SA Football Federation's Player of the Year while the Federation played, defiantly, non-racial football.

For that, it stood apart. The white NFL carried on in its vacuum while other black organisations sprung up, disbanded, struggled with the divisive nature of apartheid. At various times, Smiley Moosa played for clubs based in black townships, 'Coloured' areas, Indian suburbs, white districts, his career a whirligig of the game's shifting alliances. As we talked through his career, we counted his myriad clubs – Swaraj, Bluebells, Sundowns (who became Mamelodi Sundowns), Berea Park, Durban Aces, Adriatica, Benoni United, Pretoria Callies – and we totted up the various different organisations under whom he had played: the NSL, the NPSL, the NFL, The Federation, each of them formed around, or set up to oppose, the principle of segregation with various degrees of commitment.

All this time Smiley Moosa – black enough to be disenfranchised, pale enough to pass as Arthur Williams, classified as Indian, from a 'Coloured' background – just wanted to belong. 'I think I suffered the most because I was classified as an Indian and I played my career playing with and against blacks. That's where I made my name. Then after I'd made my name, I took the opportunity to make it against the whites. I was told "Look, you can't play for the whites because you're not white." I got kicked out.' Soon after the Arthur Williams affair, Moosa would be confronted by a fracture within the main non-white organisation, the NPSL. Moosa remembers: 'The guy who was in charge of the African Football Association – or whatever it was called in those days – made a statement saying "We don't want any more Indians or Coloureds to play in our league." That stopped us from playing against clubs like Orlando Pirates and Moroka Swallows. And that was where I enjoyed my football most. The supporters were fanatical, there was an atmosphere that you wouldn't get anywhere else. In the old days if two "Indian" teams played or two "Coloured" teams it was just not the same. I would look forward to playing for and against the so-called "black" teams. What fascinated them was that I was an Indian. They would say that I played football like an African. They would wonder, the same as they did with my brother, Zane, where I got all this skill from. But when the black association said they didn't want us, we said: "What future have we got? Where must we go and play? We can't play for the whites and we can't play against them. Now we can't play against the 'Africans' and we can't play for them." And I have to use the word "African" here, because we, all the non-whites, were classified as black. That was the situation.'

Confused? Everybody was. Things became more muddled as new euphemisms for state racism entered the vocabulary. A sports fixture including different, non-white, racial groups went from being called 'international' to being known as 'multi-racial'. Now, multi-racial might *sound* a good idea: it actually denoted a vicious sort of division. It meant black versus white, not black with white. Yet, given the schisms of the 1970s, multi-racial football asked intriguing, tempting questions. A black fan with a little disposable income could sit – in his segregated area – and watch a NFL game one day on the green, well-tended surface of Johannesburg's Rand Stadium. The next day, he might take a seat on the crowded wooden bleachers of Orlando stadium to see Orlando Pirates take on Moroka Swallows in a Soweto derby. Then he wondered: Whose standards were higher? What might it be like if, say, Pirates were to meet white Highlands Park?

Promoters scratched at the idea as hard as they could. Why not take such a collision outside the apartheid's jurisdiction, take it abroad? Highlands Park, dominant in the NFL, arranged with Orlando Pirates, kings of the SASL, to meet in neighbouring Swaziland. Passport applications from fans in Soweto soared in anticipation. But when the players asked the Home Office for exit visas, they would be uniformly rejected. A new prime minister, John Vorster, had become jittery about sport as an expression of black excellence. The US athletes Tommie Smith and John Carlos had recently raised and clenched their fists in recognition of black power on the medals podium at the Mexico Olympic Games and there was the D'Oliveira affair, when a scheduled England cricket tour of the republic would be cancelled because of the inclusion of a man born in South Africa and marginalised there as 'coloured' in the English tour party.

■ ■ ■

Banned from the Olympics, estranged from Fifa and exiled from international cricket, by the beginning of the 1970s, sports sanctions were hurting white South Africa, where men are brought up macho. At home, resistance movements became stronger, marches more numerous, culminating in the violent, brutal and murderous clashes in Soweto in 1976 between police, army and children protesting against the compulsory teaching of Afrikaans in schools. Gradually, the government altered its stance on sport. Vorster resolved it could be turned into an ally before his white electorate, and a desperately needed PR opportunity towards an outside world shunning his policies more aggressively. In March 1973, a quarter of a century after the National Party had introduced the word apartheid and made it its central, defining tenet, it allowed a tournament to take place called the South African Soccer Games: four teams, twelve fixtures, a round-robin between The SA Whites, The SA Blacks, The SA Coloureds and The SA Indians. It excited interest, though not everywhere. The Federation, the organisation most fiercely opposed to discrimination on the football fields, saw that to participate would amount to emblazoning the words 'Uncle Tom', or 'sellout', on their chests. Smiley Moosa felt clear: 'I said "No, I'm not going to represent an 'Indian' team. Yes, I'd like to play for my country but not as an Indian for an Indian team against a 'coloured' team or against a white team or a black team".' He wanted to play for a colour-blind team.

The best black players mostly answered the call to form a 'Black XI'. Likewise whites. The White XI, at full strength, won the tournament; the blacks finished third; the coloureds, even without a large number of refuseniks, came second; the Indians, many of whose best players declined to take part, lost all their games and did not score a goal. Sponsors and the outside world took notice. Some 45,000 spectators had watched black versus white, and some of Vorster's aims had been rewarded. The US magazine *Newsweek* put a picture of Nicky Howe, skipper of the whites, on its front cover to illustrate a piece about where South Africa's colour-coded system of rule might be going. Howe was embracing the captain of the Black XI, Jomo Sono.

Now, Ephraim Matsilele Jomo Sono did not need *Newsweek* to make him a star. He was probably and may still be the finest football player South Africa has ever known. He'd certainly be its most protean football man. By the time he had reached 50, Jomo owned one of South Africa's most enduring clubs, modestly called Jomo Cosmos; he had coached the South African national team to their first ever victory in a World Cup tournament; he had a range of businesses from restaurant franchises in Soweto to directorships in black empowerment enterprises across the New South Africa. Jomo could and is often called many things, but to call him an 'Uncle Tom' because he participated in the first cross-colour football matches under the apartheid regime would not be best advised, nor even whispered anywhere within his earshot.

Jomo is the son of a football man, the former Orlando Pirates player Eric Sono, whose nickname 'Scara' inspired choruses among crowds in Soweto in the 1950s. After Eric Sono died in a car accident, reports had the congregation at the wake numbering more than for any funeral in the history of greater Johannesburg. His son would almost be under obligation to continue the pioneering. Ephraim Matsilele Sono quickly became Jomo Sono: 'As a kid, people started calling me Jomo after Jomo Kenyatta,' he explains. (Kenyatta had led Kenya's fight against colonial rule in the 1950s and 60s). Jomo the footballer in turn became The Black Prince of Soweto, a real-life Roy Race, a superhero. Myths grew up around him: the guy who scored too many goals for Orlando Pirates for archivists ever to agree on the actual figure; the man who, hearing that Pirates were a goal down on his wedding day, left church to rush to Orlando stadium, ditch his tuxedo, put on the all-black strip of the Buccaneers and come on as half-time substitute to win the match.

Jomo Sono was the face of South African football for the best part of 20 years. There is a vivid black and white photo of Jomo Sono celebrating a Pirates goal at Orlando Stadium in the mid 1970s, five feet off the ground, his back to the camera, black shorts, black shirts, white socks, arms and legs splayed in a star shape, the number 110 on his back and if you look very carefully in the background, there are four, five, six, seven white faces in the predominantly black crowd in the packed stands behind the goal. And above them, there's a huge billboard poster for the invention that had revolutionised the rest of the world 20 years earlier. 'Blaupunkt TV' it reads. It might as well say: 'Now you too can watch this great game of yours at home.' Television had only come to South Africa in 1976, and it caught Jomo Sono's career just in time to make him an icon for the nation.

In middle-age, Jomo retains the charisma that made him a young superstar. He is big man, stout around the belly and with a wonderfully expressive pair of eyebrows. He was pretty stout the last time he played for Jomo Cosmos, too, into his 40s, but could still land a 50-metre pass onto a pinhead and still make the ball curl and spin off the outside of his boot. How good had Jomo been at his peak? Good enough to have been a team-mate of Pelé, Brazil's finest footballer, and Franz Beckenbauer, Germany's best, for a long period in the late 1970s at the New York Cosmos, at that stage the most glamorous, if showy, team in the world. He had been at Sporting Lisbon too, and had been invited to join Juventus in Italy. At both places, visa obstacles prevented him signing long-term contracts.

After America he went home to apartheid South Africa. He now says he felt obliged to stay, not because the regime was vaguely hinting at non-racial sport, but because being a folk hero meant certain responsibilities. 'In that time, I was the country's number one soccer player,' Jomo reflects, 'which, let's be frank, meant the nation's number one sportsman and I made a specific choice to stay in South Africa. I could have gone to Canada after New York Cosmos and they offered me heaven and earth to relocate. But I looked at our sports heroes who went on to represent the USA or other countries and I thought: It's not fair to leave. I owed it to the children of South Africa to stay. They needed role models, they needed people who made it in spite of the apartheid regime, so I can do it too. Was it a sacrifice? Nelson Mandela spent 27 years in prison. That's sacrifice. Me, I played football.'

With figures like Jomo Sono involved, the 'multi-racial' Soccer Games of 1973 had set a momentum. Three years later, Pretoria unveiled a revised sports policy, headed by a more 'enlightened' Sports Minister Piet Koornhof, a man who, it would later be gleefully revealed, took a flexible attitude in one area of his private life – his bed – to some of apartheid's laws regarding the mixing of races. His Ministry reiterated that 'white, Coloured, Indian and black sportsmen should all belong to their own clubs' but that 'wherever possible, practical or desirable, the committees or councils of the different race groups should consult together or have such contact as would advance the interests of the sport.' Football, white and black, listened and heard one sound very clearly: Ker-ching! Bigger crowds, bigger markets. There were rands to be earned here.

Sponsors climbed aboard. The car manufacturer Chevrolet put their name to a Cup that invited two clubs from each of the four race groups to participate. Kaizer Chiefs, from black South Africa, reached the final, so did Hellenic, white and from Cape Town. A cliffhanger? Hardly. The first 90 minutes of the first Black versus White club final had ended with a 4-1 triumph for Hellenic. Even the anticipated inflammatory atmosphere that had led the organisers to hire the world's highest-profile referee, the Englishman Jack Taylor, had not materialized, at least in the Cape Town leg, the site the middle-class white suburb of Hartleyvale. The government's PR machine ensured the world's press knew that players of both sides had stayed in the same Cape Town hotel, and photographers obligingly recorded they'd had drinks together in the bar. The only social distinctions on the eve of the game had been those imposed by the Immorality Act, a notorious tool in apartheid's workshop: black men being prohibited from dancing with white women, none of the Chiefs players had been allowed into the hotel nightclub.

Back in Johannesburg for the second leg with more vocal support, a different Chiefs emerged, although too late to reverse the outcome. Hellenic scored early, 5-1 leaders on aggregate, although there would be enough suspicion of offside for the Chiefs goalkeeper to protest against Taylor's judgement by seizing the ball and sitting, holding it, with his back against his goal net, refusing to play on. Behind him, supporters threw cans and missiles on the pitch. The Hellenic players fled to the dressing-rooms of the Rand stadium. Referee Taylor followed. Only after an interlude of 20 minutes did they return. Chiefs scored twice on the resumption, and that, a 2-1 victory on the night, was enough to keep the peace.

The divisions may have narrowed, but the skirmishes continued, in and outside stadiums where black versus white was still a novelty. Gordon Igesund, a player for NFL club Highlands Park, remembers a volatile mid-1970s evening in Durban against Amazulu. 'It was a full house, the majority were Amazulu supporters and in those days they had those wooden stands. The referee gave us a penalty and suddenly there was this big banging sound, fans stamping their feet and fists on the seats. They felt like the penalty was for us, the whites against them, the blacks. So the fans cut through the fence and ran onto the field and chased the referee and as he was running someone was stabbing him in the back with a screwdriver. Eventually the game was stopped and the players were sitting in the middle of the field, big fights all over the place. They sorted it out with police and dogs and the fans went back to the stand but they started making the banging noise again when they were sat down. The linesman and the officials said the game can't go on, that people could die. The match commissioner said the game had to go on. Our player took the penalty and on purpose hit the corner flag. The game finished 0-0. That referee became known as "Screwdriver". It was my first experience of that kind of situation. It was part of us growing. When I think of those days I realise that we have grown incredibly.'

If the collision of white and black teams was noisy, and sometimes turned riotous, the arrival of a black player in a white team, a watershed moment, provoked an eerie silence. In an echo of the Arthur Williams affair, a non-white man took the field for the NFL club, Arcadia Shepherds, one day in 1976 against Highlands Park. 'You could have heard a pin drop,' according to the Arcadia coach Kia Johaneson. The player's name was Vincent Julius, and, unlike his good friend Smiley Moosa, he used no pseudonym. Nor, under any circumstances, could Julius pass for white. The opposition protested his presence; the NFL turned down the protests. The Home Office took no action. Arcadia had warned them of their intentions and rather than fight them and create an incident to be reported around the world, the government raised a cautious white flag. For Julius, one obstacle remained:

convincing his taunters. Smiley Moosa remembers: 'Vincent commented that some Highlands Park players had called him a "Kaffir", which is a very rude insult towards a black person. Now, Vincent's a very humble guy, always full of humour and you rarely find him in a bad mood. So he didn't say anything until after he had scored the winning goal. Then he ran to one guy who called him a kaffir, just to say: "So, what did you think of the goal the kaffir just scored, eh?".'

There would be battles ahead, but the war against compulsary segregation was effectively over in South African football. In 1978, a full 12 years before Mandela's release, most of the white NFL and the black NPSL's leading clubs united in a new league that had discarded colour restrictions. Attitudes would be changed across communities. Phil Venter was one of the first whites to join Orlando Pirates. 'I came from a right-wing, National Party background,' Venter recalls. 'My grandfather and father belonged to the Party, and for a year after I joined Pirates, my dad would not speak to me. Then the black guys in his company, Pirates fans, started telling him about me, and he accepted it. I like to think his relationships with his black colleagues also changed. Mine did.'

■ ■ ■

These sorts of epiphanies might have disturbed the government if they heard too many of them. Comforting stories of integration were hardly the country's theme tune. By the 1980s, football's gradual miscegenation would look more and more at odds with the oppressed life of South Africa's vast majority. The country had become horrifically violent, and very angry indeed. The regime had turned ever more sinister, programming assassinations of its enemies, funding armed conflicts around southern Africa. Sport?

It was a mess. State companies funded rebel tours by Australian, English and West Indian cricketers to South Africa in spite of sanctions. As for the favourite game, by the late 1980s, South Africa's best known 'football' team to the outside world was neither the racially diverse and admired Chiefs or Pirates, it was something called The Mandela United Football Club, a notorious collection of toughies whose principal activity had very little to do with sport. They were about administering the law of the township, and had originally been brought together by Winnie Mandela, whose husband had entered his second decade as a prisoner of the state.

Nelson Mandela's African National Congress, ANC, had urged the people to accelerate the struggle by 'making the country ungovernable' and in a land where a sub-machine gun could be purchased almost as easily as a second hand TV, violence reached stadiums, spectacularly, on the opening day of the 1986 league season. The legacy of different and conflicting organisations – the alphabet soup of NFL, NPSL, and so on – had left fissures throughout organised football and on the first afternoon of the new campaign, two teams, both claiming to represent Orlando Pirates, both kitted out in Pirates strips, walked out in front of tens of thousands at Ellis Park in Johannesburg to meet a bewildered Jomo Cosmos. Leading one of the 'rival' factions in the Pirates split was a Soweto businessman, China Hlongwane. Television covered the game live, so in the lead-up, millions witnessed a group of men crowd around Hlongwane on the side of the pitch and repeatedly stab him until he was carried away, unconscious. He survived.

The country's best young footballers were meanwhile dodging bullets. In Soweto a young man named Lucas Radebe, from a family of 11 children, had returned to the township from the homeland of Bophutatswana to pursue his big chance with Kaizer Chiefs. He was also an activist, a member of a student movement and a vigilante. Radebe carried a knife and he used his fists, and sometimes a sjambok whip against 'sell-outs', allies of the regime. A decade later, Radebe was helping England's Leeds United to a European Cup semi-final, captaining his country and keeping quieter about his angry years. 'During the riots of the 1980s,' he now recalls, 'I did some really rough stuff. We'd stop people driving to work, and we'd hijack company cars because we were taking them from big business not from individuals. If there was a crime locally, we'd go and punish the guy who did it. You see you couldn't trust the police. They were not just useless, they were the enemy. You had to take care of things yourself.' Radebe was lucky. Football would guide him away from that life, though he still occasionally wonders whether the bullet that entered his back, came out through his right thigh and stuck in the driver's seat of his BMW in Soweto might have been fired by someone who had known him in his teens. An inch either way, and that would have been the end of Radebe's ability to walk again, let alone his career.

Violence touched everybody. Benni McCarthy was a bumptious kid growing up in the Cape Flats, in the township of Hanover Park, where gangsters governed. McCarthy recalls sitting on a street corner when he was 10 and a stray bullet ripping into his friend Reginald's skull. 'That was it for him, shot in the head by a guy maybe 10 metres away,' remembers McCarthy. 'You grow up in a neighbourhood like that, and you never know if you're going to see 15. We would wait behind at the school most days because there was some sort of commotion outside, gang wars, shootings. You'd hear gunshot every day, especially Sundays. You see, Sunday afternoon used to be fighting day, and being kids you'd be scared and running home, but part of you also wanted to see who was winning.' McCarthy reckons he joined the winning side, turning to sport because he 'had something that stopped me becoming a gangster, or drinking booze, or taking mandrax and ecstasy.' He had football. By the end of his teens he was playing for Ajax in Holland. By 26 he had won the European Cup with Porto.

If football gave a man status in the townships, or a way out of them, in white South Africa, the sport could be met with a sneer. Mark Fish, a schoolboy who would grow up to play for Jomo Cosmos, won the African Champions League with Pirates and then perform in the senior leagues of Italy and England, remembers that at conservative Pretoria Boys High School, 'they barely gave prizes for anything you achieved in football. They'd be more likely to announce in assembly that some kid had been picked for the regional Jukskei team.' (A gloss here: Jukskei is an obscure sport that enthuses few, most of them rural Afrikaaners). Gary Bailey, a goalkeeper who returned to his native South Africa after 10 years at Manchester United and joined Kaizer Chiefs in the late 1980s, found that while the sport had changed, become genuinely mixed, many attitudes had not. 'I just thought: The gap between the whites and blacks is still massive. I'd go out in a social group with white people and they'd ask me: "What do you do?". I'd say "I play for Kaizer Chiefs". And they'd say "Kaizer Chiefs? Oh, is that a soccer team?" And then they'd look away. They had no interest. Some of them, the moment you mentioned it, just walked away. It was a strange time for the country. People were all wondering: "Well, what is the next step after apartheid?"'

With Mandela's release in February 1990, whites got some pleasing answers to that question. With the death of apartheid, they'd get their sport back, sanctions lifted, the cricketers could take on the world again. So could runners and rugby players. For South African lovers of football, the end of international sanctions was only part of the story. Most clubs did not have their own stadiums because of apartheid's restrictions on black ownership of almost anything. Kaizer Chiefs used to practice each day at a sparse arena just off the highway that runs up the east margin of Johannesburg. The George Goch stadium had been built to provide a recreation site for the miners housed in the grim dormitories of the nearby hostel. In evening, as the workers trudged in as the sun set on the flat-topped, sandy mine dumps and made them glow a rusty orange, the country's most glamorous footballers would drive past them in their smart cars to train. Each Saturday, Chiefs would drift from ground to ground, one weekend a 'home' fixture in the Rand stadium, a fortnight later a 'home' match in somewhere like Katlehong, an edgy township where the nights were often violent.

Chiefs jumped around because they had no permanent abode and yet could fill any stadium anywhere, short notice or long. In the early 1990s they were the serial NSL champions, and from numbers one to eleven on the teamsheet, a happy reflection of how racially unselfconscious the national sport had become. They usually had two white players in the team, another from what was still called the 'coloured' community, who partnered the outstanding Lucas Radebe in defence. The rest, like Radebe, were black. And if you bothered counting the colours like that, you would have been one of the very few people in the stadium who did.

Supporters had other things to worry about: like what nicknames to give to the players. Borrowing from the lexicon of the times, Chiefs had, at right back, Trevor 'AK47' Mthimkulu, named after a Kalashnikov for the vigour of his tackles. They had 'Doctor' Khumalo, a scholar of close control, backheels and stepovers and something of a heartthrob. They had Fani 'Saddam' Madida, so-called for his ruthlessness in front of goal. And soon they had a new nickname for their reliable, angular midfield player Neil Tovey, who is white. He became Neil 'Codesa' Tovey: Codesa was shorthand for diplomacy, it was the acronym for the Council for a Democratic South Africa, for the talks going on between the National Party, the ANC and others about the future of the nation.

■ ■ ■

In June 1992, the Fifa Congress readmitted to international football the nation it had expelled from all international competition almost 30 years earlier. Delegates in Zurich whooped as the announcement was made. So began the frantic process of building a national squad, a process that over the next two years would mirror and track South Afirca's awkward, sometimes chaotic and often heartbreaking transition to a one-man, one-vote democracy. People asked nervous questions: Did it matter if the SA football captain was white, black or brown? For some it did. Neil 'Codesa' Tovey got the job first but by the time South Africa's first competitive international arrived, he had lost it to the schoolmaster from QwaQwa, Steve Khompela. Did the head coach have to be native? An Englishman named Jeff Butler, who had guided Chiefs to the NSL title, was first given the job. He lost it when enquiries at the English clubs he claimed to have played for in the 1950s exposed some tall stories on his CV. Were South Africa any good? The first few months of their international life would give contradictory answers.

On a rainy, chilly July night in Durban, the inaugural match of the non-racial, Fifa-recognised, South African national XI took place. The guests were Cameroon, fresh from Italia 90. The demographic of the crowd would be a happy mix of the country's ethnicities, and the vast majority raised their right arms and clenched their fists at head height for South Africa's turn at the playing of the anthems. And they heard not the official national anthem, the Afrikaans dirge 'Die Stem', but the rousing 'Nkosi Sikelel iAfrica', God Bless Africa. With the crushing emotion of that song, on that watershed night, people cried and barely noticed that along the line of 22 men standing to attention on the pitch, the 11 wearing the green of Cameroon seemed to measure about a foot taller, and appeared twice as muscular as the 11 novices wearing a rather racy gold and white kit designed for the Rainbow Nation, soon to acquire a new nickname that had nothing to do with a Springbok. South Africa became known simply as Bafana Bafana, Zulu for 'The Boys'.

Bafana's debut was feisty, and it was proud. Within minutes of kick-off, the Kaizer Chiefs' pin-up and midfield show-off 'Doctor' Khumalo got involved in some pushing and shoving with the dreadlocked Indomitable Lion, Jean-Claude Pagal. By the end, Doctor had scored the night's only goal, a penalty. It had not been a vintage game but it felt like a glorious coming of age.

Bafana Bafana played Cameroon again in Cape Town and lost, and again in Soweto and drew. Almost everybody over-reacted to a promising trio of friendly results. Could South Africa, at the first time of asking, reach the finals of the 1994 World Cup? Would they take the African Cup of Nations by storm? The first qualifier, the competitive debut of a 'free' South Africa would, by happy coincidence, be a trip just over the border to Zimbabwe. Bafana Bafana were thumped 4-1. Khompela, Radebe, another reporter and I went out to dinner in Harare after the game and dissected the details of what had been a glum day. We asked Doctor Khumalo to join us. He declined. He didn't fancy too many more encounters with Zimbabweans, several thousand of whom had spent the afternoon shouting, 'Hey, Doctor, you play like a Nurse!'

More mirth from a worldlier Africa followed Bafana to their World Cup qualifier in Nigeria. Before the game the South African striker Bennet Masinga found himself in a hotel lift with the towering Nigeria captain Stephen Keshi. Witheringly, Keshi asked the 5ft 6in Masinga whether he was one of the ball boys. Before kick-off in Lagos's Surulere stadium, the Nigerians blasted the wrong South African anthem over a tinny PA. Specifically told to play 'Nkosi Sikelel iAfrica', they played 'Die Stem'. The Super Eagles then walloped the upstarts 4-0. So much for the suffragette soccer team, Bafana Bafana, as beacon for the Rainbow Nation.

Things would improve, dramatically, especially once the penny had dropped that the team could play very well indeed, as long as Mandela came to watch. The Codesa talks finished their work, the ANC won the April 1994 general election and on 10 May, the former prisoner took his oath as the country's first black head of state. Mandela decided the way he would most like to celebrate his inauguration that evening would be by watching a football match. So he dutifully excused himself from the company of the Clintons, Mikhail Gorbachev, Fidel Castro, Muammar Gaddafi and several thousand VIP guests at Government House in Pretoria and set off to watch Bafana Bafana play Zambia at Ellis Park, Johannesburg. It being a busy day for Mandela, he didn't quite make kick-off, but he arrived in time to visit the South Africa dressing-room at the interval, an apparition that left several players overcome. He made a point of saluting Doctor Khumalo, who a few months later was reported to be dating Mandela's niece. Bafana then took the field utterly transformed. Within three minutes of the restart, they had turned 0-0 into 2-0. Doctor Khumalo got sent off, but only after he had scored Bafana Bafana's second.

The New South Africa was on its way. Less than two years later, Doctor Khumalo, Neil 'Codesa' Tovey, Lucas Radebe, Mark

Fish and others were sprawled on the pitch at Soccer City, Soweto, celebrating with their septugenarian president, Mandela, dressed in his Bafana Bafana jersey. The Rainbow Nation had just won the African Cup of Nations. They were the champions of Africa.

CHAPTER NINE

THE BUFFALO AND THE PHOENIX

It was a late spring morning in 1993 when Kalusha Bwalya received the call. He was about to set off in his car to his favoured jogging spot along the flat Dutch countryside. It was his usual drill on the morning of a day off from club practice and a necessary preparation for his next 48 hours, where he knew the likely routine: stuck in airport lounges; squeezed into economy class aeroplane seats; checking into a hotel where his room may not be ready; probably hemmed in on a bus in a Dakar traffic jam.

Bwalya had started the engine of his car when the telephone rang inside his house in Eindhoven, Holland. He left the motor running while he darted back inside. A compatriot was on the other end of the line, calling from Lusaka, the Zambian capital. He was ringing on behalf of the country's Football Association, said the unfamiliar voice. Bwalya felt puzzled to hear from this particular official because he was not the man with whom Bwalya, as national team captain, normally had dealings when he spoke with the Football Association of Zambia, FAZ. Bwalya's heart stopped as it was explained to him there had been an accident, that he should not, as planned, fly to meet his team-mates in Senegal, where they had an important fixture that Sunday. An aeroplane carrying most of the rest of the national team had gone down. Nine of the 30 on board, it was thought, had survived.

That information, it soon became clear, was badly wrong. The Zambian National Broadcasting Corporation confirmed in their lunchtime radio news that a De Havilland C5 Buffalo military aircraft transporting the national team to their World Cup qualifying fixture in Senegal had crashed in the Atlantic Ocean off the coast of West Africa shortly after a scheduled refuelling stopover in Gabon. Nobody had survived. By the end of the next day, 24 bodies had been pulled from the sea, and by the time the remains were placed in coffins in a Libreville hospital and mortuary, only 13 could be identified. Eye-witnesses, still awake and outdoors in the moments approaching midnight in Libreville on the Wednesday, spoke of a dramatic, bright, fiery explosion in the sky. Pieces of the fuselage spread over a large area of the water. Photographs of the recovery made it horribly clear why rescuers had such difficulties in putting names to corpses. Many had been dismembered in the crash.

In Lusaka, office workers stepped onto the pavements and looked, forlorn, up at the sky. In between bulletins, the ZNBC played mournful dirges. President Frederick Chiluba declared a week of national mourning and, in the home of his predecessor, whose 27 years of uninterrupted government had only recently come to an end, Kenneth Kaunda's 69th birthday celebrations came to an abrupt halt. Zambians had grown to recognise Kaunda, or 'KK', as an emotional man, and he apparently greeted the news with a deep moan: 'What? How? Oh, no, no no!' Among the 30 who died were many who had born his name proudly. Zambia's national team had a nickname out of keeping with the popular tradition of many African national sides. They had not taken on as an emblem one of the brave or the mighty or the elegant animals of the country. They were known as the KK XI, Kenneth Kaunda's men. Theirs was a project in which the ex-president had taken a strong, genuine interest. Many had developed as footballers on the salaries of his nationalised industries, notably in Zambia's abundant copper mines. This lost KK XI were special, too. They were the finest football team Zambia had ever known.

The coffins returned to Lusaka on the Sunday, at about the time the players should have been kicking off in Dakar against Senegal, pursuing their favourable prospects of a place at the World Cup finals in America the following year. Kalusha Bwalya had returned home to Zambia. He was among thousands at the airport. Tens of thousands more had assembled at the Independence stadium. Others jostled for a place on the 16-mile route between the airport and the centre of Lusaka, bearing photographs of the dead, placards praising the players, waving the dark green national flag. The dead would fly home in a better aeroplane than the living had departed in, it was noted. As the Zambia Airways DC8 touched down, some members of the crowd wailed, a brass band began its solemn tribute.

Then a kaleidoscope of memories turned in Kalusha Bwalya's mind: 'Everything was so still. I looked at the plane and there was no movement from inside, nobody looking out of the windows. That was when I realised I'd never see the boys again.' There were many eerie echoes that day: of the match that should have been taking place on the other side of Africa, Senegal against Zambia; the safe landing of a DC8 instead of the fatal plunge of a worn old military crate. Bwalya and many of the fans who turned out at the airport found themselves reminded of the last time such numbers had gathered to welcome home the KK XI. When Bwalya thought of 'the boys' – he still calls them boys, though some would be in their late 40s by now – he recalled their trotting down the steps of an aeroplane just like this DC8, four and a half years earlier, bowing to have garlands of flowers put around each of their necks by shy schoolgirls, and the great ovation they received. That day they had just returned from Korea, celebrated as the heroes of one of the continent's outstanding feats on the football field.

■ ■ ■

The Olympic Games in 1988 had put Zambia on the game's global map, suddenly, refreshingly, as if from nowhere. They reached the Olympic quarter-finals and the way they did so had caught the eye, particularly during their second match against Italy. Olympic football tournaments then were not played under the age restrictions imposed in later tournaments, and this was a strong Italian side. Zambia destroyed them. Kalusha Bwalya opened the scoring with a left-footed finish of startling power just before half-time. By the end, he had curled a free-kick around the Italian defensive wall and goalkeeper and with a cool finish, completed his hat-trick. Johnson Bwalya, an all-terrain midfielder, had thumped in another. Final score: 4-0.

In Italy, they called it a shock to rival their national team's defeat to North Korea at the 1966 World Cup. For the KK XI, it felt like a seismic coming of age. 'Zambia before those Olympics had played some good football,' remembers Kalusha Bwalya, 'but we surprised ourselves really and we made history. At that particular time, Algeria, Cameroon and Morocco had been to World Cups and made a good impression, but in a way this was the first really big African victory that was widely recognised over a major European power. And we had beaten them at their own game. We were playing a type of football people wanted to watch. We were a committed, confident team, with very good discipline. I had had a wonderful year for my club in Belgium in 1987. So we felt strong going to those Games. The Italy result still felt like a dream for everybody. It was the arrival of Zambia, the announcement of Zambia as a major international team.' It seemed to haul the momentum of African football a long way south, too. 'Most people had looked at the North of Africa and the West of Africa. Below the equator nobody suspected a great team would emerge.' Or at least, they had not in the economic climate of the late 1980s.

Zambia's football health had been tied strongly to the strength of the country's major industry, copper, since independence from Britain in 1964. Kaunda, the leader of the nation since then, oversaw relative prosperity for his first decade, helped by a buoyant world market for copper, mined in the north of the country. From there some good clubs emerged, often tied closely to specific mining houses, and in 1974, Zambia and their neighbours, Zaïre reached the final of the African Cup of Nations in Egypt, separated only by a replay, won 2-0 by Zaïre. That had also been taken as marking a new, southerly, line of latitude for the kingdom of African football. It turned out to be an illusion. Zaïre's peak was shortlived, Zambia's ascendency brief. Prices of the ores mined in both countries fell sharply during the next decade and the football might of those two countries seemed to track the same graph.

Yet the class of the mid-1980s seemed especially promising. Kalusha Bwalya had indentified himself in their vanguard as a teenager. He comes from Mufulira, very close to the Zaïre border. As did an excellent, outgoing goalkeeper, Efford Chabala and the upright midfielder from the Olympic team, Charles Musonda. So did the second Bwalya on the scoresheet against Italy, Johnson Bwalya and indeed Kalusha's brother, Joel Bwalya. Almost all the better players of their generation came from Copperbelt towns and cities. Several of them happen to be called Bwalya too, so from here on in we shall refer to the greatest of them as simply Kalusha. Most Zambians do, and even in 1980s Mufulira, where Kalusha combined his early career at the Wanderers club with a clerical post at the state-owned mine, he was beginning to hear himself talked of as the 'Great Kalu'.

Before he had reached 20, Kalusha had been whisked off to Europe, offered a professional contract in Belgium by Cercle Brugge. He was something of a pathfinder for that. Musonda joined Kalusha in Belgium a year later. So the Olympic team assembled for Seoul had some seasoned voyagers among its young men, some professionals with the amateurs. The Korea campaign would advance Kalusha's reputation further. He scored six goals in Zambia's four matches – they lost to Jürgen Klinsmann's Germany in the last eight – and joined PSV Eindhoven, the then European champions. Exile of course meant financial rewards and status for Kalusha and a handful of Zambian players scattered across Europe and the Middle East by early 1993. Residing abroad would also save their lives.

The Olympic adventure gave Zambian football a thrust, and in the next five years, its clubs had some good runs in the continental competitions. Nkana Red Devils reached the Champions Cup final in 1990, Power Dynamos won the Cup Winners Cup in 1991. But the patronage they had enjoyed from the state, directly and through nationalised industry, was cutting back. Zambia's economy was struggling. The country had been due to host the 1988 African Cup of Nations, but withdrew for want of funds. Kaunda came under domestic and international pressure to adjust his Cold War system of socialism and would lose his position at the 1991 elections. The mines, more and more in private hands, became less willing to support football clubs. The KK XI was backed by an FAZ struggling to make ends meet. The team now bore the name of an ex-head of state.

President Kaunda was not unique among African presidents for appreciating the afterglow of a good show by the national football team but, more unusual, he visibly enjoyed the sport. Stories are told, and not only by his acolytes of his turning up to watch insignificant lower-league matches, just for fun. Mostly, the national team's players had been happy to be identified with the man who, twice imprisoned by the British, had fought for independence. 'The KK XI was a good nickname,' says Kalusha. 'It meant we had some fight. And he had been there for 27 years. We were the KK XI because of the foundation he built for Zambia, for liberating the Zambian people. Our team has always had that drive to it. We were like a train, always moving forward.'

The Zambian Air Force's transport, alas, moved forward more and more crankily. The ZAF fleet had suffered some notable setbacks before the Gabon tragedy. They were not to do with any war. In 1982, minutes before the arrival on a state visit to Lusaka of the Tanzanian president and Kaunda ally Julius Nyerere, an airforce plane crashed on a runway at Lusaka airport during a routine test flight. Eight years later, a ZAF passenger aircraft en route from an airfield in Mbala to Lusaka crashed in Ngwerere, just outside the capital, leaving all 28 people on board dead.

By the beginning of the 1990s Zambia's best footballers were reconciled to travelling rough. They were not unique for that. Twelve African countries had withdrawn in the seven months between the start and completion of the first stage of World Cup qualifying, most of them citing costs. Central Africa seemed hardest hit. Zambia's neighbour Malawi withdrew from their campaign, so did Tanzania, Uganda and Sudan. Fewer and fewer reporters travelled with the team, and even Dennis Liwewe, the voice of football in the region, the star Zambian commentator, would often be told late in the day that the Zambian Broadcasting Authority could not afford his ticket to distant away games. The KK XI stoically accepted that before each long-haul expedition, either for Nations Cup qualifiers or matches for a place in World Cups, came the added suspense ahead of the trip over whether or not the FAZ would find the money to charter a passenger plane, pay for enough seats on a scheduled flight, or turn, often at the 11th hour, to the Air Force to ask them for one of their ageing military jets. And the FAZ's coffers were usually bare, sometimes through every fault of their own. In August 1992, just as Kalusha's promising squad embarked on the programme that they believed might take them to a first World Cup finals, FAZ chairman Jabes Zulu and his sidekick, Wilfrid Monani were suspended after the disappearance of funds earned during the national team's friendly tour of Korea the previous month.

Just before Christmas, Zambia had to play Madagascar away in the first group stage of the marathon World Cup qualifying programme. On the ZAF Buffalo, it would mean a five-or six-hour trip across the Indian Ocean because of the aircraft's short-haul specifications. Logically enough, the crew planned a refuelling stop in Lilongwe, Malawi. There, a dispute arose between the crew and officials at Chileka airport over the currency used to pay for the gasoline. The Malawians would not take the unstable Zambian kwacha. It turned into a minor diplomatic incident during which the players stayed stuck on board, prevented from even using the airport lavatories. After the long delay, acceptable banknotes handed over, the Buffalo lurched into the sky and over the sea. During the journey, the captain requested the passengers to wear their life-jackets. Johnson Bwalya took some photographs of his team-mates in the puffy inflatable life-vests, and some jokey routines started up among the players about the reliability of the plane. 'We always got away with it, basically,' says Kalusha. 'Because I was usually coming from Europe, I was not often on those flights, but I did go to Madagascar on the Buffalo. The boys always used to say: "This plane will kill us one day".'

The grumpy Buffalo simply formed part of a list of inconveniences that wearing the Zambia jersey in tough times demanded. On reaching Antananarivo, the island's capital, Zambia's first training session would be disrupted when Madagascan schoolboys stole a number of their footballs. They were still waiting for two players, Derby Makinka, one of the Olympic heroes, and Kelvin Mutale, a young striker of promise, who had missed a connecting flight in Kenya on the way from their clubs in Saudi Arabia. They made it just in time. Then Zambia lost. They promptly sacked head coach Samuel 'Zoom' Nhdlovu and replaced him with Moses Simwala, who promptly fell ill, his place in turn taken by one of the stars of the 1974 Nations Cup team, Godfrey 'Ucar' Chitalu. The World Cup campaign seemed to be unravelling barely after it had begun.

■ ■ ■

Under a new coach, the team recovered. They won their next three World Cup games, as they needed to in order to reach the next stage of qualifying for USA 94. Their first examination would be in Senegal, four months hence. Yet before that there were more journeys for the players, more revolutions for the tired propellers of their transporter. In those days, World Cup qualifiers spliced themselves in between a separate programme of matches to decide the finalists of the Nations Cup. For that, Zambia had to go way out into the Indian Ocean again, to play Mauritius, the week before heading off to Senegal. The FAZ hoped that a date on the tourist island meant they might gather funds from wealthier Zambian supporters to charter a passenger airline to travel to the match and return with the team on board. They could not. So they summoned the Buffalo: a 10-hour flight to Mauritius, with two stopovers. At the first, further administrative problems. The Buffalo refuelled in Lilongwe, took off and was then ordered to turn back. The next destination, Madagascar, had closed its airport for the night, so the plane would not be able to land there and refuel for the final leg to Mauritius. So the players spent the night on board the Buffalo, grounded in Malawi. Only when they reached Madagascar could they disembark and stretch their legs. The Buffalo finally hit the runway in Mauritius a full 24 hours after it had taken off from Lusaka. The footballers' complaints would be assuaged by a hike in their daily allowance for the trip, an extra $20 a head, so they were on $100 a day.

Zambia walloped the islanders 3-0 in the George V stadium, the young Mutale scoring a hat-trick. On the long flight home, Mutale gave an interview to the one travelling journalist, Beauty Lupiya, who remembers the 24-year-old's preoccupation with the safety of the aircraft. 'He told me: "You know, Beauty, even if we were to crash, this plane floats. We could survive. They keep life jackets on board. We'd have a high chance of surviving". "Cut the topic, I told him, it's not good".' Lupiya had nevertheless noticed the low altitude at which the Buffalo crossed the Indian Ocean, its 'snail's pace', the constant noise of the engines, 'the hard, straight seats' and how 'the wind blew inside the plane and down our ears.' At one point, the effervescent Chabala, the goalkeeper, turned to her. 'He told me that as national team players their interest was to play and win for Zambia no matter the hardships,' recalled Lupiya. 'Writing about their complaints at the time was not a good idea.

"We have jobs to keep. Don't write anything please," he pleaded, "but if we crash and a miracle happens that you survived, tell the nation the Buffalo is not the best plane to use".'

Those who missed the flight to Senegal, relive the days and hours ahead of 27 April 1993 and wonder. Beauty Lupiya had been assigned both the trip to Mauritius and the away game in Senegal. Checking in at her Lusaka office in the 24 hours between, her editor told her the long journey east looked as if it had tired her out, and besides, he wanted her to cover some tennis locally. Another journalist, Joe Salimu, would take her place with the team. The chairman of the FAZ, Michael Mwape had discussed with his wife taking their young daughter on the trip to Senegal. She had been pestering him to come on one of his trips abroad and they had agreed this would be an exciting one for her. On the morning of departure, though, she seemed a little under the weather and sleepy. So she stayed at home. As for Kalusha, he had been obliged to select carefully his commitments to Zambia where they clashed with his employer, PSV Eindhoven's important end-of-season fixtures. The Zambia captain had missed the Mauritius game, a less daunting Nations Cup qualifier for the KK XI than Senegal away in the more important competition, the World Cup. Charles Musonda, of Anderlecht in Belgium, was under pressure from his club to be sparing with his absences. So a small group of the European-based players had booked flights to join up directly with the team in West Africa in time for the Sunday match.

Others would have been on board but for caprice, circumstance, illness. At the practice ground of the South African club Kaizer Chiefs the day the news broke, the Zambian striker, Albert Bwalya turned up for training, having driven the widow of Sam Chomba to Jan Smuts airport for her return to Lusaka. Albert Bwalya stewed with emotions: guilt, grief and anger. Bwalya had been called up for an international in Tanzania in January and withdrawn, suffering from malaria, his reputation as somewhat headstrong counting against him when the FAZ considered his case for a recall. They had not invited him back for the Mauritius and Senegal squads. The malaria, or else his maverick streak, had saved his life. 'I was supposed to have been there,' he told me that day. 'And the last time I was with them in Dar-es-Salaam, I was surprised at how badly we players were treated. Zambia wants a successful team but it isn't prepared to look after them.' He knew the Buffalo well enough. 'You don't take a small plane like that all that way. They wanted to save costs. Any other country would have taken connecting flights with commercial airlines. I blame the FAZ for this. I can't forgive them for what has happened.'

What had happened was that as the 30 passengers, made up of players, pilots, FAZ officials and reporter gathered for take-off, they felt a tiresome déjà vu. There were problems, explained the flight captain, Feston M'hone. His preferred plan, with stop-offs in Brazzaville, Congo, then Libreville, Gabon, and finally Abidjan, Ivory Coast had been complicated because the Buffalo, being a military aircraft, had been refused permission to cross Congolese airspace. So take-off was delayed until the decision had been taken to fly direct to Gabon. That leg of the journey it managed. The plane reached Libreville's Léon Mba airport in the evening of 27 April. It refuelled and the bill had been paid in cash. According to the Gabonese Minister of Transport, the aircraft then underwent routine checks and took off normally. It was in the air for about two minutes when the reported explosion lit up the sky above the Atlantic coast and the Buffalo made its final plunge.

■ ■ ■

It would take 10 years for a report to be released into the causes of the accident, and it remained partial, inconclusive. In that time, the government of Zambia would be sued by the families of the dead, and the diplomatic relationship between Anglophone Zambia and Francophone Gabon came under strain. While Gabonese mourners took to the streets in ceremonial numbers as the coffins departed Leon Mba airport four days after the crash, there had been distasteful protests from local bereaved about the diverting of local resources at a Libreville mortuary and hospital towards the Zambian disaster. Some of the stories surfacing via bush telegraph inflamed both countries.

One tale had the Buffalo forced by a Gabonese rebel militia to land on a tiny Atlantic island, mistaken for a plane carrying government ministers whom the rebels wanted to take hostage. Another had the Zambian aircraft hit by a missile launched by the Gabonese army, suspecting the Buffalo was part of an airborne attack, perhaps backed by South African mercenaries, against the regime of the long-serving, despotic Gabonese president, Omar Bongo. The idea caught on. Schoolchildren at Libreville's Lycée D'État were by early May singing a playground rhyme: 'Papa Omar, il a tué la Zambie/Si vous n'êtes pas sage, il va vous tuer aussi!'. 'Papa Omar killed the Zambia team/If you're not careful, he's gonna kill you too!'. The reporter from the Mauritius trip, Beauty Lupiya remembered how the players had told her they felt uncomfortable jetting over Africa's war zones in a military plane. When Brigadier-General Joseph Musonda of the ZAF, leading the Zambian investigation into the disaster announced that whatever happened 'must have happened in a flash', some Zambians at home demanded political reprisals against Gabon, the more extreme called for a declaration of war. Investigators from the two countries frequently clashed, encouraging suspicions of a cover-up on both sides. President Bongo took the opportunity to make a special broadcast to his people that no stone would be left unturned in their efforts to put a rapid end to speculation. In early July, Vernon Mwaanga, the Zambian Minister, of Foreign Affairs, wrote to Pascalina Bongo, Gabon's Defence Minister complaining about a lack of co-operation. Two months later, he asked the Organisation of African Unity to step in and push the Gabonese authorities to stop 'throwing roadblocks at every turn of the investigations.' Gabon replied that it could not be expected to bear the cost of what was proving a complicated search for clues.

Being a military plane, there was no black box, the device that records information on modern passenger flights. The debris had also spread over a very wide area, a propeller retrieved some seven miles from the fuselage. ZAF pilots who had flown the plane in the weeks before 27 April testified they had found no problems with it. De Havilland said the aircraft was young enough still to be in service. Gabon air traffic control had heard nothing irregular from the pilots in the two minutes after take-off, and although Zambia's *Sun* newspaper reported, a full 20 months after the crash, that technicians at Leon Mba had alerted the crew to a possible fault in the left engine, they never named their sources.

In Zambia, the grief became overwhelming. Among the thousands who gathered to receive the bodies and pay respects at the Independence stadium, where the players would be buried in a site reserved next to the ground, were the widows and parents. Cleopatra Mwitwa, whose husband Timothy had been on board the plane, went into labour on the day of the burial, and, ferried through the crowds to hospital, gave birth to a son. Timothy Mwitwa had been 24 when he died, the average age of the players on board the Buffalo. Derby Makinkwa, 26, left two children, the second a month old. He was one of six members of the Seoul

Olympic squad to perish in a tragedy that ripped across two generations of Zambia's best footballers. Moses Chikwalakwala, the country's Young Player of the Year in 1992, died short of his 20th birthday, goalkeeper Chabala was 32.

To look over the roll-call is to be reminded of similar tragedies that have marked football history. In 1949, the entire Torino team were killed when their Fiat G-212 aircraft crashed into a hillside at Superga, near Turin. They were already known as Il Grande Torino, and the dead formed a team unmatched for talent by any other in the club's existence: they were closing in on a fifth successive league championship, an achievement they would never repeat after the tragedy. In 1958, the plane carrying the Manchester United team back from a European Cup tie crashed soon after refuelling at Munich airport. Among the eight of the so-called 'Busby Babes' who died was 21-year-old Duncan Edwards, around whose brilliance the England World Cup-winning side of eight years later might have been built. Bobby Charlton, central to England's 1966 triumph, would be among the survivors and, like Zambia's Kalusha, no player would become more significant a figurehead for a future renaissance.

For the Zambian widows the struggle both to receive compensation, initially promised by their government, and to preserve it for the immediate dependants of the dead men would be painful and long. The period of mourning suffered a tawdry interruption only weeks after the disaster when a group of widows complained at the number of relatives claiming part of the emergency fund. *The Times* of Zambia detected a wider social injustice in the scandal. 'This nation is still bogged down in a primitive culture which condones harassment of widows and children,' it commented. 'Spouses of the Gabon crash victims are going through a traumatic experience, perhaps much worse than the ordeal they endured after the demise of their loved one. Nobody wants to intervene to halt the wanton plunder of the deceased's goods that began shortly after the funeral. The law of succession needs to undergo a radical change.'

For the lucky men, those who had escaped being on board, the sense of succession became urgent. If the spine of the KK XI had gone, the best they could to do to honour their memory was to make Zambia great on the football field. For Kalusha, it would become a raison d'être . 'There's not a day that passes without my thinking about what happened that night,' he says. 'It changes your life. And not just me. I think all Zambians felt we were at a point of history-in-the-making, that this team had been ready for something big. When you're young you feel you can do everything you want in your life. You feel that because you're young. Suddenly, you learn life is short, that you can't know exactly what is going to happen the next day. It taught me that you have to do your things today. Don't wait for tomorrow, because maybe tomorrow will never come.' He passed through anger, frustration and weary reconciliation that no perfect set of answers would come from the wreckage. 'For me the investigation could go on for one year, two years, ten years. Nobody will know exactly what happened; nobody from on board the plane will ever be able to tell us what happened.' His task was to let rest the Buffalo and find the phoenix.

■ ■ ■

The Zambian football team's plight triggered sympathy across the world. The West responded in a very 1980s way, as if this were an African famine in miniature, a refugee crisis with victims to re-house and sustain. A few wanted to play Bob Geldof and make this their Band Aid. Many were generous. At the front of the queue were the habitual givers, like Holland and Denmark, countries without a colonial past on the African continent, European nations who consistently make the highest budgetary commitments to African aid. Once the FAZ had announced their intention to continue with their qualifying campaigns for the 1994 World Cup finals, and for the 1994 Nations Cup in Tunisia, and Fifa had granted permission to reschedule fixtures, the Danes offered sanctuary and expertise. A rebuilt Zambian squad would be guests of the Danish FA's practice facilities in Copenhagen and Jutland while two Danish coaches, Roald Poulson and Emil Pakkendorfs, would be at the FAZ's disposal. The Dutch offered training sites, too, as did the French. A British manager, Ian Porterfield, recently dismissed by Chelsea, made himself available for the post of Zambia head coach.

For some, the haste to rebuild a squad felt unseemly. Some who had escaped being on the flight still felt angry, like Albert Bwalya of Kaizer Chiefs. Charles Musonda, the midfielder from Anderlecht, declared he would never again play for a Zambia national team other than in matches to raise funds for the bereaved. His mind would be changed but he was not involved when, less than three weeks after the bodies had been buried outside the Independence stadium, a Zambia team lined up in a friendly against Malawi. Many of the players were only vaguely familiar to the crowd, some had been selected on the basis of regional trial games over the previous few days. As they took on Malawi three times in the space of five days, in Chingola, in Kitwe and in Lusaka, a new identity began to form around the team. They looked different, and above all their matches sounded different. Crowds began to chant 'Chipolopolo', and the 'Chipolopolo' song, upbeat, with a squealed refrain, 'Ayeeeeee, Chipolopolo!' became the team's unofficial new anthem. The word means 'bullets'. Zambia were no longer the KK XI. They were Chipolopolo.

Naturally, they were a little ragged. The New Zambia drew and then lost to Malawi in Kitwe, and though they defeated them in Lusaka, it had been a display full of errors. They missed Chabala's authority in goal. Before an emotional, demanding public, the stand-in coach, Fred Mwila, reminded them of the context in which the team were being reassembled: 'People seem to have forgotten the boys they are seeing are just babies.' And they were being asked to prepare for a challenge that a Zambian national team had never taken on so far: the closing stages of World Cup qualifiers. The demand was daunting. In close to 30 years Zambia had barely produced a first XI capable of touching the summit of African football. Now they were being asked to find a second XI that would do so.

Then there were the ghosts. 'Emotionally it wasn't easy,' remembers Kalusha, who met up with his new team-mates in Denmark for an intensive get-to-know-you month of training. Being away from Zambia had its advantages: it gave the team a distance from the grieving, the familiar dressing-rooms no longer filled with Efford Chabala's chatter. Or by the rapid banter of companions the defender Eston Mulenga had described during the Mauritius trip as 'a tight unit, more like a family', with their nicknames – 'Yellowman' Mulenga, Wisdom 'Weez' Chansa, Timothy 'Teacher' Mwitwa – and their in-jokes. In the New Zambia team, they had a legacy, but it should not suffocate the efforts of their successors. 'Nobody really talked about it before games,' says Kalusha. 'That was not part of the game-plan. But of course, it was something you could see in someone's eyes some-times, and we felt it. But what could you do? What could you say? The spirit was with us. There was no need to state anything about it. We just knew they were there.'

The hothouse preparations in Europe had fraught moments.

The aid effort could seem claustrophobic, the squad over-supplied with coaches: the two Danes, Poulsen and Pakkendorfs, the Zambian Mwila, and, later, the Briton, Porterfield. Kalusha's figurehead role, already there in the KK XI, grew, and that made others uncomfortable. When Kalusha's brother Joel was promoted to the first XI, Joel became sensitive to criticism that he had enjoyed a fraternal advantage to be there. But by the time Zambia approached what would be their first match in the three-team Group B of World Cup eliminators – Senegal and Morocco the rivals – they had grounds for confidence. The phoenix had risen with extraordinary speed.

Morocco arrived in Lusaka in early July, clearly the group favourites, and not averse to some cunning. As Zambian fans, wearing Chipolopolo paraphernalia arrived from early morning at the Independence stadium and paused at the crescent of tombs, a story was put about that the Moroccan players felt alarmed by playing the game so close to the graves of the dead footballers. But not so alarmed they could not take the lead after 13 minutes. This would be Kalusha's cue. A footballer of quick wits and a deceptively narrow build, he seized control. One or two swift exchanges with his brother Joel threatened and after an hour Zambia had a free-kick a little way outside the Morocco penalty area. This was Kalusha's territory. He struck it with enough curve to slip under the crossbar and zip down the back of the net. One-one, thanks to a goal with shades of Kalusha's free-kick against Italy in Gwangju, Korea, five summers earlier. When Johnson Bwalya forcefully hammered in another Zambia goal, the echoes of that triumph resonated further. Zambia had won their first competitive match since the disaster.

Their next, a Nations Cup qualifier at home to South Africa went even better, Kalusha scoring twice in a 3-0 win. To reach the finals of that tournament Zambia now needed only to draw in Harare against Zimbabwe, who could also progress for the first time in their history to a Nations Cup should they win. Zambia took a good number of fans, enough for the sound of Chipolopolo to make an impression on the watching Robert Mugabe. And they had Kalusha. Zimbabwe went 1-0 up, looking ominously secure until Kalusha outleapt the Zimbabwean goalkeeper Bruce Grobbelaar to a high ball and, untypically, scored with a header. The point would be enough to send his team to Tunisia the following year. Coming home, they had a rousing reception, applauded along the Cha Cha Cha Road on their bus and all the way to the Independence. There, they laid wreaths at the graves.

The big prize, a World Cup place, was still to be contested. Morocco had beaten Senegal, in Dakar, where home spectators rioted. That would have implications for the Zambians. Senegal were obliged to play their next match, the rescheduled, fated home game against Zambia on neutral territory, in Abidjan, Ivory Coast. The mathematics were now simple: two wins over Senegal and a draw in Morocco would get them to America.

And this time, a commercial aircraft, DC8, would fly them to West Africa. The Zambia Airways captain, Steve Mukape, alerted the passengers when they flew over Gabon and, in a moment of forgivable schmaltz, he put the Whitney Houston song 'I Will Always Love You' over the plane's PA system. Whatever inspiration the new team still carried, though, they also suffered fatigue. Kalusha joined the squad in Abidjan having played two matches on two different continents in the previous week – a friendly in China for PSV, another in Holland – and Zambia stalled against the Senegalese. Goalless, they took a single point home with them. Morale sapped. Rifts appeared between those who had a past with the KK XI and the newcomers, some of the veterans agitated that their places were threatened by novices, complaining if they had been left on the bench or substituted. The newcomers for their part felt the rebuilt team had forged its own identity. It was solid in defence, goalkeeper James Phiri shaping up an impressive successor to Chabala; the giant Elijah Litana an imposing Goliath of a centre-half.

The home match with Senegal would prove cathartic. Gibby Mbasela, the showy winger who had been among the disgruntled veterans, scored early. Joel Bwalya, the captain's kid brother, hit the crossbar, and shortly after half-time the giant Litana headed a second goal. A spectacular header from striker Kenneth Malitoli made it 3-0 and a trademark direct free-kick by Kalusha put Zambia on top of the group with one game to play. Less than five months after the crash, Zambia had moved for the first time in their history to within 90 minutes of a place at the World Cup finals. To make it, they would need only a point from Morocco in Casablanca.

They trained in Holland, guests again of the benevolent Dutch. They rallied their resources from elsewhere. The refusenik Charles Musonda, the Anderlecht midfielder, declared his availability for the first time since February. Television crews and correspondents arrived in Morocco from across Europe and the US to cover the qualifier. And the referee? The referee flew in from...Libreville, Gabon. From the moment it was announced that Jean-Fidel Diramba would officiate Morocco against Zambia, the aftermath of the crash investigation would be revisited, amplified. The FAZ protested against the presence of Gabonese officials to Fifa, who turned the objection down. It turned out Diramba had baggage beyond his nationality. He had refereed the second, away leg of a Champions Cup quarter-final the previous month between the Zambian club Nkana Red Devils and Ghana's Asante Kotoko. The Zambians grumbled about his officiating after their 3-0 defeat.

Diramba would not have a quiet afternoon in Casablanca. Nobody in the Stade Mohammed IV would. The Zambians later complained about an atmosphere not only intimidating but frightening when objects dropped from the crowd onto the perimeter track. Morocco had the better of the first hour, goalkeeper Phiri kept busy, and decisive in response to Mustapha Hadji's free-kick just before the interval. Soon after it, Morocco scored. Over the remaining 40 minutes, the phoenix stirred and retreated again and again. Mbasela, he of the jinky dribbles, found a scoring opportunity and saw his shot roll along the Morocco goal-line, hit the post and bounce back into play. Musonda, introduced from the bench, headed against an upright. The margin between defeat and a point could be measured in centimetres. But there was no equaliser. Morocco's single goal would send the North Africans to America instead of Zambia. The team and Porterfield took some flak for their strategy. 'Zambia only reacted when the chips were down,' lamented *The Times* of Zambia.

Then a nation turned to lambasting referee Diramba. They cited two 'penalties' the man from Gabon had ignored for fouls on Musonda and Kalusha. The FAZ in vain asked Fifa to annul and replay the match. Marchers converged on the FAZ's headquarters shouting 'Diramba is a criminal! We want a rematch!'. President-in-waiting Levy Mwanawasa welcomed home the defeated players with a speech denouncing 'a conspiracy concocted with the Gabonese referee'. *The Times* wrote that 'innuendoes against Gabon will continue to fly for as long as memories of the crash, the frustrated searchers, the cynical, almost triumphant grin of a referee named Diramba linger on within the Zambian mind.' The enmity between two states who had had little to connect them for the best part of a century became part of the national vocabulary.

The word Gabon became an insulting adjective. A dilapidated vehicle or a classroom misfit would be referred to as 'Gabon'.

■ ■ ■

So, all in all, it was probably a good thing that when the lots had been drawn for the 1994 African Cup of Nations, the next spring, Zambia and Gabon found themselves in separate groups, based in different Tunisian cities. Gabon would be expected to fall early in the capital, Tunis. Zambia lodged in Sousse, where they made stolid work of finishing top of a group including defending champions Ivory Coast, and Sierra Leone. Eleven months had passed since the accident, six since the agonising elimination from the World Cup, and they had settled back into ordinary rhythms – a familiar row a month before the Tunisia tournament over funds for the expedition – and plain old, arbitrary, tropical dangers: one warm-up match against Zimbabwe would be interrupted by a swarm of bees.

Kalusha, no longer with PSV but playing in Belgium's first division, sensed the squad still had the drive to do what no Zambian team had ever done: bring home the championship of Africa. By the time his side had reached the final in Tunis he saw that Zambia's second XI had some qualities the KK XI had not. 'We had the momentum,' says Kalusha. 'We felt: "Let's do it for boys who are not here". In the end somebody has to make that judgement, to say: "What are we going to do?" We had to seize that momentum and the momentum carried us. Credit to the coaches, to the players who came in. Credit to the guys who had been nowhere near the national team who came in and became the main players. Credit to all the boys who were able to bring back the memory of the fallen heroes.'

By now, half a dozen could be singled out. Zambia had created from depleted resources a formidable defence, who had conceded no goals in the four matches that guided them to the final. In the semi, their flair returned too, in a 4-0 win over Mali. The suspicion remained, though, that their progress in Tunisia had been at the expense of middleweight West Africans. In the final, they had to play Nigeria, three months away from their debut World Cup, buoyant for that, fast and muscular. The Nigerian Super Eagles held the Zambian team in high regard, too, and sympathised with what they had come through. 'There were so many instances like theirs,' recalls Sunday Oliseh, the Nigeria midfield player. 'We knew we were sometimes risking our lives flying all over Africa when we took some planes that had no lights in them, and would be shaking all over the place.'

Nigeria brought their brass bands to Tunis; Zambia had sufficient backing to rouse a good chorus of Chipolopolo. Three minutes into the 1994 final of the African Cup of Nations, it reached a crescendo. Litana, the big defender, had headed Zambia in front. The singing lasted little more than two minutes. Nigeria equalised. The Super Eagles scored again just after half-time. In their minds, the Zambians were back in the Mohammed IV stadium in Casablanca, so near yet so far, and galvanised by it. At 2-1 down, Kalusha hit the post. Nigeria cleared two Zambian attempts off the goal-line. Then it was over. The phoenix, the Zambian Second XI, had finished a very close second, again.

Over the next 15 years, Zambia would never come as close to a big prize again. The Chipolopolo reach Nations Cup tournaments regularly enough, but not the gold or silver medal positions. As for a World Cup, Kalusha kept plugging away. He captained Zambia's failed campaign to reach the 1998 tournament. He kept on into his mid-30s in the qualifiers for 2002. He even stepped out of retirement to play, middle-aged, and to score for the Chipolopolo in the vain bid to make it to Germany 2006. He became the national team's head coach. He then became president of the FAZ. To all these positions, Kalusha has taken remembrance of those aboard the Buffalo. 'People cannot help think about what might have been. We were a team with confidence, who really wanted to reach the World Cup and that was ready for it. And then you look at the rebuilding process. Every Zambian wanted us to come back to the same level, almost overnight. We desperately want to achieve something still, and if young men can believe, like we did, they have everything going for them. Well I hope one day we can reproduce that effort, to get to a level we can compare with what those boys did. If that same effort could be put together again for Zambia, I'd be the happiest man alive.' He already knows how lucky he is, just to be alive.

CHAPTER TEN

THE SWOOP OF EAGLES

When the world's most diverse sporting spectacle arrived in America, it was hard to keep your eyes off the Nigerian football team. As they closed in on their medal positions, The Eagles lurched from cliffhanger to cliffhanger. In the semi-finals, Brazil were beaten, via an extraordinary comeback. Trailing 3-1 after half an hour, Nigeria scored 13 minutes from full-time and equalised for 3-3 in the 90th minute, thanks to a goal from Nwankwo Kanu. An impudent piece of work it had been too, Kanu, with his back to the goalkeeper, pirouetting 180 degrees while flicking the ball up to tee himself up a volley. The same gangly figure then won the game in extra-time, with a drive from longer range. That made history for Africa, putting one of its teams into a world championship final at a senior global event.

A curious US had been already wowed by what the *Los Angeles Times* dubbed 'their colorful soccer' and Americans turned up in plentiful numbers to see Nigeria play Argentina. West African expatriates, robed in green and white, took quartets and quintets of brass musicians into the campus lanes around the venue for the final and there pulled up their minibuses and cars in the same resourceful parking style that you see around Surulere, in Lagos. Inside, many neutrals among the 80,000 gamely rose to their feet to sway to the sound of trumpets and tubas. Again, Nigeria fell behind: 1-0 down after barely a minute. Their firefly of a full-back, Celestine Babayaro sprang up to head in an equaliser and, unusually for him, resisted performing his multiple cartwheels in celebration in favour of a dance parodying a drunkard's gait. Nigeria's Hercules of a centre-half, Taribo West then conceded a dubious penalty for 2-1. Daniel Amokachi's drive made it 2-2 with extra-time approaching. Poised on another precipice, Nigeria had a stroke of luck. Attacking the ball from a gaping, offside position, the speediest of The Eagles, Emmanuel Amunike volleyed in the fifth, decisive goal, as aghast Argentinian defenders pointed hopelessly towards the referee's assistant. The goal stood. As they bent forward to accept the gold medals, Nigeria's players demanded the glitter be spread wide. 'This is for Nigeria, and Africa,' declared the striker Victor Ikpeba, 'and for the whole black race.'

For African football, it marked a genuine watershed. Unfortunately, it was not quite the World Cup. These golds were Olympic medals, the venue Athens, Georgia, the event an annex of the 1996 Atlanta Games, the final contested mainly by players under 23 years old, according to the Olympic rules (naturally opponents muttered that Nigeria had understood the age restrictions flexibly). Their exploits were squeezed into a day when a female long-jumper won another gold for Nigeria, and the footballers shared a stage with archers and wrestlers, rowers and walkers. The Nigerians' dramatic comebacks had been genuinely exhilarating, yet something about the glory felt overdue. The might of Nigeria had been battering at the gates of World Cups, unfulfilled for three decades before they reached one. Here in Georgia, they conquered the Olympic Games as if it were unfinished business from a World Cup adventure in the same country, the United States, 25 months earlier.

The Olympic champions had much in common with the Super Eagles of 1994 and hoped, in turn, to give impetus to the Nigerians who led Africa's enhanced, five-team complement at the 1998 World Cup in France. The period is Nigerian football's golden era. The mid-1990s hoisted Africa's most populous country to the continent's vanguard; yet at the same time football had focused on the pariah nature of Nigeria's state. The Confederation of African Football banned the Super Eagles from the 1998 Nations Cup after they failed to turn up and defend their title at the 1996 event in South Africa. The background was a spat between Nelson Mandela and the Nigerian dictator Sani Abacha which escalated after the execution of the Nigerian human rights activist Ken Saro-Wiwa, to the point at which Abacha withdrew the Super Eagles from those finals. It left Nigeria's public and their players nursing a keen frustration, though obliged to do so quietly. 'We had a military government,' remarks Sunday Oliseh, who captained Nigeria, 'and it was not something that we could really discuss.' What Nigerians could talk long, loud and proud about was their status. 'When you are one of 11 on the field and you know you have 120m or more people behind you, you develop an ego,' smiles Oliseh. Nigeria's class of the mid-1990s, he reckons, ticked most of the right boxes: 'There was strength, speed, craftiness. We were African champions in 1994, and we went to our first World Cup that summer with a team that had ambition. The players were hungry. That World Cup then gave the Olympic team its momentum.'

Cameroon had already given Africa's World Cup saga its new momentum, thanks to their adventures at Italia '90. The Super

Eagles looked equipped to make an even better impression. The strength, speed and craftiness Oliseh identified were assembled by two Dutchmen. Clemens Westerhof, an abrasive sort, coached the US World Cup team and his former assistant Jo Bonfrere the US Olympians. Westerhof promoted tyros like Oliseh, and the trickster Jay-Jay Okocha, whom he knew as a show-off but whose feathery skills and fierce shot would be significant tools for the Super Eagles for more than a decade to come. Westerhof had the rapid Amunike on the left wing, the clever Finidi George on the right. Up front, Amokachi would give them industry, Rashidi Yekini, the 'Bull of Kaduna' furnish power. 'Yekini is the greatest Nigerian striker I ever played with,' says Oliseh. 'His strike was unbelievable. He was always asking for the ball and he was always easy to find. All you had to do was drop the ball between the lines of defence and he didn't pose. He just struck. And usually high quality strikes.'

Some of the players did not care at all for Westerhof; Westerhof did not care much for his deputy, Bonfrere, but they had not been thrown together to play happy families, and the Dutchmen came from a football culture with specific dogmas with which several Nigerians empathised. 'The Dutch mentality is very close to the Nigerian mentality in the sense that football has to be good,' argues Oliseh, 'it has to be beautiful, there has to be goals and offensive action and all that. Westerhof came and he also encouraged players to go abroad, even at a young age. We had all by then started to look at playing in Europe.' Europe paid better than Nigeria and, some of the Eagles discovered, it could be fun. In the build-up to the US World Cup, the squad prepared in the Netherlands, where Westerhof recalls having to 'fish some players back to the hotel' from an establishment enjoying Holland's liberal by-laws. He also recalls the Nigerian Federation maintaining its fame for disorder:

Westerhof was flown to Fifa's pre-tournament conference for all 24 participating national coaches in New York. On landing, he realised the seminar was already over. He had been sent there a day too late.

Happily, Nigeria made the main event on time and set about their work in a hurry, Bulgaria demolished 3-0, quite a debut for the World Cup newcomers. For many Nigerians, it felt like the dam had burst. After Yekini scored the first goal, he charged after the ball into the goal and pushed his thick forearms through the netting, eyes closed, mouth wide open, a portrait of high-strung ecstasy. The photo of that moment would become one of the most published images of the tournament. Daniel Amokachi's goal that followed would be as spectacular. Amunike headed the third. Next up: Argentina. Unbeknown to the Super Eagles, they were to be guests at the last rites of Diego Maradona's international career. Maradona sampled positive in a routine dope test immediately after the match.

During the 90 minutes, Oliseh had policed the Argentinian number 10 impressively for all but the moment when Maradona set up Claudio Caniggia's winning goal. 'I played him so hard the whole game, and afterwards I was thinking to myself: "Yeah, if I can play hard against this man then I can play against anyone in the world". It was a test for me personally. In that game I'd seen many things that I'd never seen before. Maradona's ball control was always precise, and he was as strong as a wall as well. Westerhof said to me afterwards: "Great game, you did your thing."' Nigeria had taken the lead, Samson Siasia scoring after eight minutes, and ended up losing 2-1, a harbinger of what was to come the next time they met one of the sport's heavyweights.

Once the Super Eagles defeated Greece in their final group match, through goals from Finidi George and Amokachi again,

Senegal's players jive around the corner flag after Papa Bouba Diop's goal against France in the opening match of the 2002 World Cup. Senegal beat the then world champions 1-0 and progressed to the quarter-finals, Bouba Diop giving himself two further opportunities to perform his 'mbalakh' dance routine.

A supporter of the host nation, Mali, keeps his cool under the hot sun at the 2002 African Cup of Nations, where Cameroon successfully defended their title, beating Senegal in the final.

A teenager practices his skills at the Akodessewa fetish market in Lomé, the capital of Togo. Behind him are some of the dried animal parts used in strength- and stamina-giving rituals, and sometimes given to footballers to 'boost' their performances.

Cameroon's assistant coach, Thomas Nkono, tries to struggle free after he is handcuffed and arrested by Malian police officers just before Cameroon's African Cup of Nations semi-final against Mali in 2002. Nkono had been accused of throwing a 'magic' object onto the pitch and was banned from touchlines in Africa for a year for his 'provocative behaviour.'

Ghanaian boys practice during a misty morning at the Right to Dream football school just outside Accra. The academy is one of hundreds in West Africa that attract young players aspiring to a professional career in the sport. Right to Dream is one of the noble ones; many others draw in young children, exploit their ambitions and later discard them.

Nelson Mandela clutches the World Cup trophy moments after Fifa, football's governing body, had awarded the hosting rights of the 2010 World Cup to South Africa, giving the African continent its first chance to stage the tournament. 'I feel like a young boy of 15 again," said Mandela, who was 85 at the time.

A Nigerian supporter summons extra help from above for his team during the 2008 African Cup of Nations in Ghana. Nigeria's Super Eagles were knocked out of the tournament by their oldest and fiercest rivals, Ghana, in the quarter-finals.

Ghanaians rejoice at their team's success during their first appearance at a World Cup finals, in Germany, in 2006. Ghana's Black Stars reached the second round of the competition, with victories over a strong Czech Republic and the USA.

Fans of Al Ahly, the multiple Egyptian and African club champions, prepare a typically intimidating reception for visitors to Cairo. Al Ahly, founded in 1907, have won a record number of African Champions Cups and supplied the backbone of the Egypt team that won successive African Cup of Nations titles in 2006 and 2008.

Mohammed Aboutrika, Al Ahly and Egypt's star playmaker in action at the World Club Cup in 2006, where the African side finished in the medals, just behind Barcelona of Spain. Aboutrika was named runner-up as African Footballer of the Year in 2007 and 2008.

Samuel Eto'o Fils, three times African Footballer of the Year and spearhead of Cameroon's attack since the late 1990s, fends off a Ghanaian challenge. In the five years after Eto'o joined Spain's Barcelona in 2004, the club won three league titles and two Champions Leagues, Eto'o scoring in both their victorious finals.

Emmanuel Adebayor, African Footballer of the Year in 2008, showing the touch that helped lift Togo from also-rans in African football to surprise World Cup finalists in 2006. Adebayor had by then joined Arsenal of the English Premier League, becoming their most potent centre-forward.

Michael Essien, of Ghana, forcefully shrugs off Badr El Kadouri of Morocco at the 2008 African Cup of Nations. With Essien galvanising their midfield, Ghana reached a World Cup for the first time in 2006, and his English club, Chelsea won the Premier League.

Didier Drogba, captain of the Ivory Coast, also led his country to a debut World Cup in Germany in 2006, while his goals spearheaded Chelsea to successive Premier League titles. He was one of five African-born players regularly appearing in Chelsea's line-up in the 2008-09 season.

A fan of Orlando Pirates, Soweto's oldest major club, crosses his arms in the traditional 'crossbones' gesture to show his allegiance to Pirates, the so-called 'Buccaneers'. He is clutching a vuvuzela, the buzzing trumpet whose sound dominates football in South Africa, and will ring around stadiums at the 2010 World Cup.

Under the gaze of Table Mountain, Cape Town's famous landmark, construction speeds up on the new, state-of-the-art Greenpoint stadium, one of several new venues being built to host the first World Cup to be staged in Africa. The Greenpoint arena will be the site of one of the semi-finals, in July 2010.

and finished the first round top of the group, their displays had ushered them to the top of a US poll for the World Cup's 'Most Entertaining Side'. So far, so dandy. Surprise, surprise, in the ante-rooms of the campaign, money issues surfaced. First, an attempted bribe: Westerhof says he had a call from somebody offering him $1m for a Nigeria-Greece scoreline of 1-0. The Dutchman believes the would-be fixer, who asked that Westerhof's assistant remain in the team hotel to collect the money at the final whistle, was from the Far East. He said no. Then there were the arguments. When Nigeria's Minister for Sport arrived with his large entourage, Westerhof claims the players asked for double their agreed $10,000-a-head bonus if they were to defeat Italy in the next round.

The Super Eagles met the Italians in Boston at one o'clock East Coast American time, late afternoon for Nigerians watching at home on television. The players sensed a nation behind them. Just as they had against Argentina, Nigeria scored first, Amunike capitalising on some Italian uncertainty after a Finidi George corner. With Oliseh shadowing Roberto Baggio as he had Maradona, Nigeria held out, past the hour, and until they stood one minute from a place in the quarter-finals, Africa's World Cup frontier. Then, bang: Oliseh neglected his Baggio duty for a split second in order to challenge Roberto Mussi. Mussi fed the ball to a liberated Baggio, who made it 1-1.

The timing of the goal crushed Nigeria. The circumstances annoyed them. Italy were playing with 10 men when Baggio equalised, Gianfranco Zola having been sent off. Nigeria thought Paolo Maldini also ought to have departed for having hauled down the muscular Yekini. But even at 10 against 11, Italy seemed as capable of suffocating Nigeria as they had 11 against 11. Yekini felt increasingly impotent, a lonely leader of the line because

Amokachi and Amunike had both been substituted, injured. Westerhof had replaced the pair with players accustomed to deeper positions. Those decisions would condemn the coach, who had announced that Nigeria's last game in America would be his final one in charge. Despite leading Italy for well over an hour, the second round contest would be Nigeria's last at the tournament. Twelve minutes into extra-time, Augustine Eguavoen, the full-back, tripped Antonio Benarrivo. Referee Arturo Brizio Carter gave Italy a penalty. Nigeria's goalkeeper Peter Rufai dived one way, Baggio placed his shot the other. The Super Eagles's wings had been clipped.

They had plenty to say afterwards. Amokachi blamed Westerhof for the substitutions. So did Yekini, adding acidly: 'This coach has never liked me. This defeat is a lesson for the rest of Africa when they choose their managers.' Westerhof walked around the dressing-room in the moments after the defeat and shook each player's hand. 'Gentlemen,' he announced, 'there is one flight going to Schiphol, Amsterdam tomorrow and another going to Lagos. I'll say good-bye now.' The coach had saved himself a scalding, or, better put, what one Nigerian journalist described as 'criticisms bound to flow from the press and fans like red-hot lava.' The footballers received a gentler welcome. 'It was a mixed reaction,' remembers Oliseh. 'Some said we had made a good impression. We had won two games and we lost two games, mid-table form I guess. It was just unfortunate that the second one we lost was a knockout match. We topped our group, we had five or six different players who scored goals. So there were plusses.'

Oliseh, Okocha, Amokachi, Amunike and company carried those positives to the Olympics, in a squad that was probably stronger than the Super Eagles of 1994, and younger. They would be nicknamed The Dream Team, and with their gold medals most of them would hop-scotch their way around European clubs for the next decade, some of then swapping employers almost as often as Nigeria hired and sacked national coaches. Oliseh played for Ajax of Holland, as did Kanu and Finidi, who both won the European Cup in 1995. Oliseh then played in Italy's Serie A with Juventus; in Belgium and in the German Bundesliga. Jay-Jay Okocha took his tricky feet, his boomerang free-kicks and his long throw-ins to Turkey, to France, to Germany and to the English Premier League. In most of those places, Okocha was loved by supporters, but never regarded with quite the rapture that audiences in Africa devoted to him.

■ ■ ■

On the morning of 9 June 1998, Youssou N'dour, the Senegalese singer, had his final rehearsals for the biggest live performance of his career. Hundreds of gymnasts and dancers worked around him at the Stade de France in Saint-Denis, Paris, preparing for the opening ceremony of the biggest World Cup ever. Thirty-two teams would contest it, a 25 per cent rise in the invitation list. Five African countries would be there, legacy of Morocco, Cameroon and Nigeria's presence in the later rounds at the previous three tournaments. With N'dour's sweet voice at the microphone to kick off the event, France was keen to show a continent where it once acted as landlord across most of the north and the west that its bonds with Africa remained strong and benevolent.

Just outside the French capital, at a chateau that served as temporary headquarters of the Nigerian squad, one crisis overtook another. The head coach, a peripatetic Serb called Bora Milutinović, believed he might, on the eve of the tournament, be sacked, just three months after his appointment. Then a more pressing matter suddenly presented itself to the Nigerian delegation to the 1998 World Cup. General Sani Abacha, the country's ruler, had been found dead in his presidential home in Abuja. Theories soon gained currency that he may have been poisoned. A vigorous evening in the company of some prostitutes was then cited as the cause of his fatal heart attack.

Among the issues to which Abacha had devoted his attention during his last days and hours had been the national football team, the Olympic champions, and the discouraging form in the immediate lead-up to the 1998 World Cup. The competence of Milutinović had become a matter of concern at high ministerial level. Senior players, some of whom had a direct line to Abuja, had debated the matter. As Oliseh remembers: 'It was chaotic. Here we were, three days before our opening match against Spain talking about changing the head coach. He actually should have lost the job way before then because he was wrong for a team like Nigeria, but it would have been wrong to get rid of him so late. Some players said "Sack him", others said "I'm not taking the brunt of it".'

The death of Abacha may have prolonged Milutinović's stay in a job he only inherited two months earlier. Certainly, it was a distraction. Briefly, it had been suggested the team withdraw from the tournament to honour a widely loathed leader. Safe to say, like millions of Nigerians, most players felt a limited sort of bereavement for the end of a tyrant's reign. Had they grieved? 'Put it this way,' replies Oliseh. 'We topped the group, we gave some great performances.' They did so in spite of the working environment, he adds. 'If you judged us on our organisation, the tactical know-how of the people in charge, it was a miracle that we got to the second round. It was because we had the players. It was just the players' will and fighting spirit. Against Spain, it was a question of pride, like always.'

Against Spain, on the first Saturday of the 16th World Cup, Nigeria produced what had become the African continent's traditional first-match blitz. They felt motivated, their pride had been piqued. 'The Spanish players gave big interviews saying that they had to beat us with a lot of goals because it might be goals that decided who would be first in the group,' recalls Oliseh. 'Our coach got hold of this and he put it up on the wall in the dining room. I really think that if they'd have shut their mouths up, the Spain team and their trainer, they would have won the game. Instead, we came out for war that day.' It would turn into an epic. A goal down after 21 minutes, Nigeria's Mutiu Adepoju equalised quickly. Just after half-time, a 20-year-old Raúl González gave Spain the lead. Nigeria pressed, Spain became anxious. Garba Lawal scored a second goal with just over a quarter of an hour remaining: 2-2. Cue Oliseh in the 78th minute. He sensed Nigeria were growing in strength, Spain fatigued. 'I'd been keeping an eye on their centre-forward, Kiko, and after he took a few knocks, he was retreating so I could move forward. Okocha took a throw-in, the ball got headed out, coming towards me. Now, I had scored many goals from this sort of position, a long way out, for Ajax. I was well outside the penalty box, but in my mind was just hit the target, keep the ball down. It went just where I wanted.' Boom: Nigeria 3, Spain 2.

The rest of the African contingent had hardly kept pace. South Africa, debutants, had been blown away under a Mistral wind, losing 3-0 to France in Marseille, where a beery collection of England fans burned a Tunisian flag and fought with North Africans in the streets ahead of England 2, Tunisia 0. Morocco's Mustapha El Hadji and Cameroon's Pierre Njanka scored goals as spectacular as Oliseh's against Spain as those two countries drew their first encounters and sustained the idea of progress to the knockout phase. But by the end of the group stage, from Africa only the Super Eagles remained in the tournament. They had built on the victory against Spain with a win against Bulgaria, and again they finished top of their mini-league.

The Super Eagles would meet Denmark for a place in the last eight. This time, there was no suspense, no extra-time, no Baggio to curse. All had been lost by the 13th minute, at Denmark 2, Nigeria 0. On the hour, the Danes added a third goal. Milutinović's team were wretched. 'Tactically we were gone,' recalls Oliseh. 'Players were running and dribbling all over the place and no one was saying "Look, you have to do this or that". We lost all possible shape.' And the Super Eagles' state of mind? Oliseh sighs: 'Well, like always, there had been arguments before the game.' What about? Unpaid bonuses, of course. Nigeria scored a late goal, but by then Denmark had a fourth and were in the quarter-finals.

Nigeria made the next tournament, in Korea and Japan, but lost two games and returned home with just a point. They failed to qualify for Germany in 2006. In the first decade after their ban from the African Nations Cup had been lifted, they would not become champions again. Had Oliseh felt his was the golden generation? He did. 'Sometimes,' he adds, a little maudlin, 'it looks to me as if the golden generation was the *only* generation.'

With the thrashing by Denmark, the 20th century story of Africa and the World Cup had ended with a whimper. In France, milestones would be achieved, but vicariously. A fortnight after the last Nigerian trumpet tooted its farewell notes in Saint-Denis, Les Bleus of France won their first World Cup. A Moroccan, Saïd Belqola became the first African to referee a final. He gave a red card to the first African-born footballer to win a World Cup, Marcel Desailly, a Ghanaian who as a boy had been adopted by a French father. The night's hero, the finest footballer in the world at the time, was the son of Algerian immigrants. Zinedine Zidane's two first-half goals in a 3-0 defeat of Brazil led to vivid celebrations across the Kabylie, the Berber region of North Africa. On one of the last trains out of Saint-Denis into the French capital that night, I saw an immigrant from Senegal bang his fist against the window, joyfully shouting 'Take that, Le Pen!' in reference to the Far-Right, anti-immigration French politician, Jean-Marie Le Pen. France read into the victory of its black-blanc-beur XI – black, white, Maghrebi XI – its players with antecedents in Africa, the Caribbean, Polynesia and Eastern Europe, a cultural watershed, a celebration of its own rainbow nation. As Parisians chanted 'Zidane for President' along the Champs Elysées, it sounded convincing.

CHAPTER ELEVEN

WHISPERING AT PIGEONS

Pastor TB Joshua makes miracles. Working out of his low-roofed church in Ikotun-Egbe in Lagos, Nigeria, he heals the sick, says he can cure terminal tumours, detect and exorcise the evil that turns men and women into witches, that he will show sufferers the path that leads to recovery from Aids. Hundreds believe him and thousands have witnessed his intense, mesmerising sermons. On Sundays, his parishioners crowd along narrow pews under a low corrugated iron roof at his Synagogue, Church of All Nations, their altar a simple wooden construction on a crimson rug. If the atmosphere at the start of the service feels heavy, suffocating, flat, the spiritual energy generated by the words and gestures of Senior Prophet Temitope Balogun Joshua, Master Healer, soon rouses. Congregants will rise from their seats to confess in public to witchcraft, adultery, disease, to hear his admonishments and hope for his blessings.

To his devotees, Pastor Joshua is a sort of Messiah with a microphone, among the more prominent of the Pentecostal churchmen whose following has grown rapidly across west and central Africa since the 1970s. To Lagosians not entirely moved by the greatness of his work, he is plain TB Joshua, a dangerous charlatan, not a prophet but a profiteer. It remains unclear into which category the celebrated and loved centre-forward of the Super Eagles, Nwankwo Kanu belongs.

When Kanu came to visit Pastor Joshua shortly after he had captained Nigeria to an Olympic gold medal in 1996, Africa's first such football triumph at a Games, the footballer was 20. He had just been diagnosed with a serious heart defect, a malfunctioning aortic valve and told he should never play again. That he was still skippering the Super Eagles a full dozen years later would be taken as a blessing indeed for the millions of Nigerians who have grown to love their willowy striker almost as much as any footballer in their history; the 'long, stringy thing who does amazing things with the ball,' as his first coach in the Nigerian junior team, Fanny Amun, described him, a six-foot-four giant so slender that on windy days his baggy shirt blows around his frame like a flag on a pole. Kanu's football can enchant. At his peak, for Nigeria and for European clubs as hallowed as Ajax, Arsenal and Internazionale, Kanu would use his long stride to mark out a protective area around the ball as he ran, elegant, swaying, with it, measuring the weight of his passes like golf putts, and scored goals from apparently impossible angles. Nigerians have always appreciated Kanu even when his dips in form frustrated them. They also loved him for his vulnerability, for his miracle return from sickness.

When the doctors told him his career was probably over, Kanu turned to Pastor Joshua. They met in one of the ante-rooms of the main hall of his church. Kanu wore a pale blue suit and the Pastor, a portly man in his 50s, was dressed in a long white robe. He read from an open Bible, occasionally stroking his greying beard, putting exaggerated emphasis on selected words. Kanu signed a document promising to 'attain [sic] services once a week'. Pastor TB Joshua sternly told the footballer he should be 'not just a church go-er, but a church *do-er*.' The contract made, the healing began. The men faced one another. The Pastor placed a hand firmly on Kanu's chest. He appeared to close his eyes for a moment before moving his flat palm from the footballer's heart and placing it on his own. He then broke the silence. 'This,' declared Pastor Joshua, 'is what is meant by "With Thy wound, I Thee heal".' The Master Healer then moved his body as if in a trance, stretching his arms out and swaying, his eyes shut. With a startling jerk of his right arm, Kanu then jumped two feet to his left. 'What moved you?' asked the Pastor.

The question hung in the air of the small room. The best respondents at the Synagogue, Church of All Nations tend to react with a vivid crescendo at their saving by the hands of Pastor TB Joshua. During his masses, young women jerk about as if seized by epilepsy before thanking him for delivering them from demons, while crippled septuagenarians discard their sticks, whooping. Some of the most vivid instances of the Pastor's power, like his meeting with Kanu, are carefully recorded on video and in his well-stocked editing room; along a passageway next to the main church hall across from the hall that sells religious paraphernalia, guests can watch tape after tape of it. The footage of Kanu's encounter with the mystic is genuine enough, but it lacked the pyrotechnics of some of TB Joshua's more vivid shows. Often, the reactions of the blessed and the saved look like the stunts of hastily employed actors. But the Pastor also has a stack of tapes of celebrity testimonials, oozing sincerity. The Super Eagles goalkeeper Peter Rufai gives an earnest interview on the wonder of the Synagogue, Church of All Nations. Other, powerful athletes bow down before his miracles. The Nigerian wrestler Armstrong Okere, apparently cured of excruciating burns while held in thrall to the Pastor, celebrates to camera his instant recovery from pain by telling TB Joshua 'You are the prophet sent by God!' Kanu's answer to the question. 'What moved you?' seemed understated by comparison. The footballer, frowning, told the Pastor he felt unsure what had moved him.

What saved Kanu's heart? I asked Pastor Joshua one day in early 2000, as we sat in his lounge, being recorded, as he always is, by his faithful cameraman. We were surrounded by his certificates from Pentecostal 'universities' in the United States of America. A vast television stood next to us. Helpers scuttled around. The Pastor said he did not care to dwell on specific miracles, and spoke in aphorisms and quoted psalms. He said he was merely an appointed worker. His time with me abruptly terminated, he asked one of his young attendants to give me some more videos of his work to take home.

The next afternoon I went to see Kanu. He was staying at the Lagos Sheraton, preparing, with the rest of the Nigeria squad, for the final of the African Nations Cup. I asked him about the tournament, the imminent showdown against Cameroon, about Arsenal, where he was then employed, and about his popularity among Nigerian fans. Then I asked him about his recovery from the heart condition and about his session with Pastor TB Joshua. I quickly gathered Kanu felt uncomfortable with the Pastor publicising their relationship, as the Healer tends to. So what saved Kanu's heart? The surgeon in America who operated on his defective valve? Faith? 'You can say God answered my prayers,' Kanu replied. His faith had always been strong, he added.

■ ■ ■

On the Sunday of Nigeria against Cameroon, the first Nations Cup final of the new century, a very different form of spiritualism came to a packed, heaving Surulere stadium in Lagos. Around 70,000 Nigerians had paid to be there. Lots of others had not, and still found a view. Twenty-three Cameroonians meanwhile had become anxious to the point of paranoia about how far their hosts might go to win the game. The Indomitable Lions' squad had had lunch, sitting on the floor, crammed into the home of their ambassador in Lagos, urged at late notice not to eat hotel food in case it was poisoned. They had been taunted at their hotel into the early hours by noisy Lagosians. There also arose the possibility of a hex at the stadium. A curious incident had taken place late in Nigeria's tense semi-final against Senegal when a senior official from the Nigerian Football Association suddenly dashed from the area behind the substitutes' benches at Surulere to behind the Senegal goal and removed two objects. 'They were fetishes,' Kashimaro Laloko explained after his subsequent ban from sitting near the touchline. 'I had to do it for my country.' Nigeria had been trailing 1-0 at the time of Laloko's mercy mission to the goal. The Super Eagles then equalised in the 84th minute. In the 92nd, they scored their winner.

When the Cameroon players arrived in the tunnel leading to the dressing-rooms, they sensed something was up. 'We saw all the Nigerian players standing outside their dressing-room door,' recalls the Cameroon striker Samuel Eto'o. A few quizzical looks later, an explanation: 'They said they weren't going in because we'd put a spell on their dressing-room.' The Cameroonians shot back with the same: the Indomitable Lions said they would not be going into their dressing-room either because it must be bewitched. The relevant medium was promptly summoned to, as Eto'o puts it, 'purify both dressing-rooms.' The mystic did so ritually, dropping splashes of water around the two rooms.

The die had been cast. Nigeria delayed going onto the pitch for their warm-ups. In the dressing-room, they held their prayers, led by the muscular defender, Taribo West, alias 'The Pastor', a born-again Christian who for internationals liked to weave the green of Nigeria's flag into the braids of his hair, who founded his own church in Italy, where he played for both Internazionale and AC Milan. 'Cover us in the blood of Jesus,' the players murmured in chorus as 'Pastor' West was supported in praise by Sunday Oliseh, Nigeria's captain, and by Kanu. The midfielder Mutiu Adepoju then led a Muslim prayer for some of the others. And what of the earlier sorcery? 'We were a very religious team, not into voodoo,' insists Oliseh, 'but, hey, maybe there was some voodoo on the other team?' Nigerian fans went along with that idea: as Eto'o and his team-mates performed their exercises on the field, they heard themselves taunted from the grandstands with cries of 'Juju-men!'. 'Part of their tactics,' snorts Eto'o, remembering the stifling atmosphere. 'Me, I don't believe that stuff.'

That stuff goes by various names: Faith. Miracles. Voodoo. Gris-gris. What Nigeria needed at the Cup of Nations final in Surulere was luck. Pastors? Féticheurs? Wizards? What they also needed was a cool-headed, sharp-eyed linesman. At 2-2 after 120 minutes, the Super Eagles versus the Indomitable Lions went to a shoot-out. Kanu struck his penalty weakly. It was saved. For Cameroon, the late Marc-Vivien Foé missed. Finally, the Nigerian striker Victor Ikpeba hammered his kick against the crossbar, it bounced down viciously against the turf and span out of the goalmouth. Ikpeba reacted with a forlorn gesture, hands to his face, not realising the ball had in fact crossed the goal-line. The linesman, a Tunisian, said: 'No goal'. It meant Nigeria lost, and Surulere fell into a disbelieving, petrified silence as eerie as anything during the build up.

■ ■ ■

Shortly before the next African Cup of Nations, staged in Mali, the Confederation of African Football (Caf) issued a statement from its Cairo headquarters. It was designed to draw a line under an issue that had become irritating to the sponsors, marketers and governors of football in Africa. 'We are no more willing to see witch doctors on the pitch than cannibals at the concession stands,' said Caf. The incident with the NFA's Laloko and the alleged Senegal gris-gris plot had been a global embarrassment. And not just that. Caf hoped to bring to an end a century of tales of fetishism, juju, maraboutism, muti, and any other of the terms for superstitious practices that occur in football across Africa. Caf had had enough of magic, of what it called, in inverted commas, 'team advisers' who operate in the netherland between superstition and the desire of every competitive sportsman to gain an advantage.

In Africa it is a particularly fertile territory. In many of its cultures, the idea of the oracle, the body that sees ahead, has a strong resonance. So does the figure who might influence a pre-ordained future, the harbinger of rains or droughts, of victories or defeats, the character who can tell younger, maturing men how best to avoid pitfalls and ensure their own success. Africa is full of seers and, in its most popular sport, he easily finds a place. He can be the clairvoyant who predicts outcomes, sets conditions for that outcome; he may be the wizard who then sets out tasks to malleable teenagers, accustomed to obeying their elders. 'Walk backwards into the stadium', he might say; or, 'Carry these coins or roots or cloths somewhere in your kit'; or, 'Chant the name of your opponent while dipping your feet in a bowl of cow's blood'. He might also hold the key to a frustrating, persistent injury that has baffled other doctors. The figure of the gifted healer, or the soothsayer, existed in Africa long before Islam or Christianity, and if the evangelists of both religions have declared him an enemy, they have also borrowed some of his methods to proselytise.

Players often dismiss it as hocus-pocus, but have reasons to acquiesce. Surrounded by local mystics or bible-bearing priests, what choice does an ambitious kid have? If you've won a close game that you'd expected to lose after someone put a lucky charm in your sock, you'll wear it again. You get told that 10 others in the team have performed a certain ritual designed by the mystic and approved by the manager. What do you do? You say yes if you want to keep your place in the XI.

Professionalism has done a great deal to diminish the role of the sorcerer in how teams prepare, but he remains an actor in the wider theatre of football in Africa. He might be there just as a show-off fan, dressed up in a grass skirt, with beads and cowrie-shells hanging around his neck, a leopard-skin headdress and a wide-eyed, round-mouthed mask across his face as he patrols up and down in front of the stands. He's a caricature but he's a popular one, and if he no longer inspires or frightens footballers as he once did, he's part of the culture.

In literature, the soccer sorcerer crops up again and again. In Kamenga Batukezanga's novel *Seven Brothers and a Sister*, set in Zaïre, a football match approaches its climax, the scores level after 80 minutes. 'Who was going to win?,' asks the narrator. 'Amid the suspense, some creatures weirdly dressed, all in raffia, began to draw attention to themselves. They were spitting out big blobs of chewed kola nut mixed with palm wine. Every so often out of their mouths would come a sort of mud that they directed towards the players. Word went round that these bizarre men were representing three famous "nganga nkisi", or féticheurs. Thanks to their magic, the nganga nkisi made the legs of the players they were backing move with a lightness, a suppleness and much more skill than others, who turned heavy, incapable of scoring goals.' In *Man Pass Man*, a story by Ndeley Mokoso set in colonial Cameroon, the Commissioner's Cup final is determined by supernatural forces, a 'juju-man' brutally beaten up by fans of one team on the touchline while 'the club's executive vote the sum of one hundred thousand francs, under miscellaneous expenses, for the transport and upkeep of their juju-man.' He describes 'the weird process of consulting the oracle – a little object the size of a land-crab studded with cowries. It chirped like a young chick – a language which only one man understood.' The story turns on the alarming discovery by one goalkeeper and the disturbing visions of another. 'The goalkeeper of the Coasters, standing between the posts had an eerie feeling. He walked to both ends of the uprights and inspected the corners. There was nothing. He made two brilliant saves – one, a powerful header from a corner kick, the other a shot from striker Mokoko. As he dropped after saving the shot, his feet sank into the sand. He looked down at his boots. Beneath the sand was fresh loose earth. He suspected something and continued poking at the earth with his right boot. What he saw frightened him – the hind legs of some animal. He took courage and pulled at the legs. Up came the already decomposing carcass of a black sheep.' At the other end, meanwhile, 'the Wanderers goalkeeper had one of those brainwaves. He ran up to the referee just before kick-off to protest against the continued use of the football. He swore he had seen three footballs each time Manga hit the ball.' The butt of Mokoso's satire is the referee, an Englishman named John Hilton, who in a stubborn, show-must-go-on sort of way disregards the violence on the touchlines, the dead animal disinterred on the pitch, the protests of the goalkeeper with the kaleidoscope halucinations. 'I'll have no more of this superstitious nonsense about juju in football,' insists the referee.

Once upon a time, there were dozens of John Hiltons in colonial Africa, disapproving of fetishism in the sports they sought to control and manage. The Christian missionaries involved in promoting healthy, hearty, good-for-the-soul games like football liked it even less. A note in the official programme for a 1937 annual regimental sports meeting in Nigeria felt it necessary to state: 'Any team or individual displaying a juju or anything purporting to be a juju or charm, or claiming to possess a juju will be disqualified.' In the 1950s, the relationship between Zulu inyangas – traditional seers and healers – and the football clubs of Durban, South Africa, attracted the attention of a Harvard academic, NA Scotch. Dr Scotch reported that 'each team employs an inyanga who serves the dual purpose of strengthening his own team by magic ritual and of forestalling the sorcery directed at his team by rival inyangas.' The rituals are those you regularly hear described by players active in southern Africa from the 1960s until well into the 1990s: bathing in various liquids – sometimes animal blood – on the eve of matches; standing naked in circles around the inyanga; and having ground bone solutions or other ointments applied to the body, often via incisions made to the flesh.

As international competitions took off in Africa, in the 1960s, the spectre of fetishism sometimes became part of the strategy, as host teams sought to intimidate visitors from afar. When a human skull was dug up from beneath the centre circle of Kinshasa's May 20th stadium in 1969, rivals of the club, Tout-Puissant Engelbert of Lubumbashi, unbeaten at that ground, imagined they had stumbled on an explanation for the club's domestic pre-eminence. Football in Zaïre developed a particular fame, and not simply because of the indistinct roles of many of the individuals – or 'team advisers' as Caf would call them – who joined the huge delegation that accompanied The Leopards of Zaïre to their disastrous World Cup finals in Germany in 1974. A decade later, *Elima*, the Kinshasa newspaper, reported on a series of strange events at the Lumumba stadium in Kisangani, notably that a team official had apparently poured a litre of blood across the corridor between dressing-rooms.

Some clubs still employ a mystic. Once upon a time, many did. In 1970s Rhodesia, the young goalkeeper Bruce Grobbelaar would get on his bicycle, head out of his suburban Bulawayo home and meet up with his Matabeleland Highlanders team-mates in the township of Mzilikazi to receive what seemed to him a bizarre sort of blessing. 'We would stand around in a circle at the youth centre stripped naked desperately hoping that none of the locals would see us,' remembers Grobbelaar. 'We would go into the witch doctor one at a time to have water swished over us with a goat's tail and while we were still wet, we would put on our football kit and rejoin the circle to chant'. Grobbelaar, the white son of an Afrikaaner in a team mainly of black players, had discarded his self-consciousness with his clothes. 'We would go through this straight faced and make out we believed in it. The slightest sign of doubt would have discouraged the others. If we were away from home the team would get changed on the bus because they believed the opposition witch doctor would have cast a spell on the dressing-room. Often we would enter the pitch by threading our way through the crowd and climbing over the fence.' Grobbelaar recalls an incident which might have been drawn from the pages of *Man Pass Man*. An opposition mystic had turned up to perform at the stadium of another of Grobbelaar's clubs, Salisbury Callies, two days before a league match against Chibuku. 'He had the full works, grass headdress, goats' tails and a bucket full of some strange substance. Our club did everything to keep him away, chasing him off the pitch and even putting him on a bus but he was persistent. When the big game came he was up and down the touchline more often than the linesman.' Callies won. Grobbelaar felt for the man in the headdress as he saw him 'chased down the road by stone-throwing fans.'

Some major games attracted very tall stories, retold and probably embellished over the years. Like the 1977 African Champions

Cup final. Various oracles had been consulted ahead of the collision between Ghana's Hearts of Oak and Hafia from Guinea. For the first leg, supporters gathered at the Accra Sports Stadium long before kick-off and cheered loudly when they were joined by a quartet of ravens who landed on the pitch, strutted around, pecking, cocking their heads stiffly from side to side. A senior mystic had predicted four goals that day for Hearts: one goal for each bird. Then an anxious murmur grew around the grandstands. A white dove had joined the ravens on the field. If the dark birds were omens, so the pale one must be some form of harbinger, too. The visitors from Conakry won 1-0; Hearts had missed a penalty, one Anas Seidou having blazed his spot-kick way off target. Word had it that his aim had been distracted by another mystic's terrible prediction that the scorer of the first goal would perish soon afterwards.

In Ghana at that time, football was full of mystics. Abedi Ayew Pelé remembers the briefings given to him, a prodigy at Tamale United in the north of Ghana, by the club's 'sorcerer'. 'We called them different things, depending on what ethnic group you came from: "Okompo", "Beyie", "Aduro", "Aze", "Djoka", "Vodou", "Tsofa", "Juju" or "Tim", where I was from,' recalled Pelé. 'The big clubs in the north all took what the sorcerer said seriously. You had to respect him or else you risked bringing bad luck onto the field.' Ahead of a replayed Cup final in 1981, Pelé was told to wash with a special soap each morning and evening until the big day, and to conceal talismanic objects in his boots. Once he refused a drink urged on him by the club mystic – he suspected it might contain alcohol – and was suspended for a week. These figures, says Pelé, could 'encourage you to be hopeful even in what seemed impossible situations.' They were also confidence tricksters. 'One day when we were travelling to a game with our sorcerer-man, he said he foresaw a 2-0 win. For us. The game did finish 2-0, but to the other side. So the whole team called him a liar; he said we hadn't obeyed his magic practices. When we got back to Tamale, he told us: "Okay, if you don't believe me, I'll show you my powers. You throw your jerseys on the ground. I'll get a gun, fire it at them and if I make holes in the jerseys, you can call me a fake".' Mention of guns put the players into apologetic, nervous retreat.

Mention of Lagos, meanwhile, was beginning to intimidate more and more visiting teams from around Africa, and not, it should be stressed, purely for supernatural reasons. Nigeria's bustling, biggest city had long been a feared place to make an away trip, for its raucous atmosphere. But the odd strategically-placed object or gesture also had an effect. Representing Algeria, the player Mustapha Dahleb remembers a fixture at Surulere during the All Africa Games of 1972, and a spectre in the tunnel between dressing-room and pitch. 'Right before our eyes, our opponents made a circle around what can only be described as some sort of sorcerer, shouting loudly, summoning up their gris-gris. It was a motivation for them and it was discouraging for us.' In 1981, the Nigerian Football Association called on the services of a 'parapsychologist' Dr Godwin Okunzua, after their narrow failure to reach the World Cup finals. Algeria had been their nemesis in an epic play-off, the North Africans having won at Surulere, quite a feat, a shock to the local spell-makers. Mohammed Maouche, then manager of Algeria, recalls the frenzied dancing and drumming of two men dressed in animal hides behind either goal ahead of the kick-off. When he took his players into the dressing-room, he found small neat balls of tightly bound ribbon placed precisely around the corners of the changing area. 'Some of the players were a bit disconcerted,' Maouche remembers, 'so I went around, picked them all up and threw them all into the corridor outside. When the Nigerians saw them, then they got worried. But, you know, we sportsmen are easily made superstitious, and it's not just something that happens in sub-Saharan Africa. I know Algerian footballers who will consult a marabout before a big game or about an injury. And then go about their rituals, like taking their boots down to the beach and filling each one seven times with sea water, because that's what the marabout said he should do.'

In other words, almost everyone's been at it, some of them believing, most of them make-believing, others ensuring they have something to brandish should the other team wield their witchcraft, proclaim their strength of faith, or their extra dash of devilry. It is a form of what managers call 'mind games'. Or most of it seems to be. For the proper, the really strong stuff, you have to go way outside the established capitals of African football. You have to go to Togo for the hardware, the medicine, and to Benin for the theory.

■ ■ ■

'And this,' announced Limikpo Jacob with a sweep of his arm, 'is what we use for sportsmen.' He was indicating a large wooden table on which were arranged the parts of several dead animals, most prominent the results of a series of decapitations. Just in front of a stack of vacant tortoise shells were some cheetahs' heads, long incisors well displayed. I could also see the face of a small baboon, but what Jacob, president of Le Marché des Féticheurs, was chiefly pointing out was the large face of a horse, and the skull of a cow. 'This is our sports medicine department, these are what make a sportsman strong,' Jacob went on. And he grinned: 'It's our form of "doping", if you want to call it that.' Then he showed the procedure. Powder from the ground bone of these large mammals would be made into solution, applied to cuts in the skin of an athlete, imbuing him with the strength of the animal. There was plenty more. Jacob was wearing a dark green boubou, embroidered with white circles like a long necklace of pearls, throat to toe and as he strolled around the various stalls of the Akodessewa market in Lomé, the Togolese capital, he explained a little of how things operate here. Like most of the féticheurs, he comes from Benin, the next-door state. But Togo shares much of the ancient medical tradition of its neighbour and Lomé has a market for everything: currencies, cloth, and evidently, this sort of creed. In this slender belt of West Africa made up by Togo and Benin, two long, narrow nations squeezed between Ghana and Nigeria, fetishism has its longest history, its greatest concentration of experts. From Togo and Benin sailed the slaves who brought voodoo to the Caribbean.

Akodessewa market is their biggest wholesaler, famous enough to have half an eye out for the passing tourist, but established enough to keep thriving for its principal function. Here in a large compound, its centrepiece a furnace that looks strangely like a modernist sculpture, full of iron hooks on which to hang objects and plants, are stall after stall displaying voodoo dolls of various designs, horse-tail whisks, masks and amulets, the majority made in Benin. The medicinal products are many: aphrodisiacs derived from roots; epilepsy treatments made from desiccated cats' tongues; a variety of plants that might conquer infertility. And also available are a wide range of creatures. Spread about an unshaded area of the market compound lie hundreds of mouse carcasses, whole crocodiles, and surprisingly little odour and very few flies. The hot sun does much of the preservation work here, though the traditional techniques of taxidermy are as sound as the principles they insist are followed by practitioners. 'We only work for good not for bad towards others, you must be clear,' said Jacob. But yes, he acknowledged, sometimes sports teams did seek from his colleagues instruction on how best to prepare for matches; and no, he couldn't tell me in advance the forthcoming weekend's scores.

If all this stuff really worked for footballers and their teams, then Togo and Benin would be Africa's leaders in football. Togo surprisingly reached a World Cup, in Germany in 2006, but brought to it not a display of eerily supernatural skill but a tawdry series of disputes between players and directors over money. Benin have made it to two African Nations Cups in the 21st century, but, once there, punched their proper weight and made little impression. The Benin national team do have their elaborate rituals behind closed doors, their former captain Jean-Marc Adjovi-Bocco told me with resignation more than with conviction: 'Benin is very well-known for that, so I can understand that people believe in it. I don't, I didn't really like it and as captain, they knew my views. But they did a lot of things: they had objects to wrap around their bodies, to take onto the pitch. I felt if it makes you feel well, just do it. The problem then is that football is being used in a bad way. Things are done to "do bad" to our opponents, it becomes a weapon to cause pain to the others. So, yes, do things that make you feel confident in yourself but remember, it is always more comfortable to win because you're better than the others than to have won because you cheated them.'

■ ■ ■

The South African Football Association paid a Togolese mystic who claimed to have blessed their progress to a World Cup in 1997 by hampering Congolese players in a particular qualifying match. Before then setting off for their first appearance at a World Cup finals, they went native, the South Africans receiving the blessing of a Zulu sangoma – a mystic – in a heavily publicised event enthusiastically attended by the former wife of the then president, Winnie Mandela, and the team's new head coach Philippe Troussier. Troussier, an old hand in African football, had coached in Ivory Coast, Nigeria and in Burkina Faso, from where all numbers of stories are told about the influence of 'wak', or magic on the outcomes of football matches and he has quite a collection of tales of this ilk.

On taking the Nigeria job, Taribo West – the Pastor – invited the new coach to accompany him to prayer. 'At first,' says Troussier, 'it looked like a meeting of the Ku Klux Klan, everybody dressed up in white. There were rituals, but Taribo was basically a Christian evangelist. At the same time, he would also say to me, "Philippe you must meet the witch doctor and you have to take this approach, to say we are going to win tomorrow, we will win 3-0 and we will play very well". I could see this whole situation was necessary for him.' Troussier wanted leaders like West in his side, motivating the rest. He also wanted to have an idea of what they might be up to. 'Often you don't know it's going on,' adds Troussier. 'You'll be watching a match and suddenly you see, hey, this player's got a bandage on his arm. Did he break it recently? Has he got an injury there he didn't say anything about? Then you'll see three or four players on the pitch like that. You find out that tucked under the strapping there is some gris-gris, some herb, some little twig that he has been given by the juju-man.'

Sometimes, Troussier found, new members of staff arrived with a special purpose. 'I remember one of my first experiences with the Ivory Coast national team was an away trip to Algeria, during a terrible period to go there because of the Islamic situation. We had to play the game outside Algiers for security reasons and there were many of us in the group because we had at least five military constantly accompanying us. The second day I was there, I sat down for the team meal, and suddenly there were two men at my table I had never seen before in my life: two small people, like pygmies. They said they had been sent by the Minister for Sport.'

Troussier decided to set some ground rules and, if they accepted those, to let the mystics do what they had to: there would be no messing with the players' diets, and no disrupting their sleep patterns. "Don't touch the night, don't touch the food, respect my timetable", I said to them. So we agreed we would go out before the sun went down and wash the players with their special water and we had to put a white powder on them. If I thought the players were happy doing that, it was no problem. I called the players and together said: "I respect your habit, and if you believe that tomorrow we will play better for it, okay." And we had to follow the way. It is strange. The players could say "Nah!! I don't believe in that" or "that is ridiculous" but they follow because that's part of their livelihood. So I said to the chief pygmy: "You are my psychologist, so tomorrow you need a tracksuit on like the rest of us." But then the Minister for Sport said to me "No don't touch him! Don't give him the tracksuit! He's a gris-gris man!"'

Then, recalls Troussier, things got out of hand, beyond his control. 'I try not to say "no, no, no" in those sorts of situations, but then they told me, "Okay, we need one pygmy for each player". So, I said then "Don't have them all sleeping in my hotel". And then they came with a lady, and supposedly a virgin, a beautiful lady.' Now the coach suspected he was being tricked, that the young lady might be there as a member not of some spiritual order, but, rather, of the oldest profession. 'I didn't like that. So I said to her: "Hey, you're a beautiful lady? Are you really a virgin?" I was joking about it. And I think Algeria knew our weak points too. At four o'clock in the morning I was woken up because some

Algerians had placed some stones in front of a player's room. You can't imagine the panic in the hotel.'

Panic, and a degree of weary ennui. Several members of that Ivory Coast team were already fed up with all the hocus-pocus. But it was clear to the footballers that the mystics had been acting under official sanction. They felt obliged to indulge it. 'It was annoying,' the Ivory Coast captain, Saint Joseph Gadji Celi told me. 'There was a lot of fetishism then and it was a real fight for us to get rid of it.' Gadji Celi describes how the team's favoured hotel would become home to over a hundred féticheurs ahead of international matches. Gourds full of various plants and potions would be placed in the players' bedrooms and the players would be ordered to take baths in often foul-smelling liquids. He remembers the panic when a belt, 'charged with magic', slipped off a colleague's waist during a match in which the object was supposed to ensure victory. Searching the field at half-time, there was no sign of it. Others would be instructed to wear special toe-rings and secrete various amulets in their boots or socks. Privately the players would laugh among themselves at many of the rituals, sighing wearily 'It's time to go to the laboratory', agreeing with one another what to whisper into the ear of the live pigeon that was supposed to guard their ambitions and help them to come true.

'There were actually some really hard things we were asked to do,' adds Gadji Celi. 'You get told "Drink this", and you don't know what it is, or where it's come from, and, no, it doesn't taste any good at all.' They felt under pressure to obey. 'It comes from the people in charge. What if you lose the game? And the féticheurs point to you and say: "It was him! It's his fault! He's the guy who wouldn't wash in the special water!" Also it was hard to get together and make a campaign, or unionise against these things because the authorities would automatically come down hard on anything like that. So we didn't always fight too hard against it. Eventually we beat it, after the early 1990s. I'm proud we did. You look at the Ivorian team now and you can see they are detached from all that. What they believe in is themselves.' Didier Drogba, captain and figurehead of the Ivory Coast team of the next generation, agrees that the seers and sorcerers have been sent packing: 'I've never come across that mysticism,' maintains Drogba, firmly. Drogba had heard about it, though: 'We used to call our former goalkeeper Jean-Jacques Tizié "The Pastor" and he told us how at one stage the players would go through a cemetery together to chase away bad spirits.'

In the Drogba era, Ivory Coast would reach a World Cup for the first time, with a team full of players with worldwide reputations; yet Gadji Celi's team, the one Troussier inherited, remains the most successful in the country's history, for the fact of delivering Ivory Coast's single senior trophy: the 1992 African Nations Cup. They did so in spite of all the background sorcery. Or, if you ask the sorcerers, they did it thanks to them. Their triumph in Senegal that year owed a good deal to a remarkable defensive record and finally to victory in the final via a marathon, 11-10, penalty shoot-out against Ghana. Credit over the subsequent months would be especially claimed by three senior mystics from the village of Akradio, outside Abidjan. Even a decade after the Nations Cup triumph, the Akradio sages were still claiming their share of the plaudits. And they were grumpy about it, more and more agitated their contribution had not been sufficiently acknowledged nor rewarded. As the Ivory Coast's Elephants failed to defend their 1992 title, then failed to make the quarter-finals in three of the next four tournaments, the scorned féticheurs acquired a status, the idea grew that they had now jinxed the team. So in April 2002, the Ivorian government's Defence and

Civil Protection Minister, Moise Lida Kouassi visited Akradio, and handed over 1.5 million CFA francs and a bottle of liquor. 'I ask forgiveness from Akradio for the promises which weren't kept after the 1992 Nations Cup,' Kouassi announced, 'and make this donation in order that this village, thanks to the learning of its wise men, will continue to assist our Republic and, in particular, the Minister for Sport.'

A Minister for Sport named René Deby had commissioned a number of féticheurs ahead of the 1992 Nations Cup, and by the time Ivory Coast reached the semi-finals, whoever was ministering to their defence were indeed doing a fine job. The Elephants conceded no goals in the group stage. Come the quarter-finals, they won 1-0 against a strong Zambian team with a 94th-minute winner. By the semi-final against Cameroon, they seemed charmed, their luck holding especially well when the Indomitable Lions' centre-forward François Omam Biyick, he of the mighty leap, crashed a header against the post during a fierce bombardment of the Ivorian goal. It went to extra-time: still no goals. In the shoot-out the Ivorian goalkeeper Alain Gouamene saved three out of four Cameroonian penalties. The same day they learned their opponents in the final, Ghana's Black Stars, would be significantly weakened.

Ghana's captain, Abedi Pelé, perhaps African football's outstanding individual of the time, had picked up a suspension for the final. That, the wizards of Akradio would claim, had been all down to them. As their campaign for recognition dragged on, the impenetrable shield around the Ivorian goal would be credited to Akradio abracadabra. By the time of the 22-kick penalty decider against Ghana, Gouamene had kept his goal intact for more than nine hours in the tournament. Gouamene, an engaging man whose long international career set a number of records, politely suggests he and his defenders may have had something to do with the results, and moreover, they had often achieved them after a bad night's sleep. 'We used to have to get up at four o'clock in the morning sometimes to go to the féticheur's room and do his things. It was tiring.' As far as Gouamene was concerned, it was irrelevant. 'I didn't believe in any of that stuff. I am a Christian. I trusted in God. In fact, I used to have my bible in the back of my goal with me.'

■ ■ ■

South of the Limpopo River, in South Africa, where football in the 21st century operates with a developed infrastructure and pays some of Africa's biggest salaries, the culture of the mystic lives on. Characters like Doctor Mageze, a Tanzanian who says he operates for a number of professional clubs in the Premier Soccer League, is up front enough to advertise his services in the local press. South Africa's best-known head coach, its most feted ex-player, Jomo Sono, has a habit – as footballers who have passed through his Jomo Cosmos club will testify – of calling in the muti man. On one occasion, a player felt their trust in alternative medicine misplaced. He took the gripe to court. Treswill Overmeyer versus Jomo Cosmos came before a Johannesburg Employment Tribunal in 2002 and Overmeyer's lawyers then took it all the way to Fifa. At issue had been Overmeyer's fitness and the terms of his contract with Cosmos. The employer said Overmeyer, a forward from Cape Town, had concealed a chronic injury on joining them. The player argued he had become injured under their care. The plaintiff's fine print detailed Cosmos's treatment of his injury, alleging that the club owner, Sono, had taken Overmeyer to see a traditional healer. The mystic scattered animal bones across the floor of his treatment room to diagnose the problem, and had a striking physical feature:

the healer was blind.

Overmeyer's case against Cosmos would be hard to prove. So would litigation brought by the Ivorian club Africa Sports four years earlier against their principal domestic rivals, Asec Mimosas. After local press reports had Asec players having drunk a liquid prepared by a féticheur prior to a decisive league match between the two clubs, won by Asec, Africa Sports took them to court on the grounds that the supernatural had influenced the destiny of the championship. The action stumbled on a shortage of evidence.

Tales like these pushed the Confederation of African Football to issue their 2002 ban on 'team advisers' with superstitious leanings. They were the governors of a sport growing in global profile, watched and admired worldwide but still producing what they called incidents carrying a 'third-world image'. The Champions League final of 2000 between Tunisia's Espérance and Hearts of Oak had been one such, its second leg disrupted by crowd trouble, then blemished by the operatics of the Espérance goalkeeper Chokri El Ouaer, whom investigation showed had elaborately faked a wound to make it appear he had been struck by something thrown from the grandstand in Accra. Closer inspection would have thrown up the bizarre mind games being played on the Ghanaian team's striker, Ismael Addo, ahead of the first encounter. A member of the Hearts of Oak coaching staff told me how Addo had been handed a hair from the head of a dead local man, advised to tuck it into his jockstrap for the game and assured a hat-trick would be his if he followed his instructions. When Addo scored the first of Hearts' goals in Tunis, he became so agitated, he was quickly substituted. It ended happily enough. Addo would score the last goal in the tempestuous second leg of the tie, and the Ghanaians, armed with their unusual, hidden charm won 5-2.

■ ■ ■

Come the African Nations Cup of 2002, soon after its moratorium on the muti men, the marabouts and wizards, Caf was obliged to confront the whole bizarre business head on. It was semi-final day in Bamako, Mali, with the host nation surprisingly through to the last four to meet the defending champions, Cameroon. A fair number of the capacity crowd had taken their places an hour and a half before kick-off. They would witness an extraordinary, alarming curtain-raiser: the roughing-up of one of Africa's greatest footballers.

Tommy Nkono had been African Footballer of the Year twice, he was Cameroon's first-choice goalkeeper at two World Cups. He remains a hero in Barcelona, where he played for over a decade for Espanyol. He is an urbane, intelligent, good-humoured and popular man, has been Cameroon's assistant coach for many years, a job he shares with training the goalkeepers at Espanyol. In Spain, where he works full-time, he is one of La Liga's most respected specialist coaches, famous for his rigorous, quasi-scientific approach to goalkeeping instruction, liked for his good-nature, appreciated by players for his bonhomie.

In Mali, Nkono acted second-in-command to the German coach, Winfried Shafer, in charge of the Indomitable Lions. As the two of them, a long-haired, squat blond, and the upright, towering Cameroonian strolled around the pitch of the May 26th stadium in Bamako ahead of kick-off, Nkono was suddenly set upon by Malian police officers. A fight broke out, ten officers gathered around Nkono, who is a powerful man, handcuffed him and trailed him around the stadium's perimeter track. Pulled along the rough asphalt, his tracksuit bottoms dragged down off his hips to around his ankles. It was humiliating. Nkono was reduced to tears. He had been arrested, charged with dropping 'magic' on the playing surface. He would later be released, granted an apology by the Mali president's office but also suspended by Caf for a year for 'provocative' acts.

Some three months after the event, I asked Nkono what it had been all about. Something out of absolutely nothing, he maintained. Had he ever come across fetishism in his long career? Only from opposition teams, he reckoned, although in his early years, in Cameroon, players had occasionally been asked to join a Catholic priest in prayer and been given lucky charms before fixtures. Some six years after the incident in Mali, I spoke to Nkono again about it. This time he shared a little more about the background to the incident. 'In Cameroon, we don't really go in for that sort of thing,' he assured me. 'But I think in other parts of West Africa, perhaps they believe these things.' Like in Togo? 'Perhaps,' he said with a grin. The plot thickened. Cameroon had played Togo in the group stage of the 2002 Nations Cup, beaten them 3-0 in Sikasso, seven days before the semi-final against Mali. There had, it seems, been some mischief around the fixture. Nkono saw the signs of it and had decided to play a trick of his own. 'They, the Togolese, were throwing some things into the goal beforehand,' he recounted. 'So I said to myself: "Okay, fine. What are we going to do now?" I took a bottle of mineral water and put a few drops on the ground in a little circle in front of them.' With a gesture, he then challenged the Togolese to walk through the wet zone. 'It was just a little psychological thing,' smiled Nkono. Perhaps the Mali police had got wind of that episode, and had it in mind come the big clash between their team and Nkono's? Still grinning, Nkono agreed. 'Perhaps they had.'

CHAPTER TWELVE

THE LION BITES THE COCKEREL

The Senegal national squad have a perfectly good nickname. It's a little long perhaps, but proud and, even if their choice of creature is not entirely original, the Lions of Teranga – a Wolof word for a sort of welcoming generosity – sounds nicely evocative: these big cats can roar and they can purr. But by the beginning of the 2002 World Cup, Senegal were being casually and repeatedly referred to by another name: Senegaul, with its insinuation they were half West African and half French. What was more, Africa's tournament debutants had been drawn to play France, the title-holders, in the opening match, in Korea. The Senegalese team-sheet showed every single player had an address in France, all employed by clubs in the French league; of the France XI, only one did. The other 10 Bleus worked outside the French championnat. It was a diaspora derby, a piquant one. 'There is so much history between France and Senegal,' said Salif Diao, the midfield player from the Lions of Teranga, soon after the match was over, 'colonisation, slavery and everything. France is like a big brother.'

Over the 90 minutes, France could have been mistaken for the sort of bigger brother who indulges his junior sibling, gives him a step-up from time to time. They were not. France looked older than Senegal, for sure, because they looked a good deal slower in most of what they attempted. They were the second-best team. They were second to the ball when it mattered, especially during the lead-up to the deciding goal. After just under half an hour of a humid evening in Seoul, Senegal's zippy left back, Omar Daf, dispossessed the French veteran Youri Djorkaeff and almost before Djorkaeff could turn around to regard the extent of the damage, the peroxide-headed, supple El Hadji Diouf had, with a jolt of acceleration made a statue of Frank Leboeuf. The next duel of the move would see Papa Bouba Diop reacting fastest once Diouf's low cross had been stopped close to the goal line. Emmanuel Petit failed to clear it; Diop hooked in for 1-0. Daf, Diouf, Diop, Dynamite.

And that was before the jiving. Now, Bouba Diop is a hefty man. Suddenly, we learned how light he could be on his feet. Sprinting to the corner flag, he whipped off his jersey and placed it very deliberately on the grass. He and half a dozen team-mates formed a small circle around the shirt and began to perform a dance that looked to most of the 60,000-odd in the arena like a form of can-can. The few Senegalese in the crowd recognised it as a dance tapped out in time to the mbalakh rhythms pumping through the footballers' heads while celebratory adrenalin coursed through their veins. It stayed 1-0. France hit the frame of Tony Sylva's goal twice in the match, but, after a speedy stepover routine that flummoxed Leboeuf, Senegal's Kalilou Fadiga also hit a French post. Some called it a shock victory. Africa was entitled to regard it as the continent's habitual start to a World Cup, like Cameroon beating Argentina, Algeria defeating Germany, or Nigeria overcoming Spain.

Three weeks later, Senegal were still there, France were not and Fadiga curtly announced it was time for everybody to stop being preoccupied by the whole Francophone big-brother, little-brother, Senegaul thing. 'We are not,' Fadiga announced ahead of the quarter-final encounter with Turkey, 'France's second XI. We are the Senegal first team, and we are Africa's top team at the moment. I think now people should know where Senegal is and what continent it is on.'

■ ■ ■

You can find Senegal in an atlas easily enough. Just look where the bulge of the continent reaches furthest into the Atlantic. On the map of African football, you have always had to look harder. Never, before the turn of the millennium, had the Lions of Teranga finished among the medals at an African Nations Cup. But in early 2002, they suddenly very nearly won one, beaten on penalties by Cameroon in the final in Mali. Reaching a World Cup had still to be regarded as a mighty coup, given that Egypt and Morocco both stood in their way during qualifying. When goal difference looked a possible factor in the last step of the road to Korea and Japan, they had pumped five past Namibia away in Windhoek to gain their place with a flourish.

Senegal played high-octane football, their best moments their swift, fluent counter-attacks. Witness the Daf-Diouf-Diop goal against France; or Diao's goal against Denmark, the conclusion of a sweeping move originating deep in their own half, full of bold, precise exchanges; or the run and cross from Henri Camara converted by Bouba Diop – one of his three goals during the tournament – that gave Senegal a 3-0 lead before half-time against Uruguay. Camara and Diouf brought potency when they attacked from wide positions, and Camara added a strong finish. Camara would score both Senegal's goals in the match against Sweden that carried the West Africans as far as any team from the continent had progressed in a World Cup; Diouf's nutmegging the Swedish defender Olof Mellberg would be one of that tie's more memorable cameos.

Diouf's status among Senegalese supporters swelled during his month in the Far East. El Hadji 'Serial Killer' Diouf has a rascal aspect to his personality, a hinterland that took him into petty crime and street-fighting growing up in a difficult quartier of Dakar, that brought him a criminal conviction after he moved to France to play professionally: he was arrested after a car accident and it was discovered the vehicle belonged not to him but a colleague and he possessed no driving licence. Diouf describes himself as 'a battler'. He can also be hot-tempered and sly. His elaborate fall after a one-on-one with the Uruguay goalkeeper in Senegal's third group match gained a penalty. The contact between players had been minimal.

By the time Senegal had reached the last eight, the rascal in many of them was being pointed out by opponents. The Turkey manager Şenol Güneş put down a marker for the referee ahead of the quarter-final between the Turks and the Senegalese by drawing attention to the raised elbows of the Lions of Teranga whenever they defended high balls into their penalty area. Their disciplinary record, even in a World Cup of twitchy officiating, drew attention to itself. Senegal conceded two penalties and received 15 yellow cards in their five matches, two of them resulting in the dismissal of Diao in the 1-1 draw against Denmark. The same man had scored Senegal's goal and caused the penalty that led to Denmark's.

They had their nervous moments, too. With a win and a draw from their first two matches – against France and Denmark –

Senegal had faced Uruguay in a strong position to break through to the next round. By the time Bouba Diop was introducing puzzled Koreans to the intricate moves of another of his ornate dance routines to celebrate 2-0 after 25 minutes, they appeared safe. Three up at the interval, they looked safer still. What happened next was bizarre. By full-time, Senegalese slackness had allowed Uruguay to score three times. At 3-3 and into injury time, it really ought to have been 4-3 to the South Americans and exit Senegal. Following a poor clearance from Sylva, the huge Uruguayan Ricardo Morales planted an unmarked header from within the six-yard box wide of the target. Senegal had just got very lucky.

■ ■ ■

By then, Senegal found themselves the lone bearers of Africa's World Cup hopes. Halfway through the tournament, Cameroon, Nigeria, South Africa and Tunisia were all heading home, having fallen at the first hurdle. The Lions of Teranga moved across the sea to Japan for their last-16 tie against Sweden. A fan took a live rooster into the Oita Big Eye Stadium, the fowl having become quite a motif for Senegalese supporters since the French cockerel had been plucked on opening night. After 10 minutes, alarmingly, goalkeeper Sylva added another error to the one that had almost invited Uruguay to proceed in the tournament at Senegal's expense. Advancing to grasp a corner, Sylva found himself beaten to it by Henrik Larsson. Senegal trailed. They had been weakened by suspensions from the group phase, missed the iron supplied by captain Aliou Cissé and the intelligence of Fadiga. But they still had Diouf and Camara riding on the crest of their wave. Diouf set up Camara's first goal, after the striker made himself space to angle a drive across the goalkeeper from outside the penalty area. Tied at a goal each, the match went into extra time triggering the possibility of a 'golden goal', a sudden-death decider. Sweden nearly seized it by hitting Sylva's post. Senegal capitalised. Camara slalomed past two defenders and with another precise finish, delivered the coup de grace.

When the dust had settled on Africa's joint-greatest achievement at a World Cup, matching Cameroon's quarter-final of 12 years earlier, Senegal looked around at the company they kept among the last eight. They noticed that to be the African team among the elite no longer meant being the rank outsider. Korea had reached the quarter-finals; so had the United States of America. Senegal would play Turkey, another nation far further advanced than they were accustomed to. Just as Cameroon had done in 1990, Senegal took their pursuit of a place in the semi-finals to extra time. The first 90 minutes against the Turks had been goalless, close, and anxious, particularly when Daf, the inexhaustible full-back, cleared a Yildiray Baştürk header off the goal-line. Come the third minute of the extra half-hour, Daf found himself running out of support, as he sought to cut off a brisk and well-manned break by the fit and ambitious Turks. Their golden goal was a handsome one to win, İlhan Mansiz turning Ümit Davala's cross past the uncertain Sylva at the near post.

Their adventure over, the Senegalese returned to their jobs in Europe, to find the World Cup had transformed their professional lives. Rather than being a squad of expatriates in France, they were in demand, en masse, in England, where the salaries were higher and the culture less familiar. Diouf, Diao, Camara, captain Aliou Cissé and the dreadlocked defender Ferdinand Coly had all joined the Premier League within the next few months. Others followed. But when they regathered as the Lions of Teranga, some of the magic had vanished. At the next Nations Cup, in 2004, Senegal departed in the quarter-finals, their tournament's enduring image

Diouf scowling through a foggy Tunis evening on the sidelines after his red card during the defeat against Tunisia that eliminated them from that tournament. In 2008, Senegal could not even make it out of the group stage of the Nations Cup. Later that year, they fell at the first, earliest hurdle of 2010 World Cup qualifying. In Dakar, a mob marched to the offices of the Senegal Football Federation, breaking windows, demanding explanations for how their Lions had so suddenly, so sourly turned into pussycats.

■ ■ ■

In between those punctuation marks of gradual decline, Senegal became one of several victims of events that hit African football with the force of a coup d'état. On 8 October 2005, over a period of 90 minutes spread across stadiums in the north, west and east of the continent, an almighty overthrow of the football establishment took place. In one case, it felt like a violent uprising, as anger spilled into the streets around some well-to-do properties in Yaoundé, Cameroon. In Nigeria, it provoked wailing so loud it might have been heard well beyond that nation's western borders had the noise not been drowned by long parties going on in Togo, Ghana and Ivory Coast. Senegal sank into a hollow nostalgia for their great Seoul night, South Africa into gloomy recognition that an economy capable of funding the construction of a dozen handsome super-stadiums in time for the 2010 World Cup could apparently not nourish 11 capable footballers.

The second Saturday of that October was the last day of African qualifying for the World Cup finals in Germany. It began with the promise of suspense and it delivered melodramas. It was an afternoon to remind the 21st century of the wonder of radio, the medium that reaches around Africa in a way television cannot. Five places in the Germany tournament would be contested by ten countries over an hour and a half and for eight of those teams, listening out for what was happening elsewhere would be essential. If fortunes ebbed for Angola in Rwanda, Nigerian spirits would soar in Lagos. A sticky spell for Togo away to Congo in Brazzaville would unleash a wave of joy in Dakar. Rumours spread through crowds, to be confirmed or denied by someone with a mobile phone, scorelines updated by anybody with a transistor. The list of World Cup qualifiers changed 12 times in 90 minutes. At various stages between kick-off and final whistle, nine different teams each held pole position, had a foot in the finals. By the end of it, the coup had deposed, one by one, almost all the Big Boys and Africa would be sending four first-time finalists to Germany.

Only Ghana, never before at a World Cup, made quick work of the D-day vicissitudes, finishing ahead of South Africa in their group with a 4-0 home win over the Cape Verde Islands.

In Abuja, Nigeria suffered. The Super Eagles would wallop their 17th, 18th, 19th, 20th and 21st goals of the 10-match qualifying group past Zimbabwe, all the while knowing the tight mathematics of their table meant they could win by 100 goals and still miss out to Angola by the finest margin, namely their unfavourable head-to-head record against the Angolans.

In Dakar, half an hour into Senegal's last match, Henri Camara and El Hadji Diouf had put the Lions of Teranga 2-0 ahead against Mali, goals cheered extra loud when somebody with a wireless let it be known that Togo, the upstarts who that morning led the group, were losing away at Congo-Brazzaville.

In Tunis, the pair of contestants for a single ticket to Germany fought one another head on, Tunisia a point ahead of, and at home to, Morocco; a Maghrebi rivalry abrasive enough to sharpen the blade of a scimitar. After 45 minutes, the score silenced all but the away section: Morocco held a 2-1 lead.

It all transformed in the course of an hour. On 62 minutes in Dakar, news filtered through of a Congolese own goal in Brazzaville, putting Togo equal on points with Senegal. Cheers followed the announcement of 2-1 to Congo; squeals five minutes later when Togo made it 2-2. As fans turned their eyes back to the pitch to watch Camara score a third for Senegal, they cut short their applause as word spread through the Stade Léopold Senghor that Togo had scored three goals too. In Abuja, Nigeria stormed to 5-1 up against Zimbabwe. The third, fourth and fifth would be academic. Ray Power Radio FM had told Nigerians of the blow landed in Kigali by Angola, joint-leaders of Group Four, some 13 minutes into the second half. The 1-0 win over Rwanda would be sufficient to take Angola through at Nigeria's expense. Up on the Mediterranean, Tunisia equalised, held onto 2-2 and headed to their fourth World Cup at Morocco's cost.

The heaviest emotional traffic passed between Yaoundé, Cameroon and Omdurman, the Sudanese city that extends out of Khartoum on the banks of the Nile. In these two venues, a last place in the 2006 World Cup finals would be settled either in favour of Samuel Eto'o's Cameroon, a point clear at the head of Group Three and at home to Egypt, or Didier Drogba's Ivory Coast, playing away against Sudan. The Ivorians felt pessimistic, half assumed they had blown it a month earlier by losing to Eto'o and company. 'At the team meeting, the vice-president of the Federation warned us "If Cameroon slip up and we don't win, we'll want to blow our brains out",' remembers Drogba. When the Ivorian captain stepped out onto a hard, dry pitch, he realised their own part of the deal might not be so straightforward. 'I've never known harder conditions. It felt like 50 degree heat there.' Ivory Coast sweated their way to a good lead, but barely celebrated any of their three goals. Over in Yaoundé, Cameroon had scored against Egypt just before the Ivorians went 1-

0 up against Sudan. It meant Cameroon's would have 23 points, Ivory Coast 22. But as the Ivorian players left the field at the final whistle, one of their staff rushed off the bench, clutching his mobile phone. 'Cameroon and Egypt are drawing!' the man spat out. 'They're still playing but it's 1-1. Two minutes left.' Some Ivorian players embraced until alerted to news of a penalty awarded in injury-time in Yaoundé. The spot-kick was Cameroon's. Other Ivorians knelt down to pray. Kolo Touré, the defender, shouted: 'Calm, boys, calm, it's not over.' 'It was unbearable,' recalls Drogba, 'There were no television pictures to look at. We just had to hope.'

Hope worked. In Yaoundé, 95 minutes on the clock, uncertainty surrounded who should take the penalty for the Indomitable Lions. Most anticipated Eto'o embarking on his customary, short stride to the ball and securing Cameroon's place at a sixth World Cup. Instead Pierre Womé, a full-back with a sledgehammer of a left foot, placed the ball, walked a few strides back, and promptly directed his kick against the outside of the post. For only the second time in nearly a quarter of a century, a World Cup would begin without Cameroon. That night, youths vandalised a car they thought belonged to Womé. His family asked to be placed under police protection. In Omdurman, a tearful delirium overcame the dressing-room of the Ivory Coast. Drogba summoned a cameraman from Ivorian television and said he had a message for the country. He and his team-mates knelt down together, and made an appeal for a cessation of the country's civil unrest. 'We have proved that all Ivorians can live together,' declared an emotional Drogba, 'and we can unite with the same objectives. Please, put down your weapons.'

■ ■ ■

Anybody arriving at the World Cup in Germany seven months later in search of a peace dividend from football success would have been best advised not to try to interpret the complex north-south divide in Ivory Coast, but to wonder instead at the rise of Angola. For the best part of 30 years since its independence from Portugal, the south-west African state, blessed with oil and diamonds, cursed with landmines, had been the site of a gruelling, maiming civil war. A ceasefire soon after the turn of the millennium brought immediate symptoms of urban economic boom. It seemed to lift the national football team suddenly from footnote participants at occasional African Nations Cups to the World Cup finals, where, after eliminating Nigeria in the qualifiers, they would present themselves a solid, if conservative team. The draw for group placings had come up with a resonant entry point for these unlikeliest finalists, obliging the Palancas Negras to meet Portugal in Cologne some five years after a disastrous 'friendly' between the former coloniser and the colonised in Lisbon had been abandoned with four Angolans sent off. By the summer of 2006, Angola's squad suggested a more collaborative relationship between the countries. Half a dozen of the players earned their livings in Portugal, including their captain, Paulo Figueiredo, who is white and had left Africa as a three-year-old at independence in 1975. His father had served in the Portuguese armed services there.

After four minutes, Portugal scored. But Angola bristled in response and would not concede another goal for a further 251 minutes of their debut World Cup. Narrowly defeated by the Portuguese, they held on, and on, and on, for a goalless draw against a lively Mexico, despite the late dismissal of defender André. When they then opened the scoring in their final group match against Iran through Flavio, spearhead of the serial African club champions, Egypt's Al Ahly, Angola held a remote chance of sneaking into round two. In the event, Iran equalised and the Angolans finished third in their table.

The 2006 tournament would be a curious one for Africa. On the one hand, the continent arrived there more worldly than ever. It had teams spearheaded by men who had just won the domestic championship in England with Chelsea: Drogba of Ivory Coast and Michael Essien of Ghana. On the other hand, four of its five entrants were debutants at a World Cup and the groupings had nasty surprises in store for most of the newcomers. Drogba's Elephants, nearly all of them expatriate professionals in strong European leagues, were asked to overcome the Netherlands, Argentina and Serbia-Montenegro, the so-called Group of Death. Ivory Coast found their first pair of matches too demanding. By half-time against Argentina and against Holland, they were 2-0 down. In both games they recovered a goal in the second half, but they had not done themselves justice, felt their captain. Runners-up at the African Nations Cup in Egypt six months earlier, they were also-rans in Germany, their only points achieved in a 3-2 win over Serbia once their hopes of progress had vanished. 'In Egypt we had a unit that worked well together,' reckons Drogba, 'at the World Cup, we revealed too much individualism. Our solidarity had disappeared at the worst time. Our individualism hurt us.'

In short, Africa's debutants were performing . . . well, they were performing just like World Cup debutants. Or worse. Down near the Austrian border, Togo were busy concentrating into two short weeks as many of the caricatures of a doomed, chaotic African World Cup campaign as humanly possible. The Togolese arrived in Germany with thin resources. They had a lone superstar, Emmanuel Sheyi Adebayor, recently contracted by Arsenal of the English Premier League, and his goals had been the principal springboard for Togo, aka the Sparrowhawks' improbable journey to Germany. They also had footballers unearthed from as low down the rungs as the French fourth division. They had a Federation run by one Rock Gnassingbe, son of the country's former dictator and a man whose motivational techniques extended, according to his renown in West Africa, to taking footballers to his private zoo and there showing them what happens if you throw a live chicken into the cage of a predator. Once in Germany, Gnassingbe's Federation and the footballers fell out over fees and bonus payments. Before their second game against Switzerland, the team announced a strike, a threat alleviated only when Fifa stepped in and offered to make up some of the financial differences between the two parties. Otto Pfister, the bellicose German who had been appointed Togo's head coach a few months before the tournament, quit in support of his players even before the first game, before then returning to the post. Togo's football? It seemed almost an after-thought. In their first match they had taken the lead against South Korea, only to lose 2-1. Switzerland then beat them, and though Togo contained France, goalless, for 55 minutes of what became a nervous evening for the French, they conceded two second-half goals. The Sparrowhawks flew home without either a win or a draw, having spent many hours negotiating how much they might be paid should they achieve a point or more.

Once Tunisia had made their customary first-round exit, Africa's hopes concentrated on one team. Ghana, the Black Stars, would buck the novice trend. More dynamic than Ivory Coast, far more dashing than Angola or Tunisia and rather better organised than Togo, they found their way into the second round with some room to spare. Beaten by Italy in their first game, they would be galvanised by a high-quality, well-balanced midfield including the energetic Michael Essien, the authoritative Stephen Appiah and the fine left foot of Ali Sulley Muntari.

Muntari's goal gave Ghana their first World Cup win at the expense of a Czech Republic rated among the top three international sides in the world at that time. This would be the afternoon Ghana believed they had a centre-forward of a standard to complement their fine midfield trio. The gangly Asamoah Gyan can look awkward but then surprise with the delicacy of his touch. He had the match of his life. He scored after barely 60 seconds, caused so many difficulties with his height, his running, his lay-offs that the Czech defender Tomáš Ujfaluši would lose his co-ordinates so badly he fell into indiscipline and received a red card. It was Africa's most exhilarating display in Germany, and it hung in the balance until Muntari's winner eight minutes from the end. Poor Gyan ought to have scored a second goal and believed he had when he converted a penalty. His enthusiasm had led him to approach the spot-kick before the referee's whistle authorised it. Ordered to retake it, having scored his first attempt, he failed with his second. He found himself booked for his excessive haste, too.

To secure their progress Ghana met the United States of America, Black Stars versus Stars-n-Stripes. They seemed cocky. Asked by an American reporter in the pre-match press conference what he liked about the USA, the captain Appiah answered: 'The discos.' On the pitch, Ghana had much the better moves. Midway into the opening period in Nuremburg, Haminu Dramini thundered through the American captain, Claudio Reyna, stealing the ball from him and slipping a shot across the US goalkeeper for the lead. The Black Stars would be caught somewhat square across their back line in conceding a goal, and then somewhat lucky in gaining a penalty. Appiah struck it, high and unstoppable: Ghana 2, USA 1.

In the last 16, they would meet the defending champions, Brazil. Peace FM, the popular radio station in Accra, reported on the morning of the Black Stars' knockout match against Brazil that across Ghana over the previous 12 hours, 'all-nights' had been taking place, church vigils of prayer and song dedicated to the outcome. Atukwei Okai, secretary-general of the Pan-African Writers Association, dedicated a poem to the occasion, including the verse that ingeniously united the inspirer of the Black Star symbol and the Ghana goalkeeper: 'Marcus Garvey is chanting/in the Black Star square/Richard Kingson is alight/And aflutter in the Dortmund air.' Alas, in Dortmund, the Black Stars were caught very square, their high defensive line pierced three times, for all three Brazil goals, the second of which, from Adriano, caused some justified complaints from Ghanaians for an unflagged offside. Ronaldo had already outsprinted the quartet of defenders after five minutes, and Zé Roberto would do the same later on. Gyan would be sent off for diving with 10 minutes left. Ghana had also missed Essien's thrust. A yellow card in the previous fixture meant their finest footballer of his generation watched his country's most significant match from the grandstand. He saw Ghana spoil the three or four good chances they had, and then he saw them fade. The 2006 quarter-finals would be contested only by Europeans and South Americans. Africa's World Cup glass ceiling had gently lowered again.

CHAPTER THIRTEEN

SPHINXES AND VIPERS

The generous chairman of Mamelodi Sundowns had flown 50 lucky, loyal fans from the tip to the top of Africa absolutely for free. A smaller number had paid the nearly 8,000 rands, or about £600, it cost to travel from the continent's southernmost country to its northeast corner. This was a special occasion for the South Africans and the clutch of away supporters were numerous enough to create a small fleck of yellow in the great red wraparound that circles the grandstands of the Cairo International Stadium when Al Ahly play at home in their favourite competition, the African Champions League.

The Sundowns fans had brought their plastic vuvuzelas to blow on, and entered the stadium relieved that after six separate inspections by Egyptian security guards and riot police at perimeter rings around the arena, they were permitted to take in their infernal, buzzing instruments. A martial security presence, they later gathered, is sometimes necessary at Al Ahly's home fixtures. Partisans there have a fame not only for their huge numbers, spread beyond Cairo, beyond Egypt and into the Arabian peninsula, but for the violent scuffles that sometimes surround their derbies with Zamalek. Cairo itself had come under scrutiny for the way it manages its football throngs after some overcrowding at the African Cup of Nations the previous year. Above all, this was a big month for Al Ahly to behave themselves. They were celebrating 100 years since their foundation in April 1907.

Al Ahly are sometimes referred to as the Real Madrid of Africa, for the huge reach of their following, their profile in Egyptian life, their mix of patriotic punch and an appeal through the Arabic-speaking world. In their centenary year, there had been many reminders of their particular history: that it had been founded to give Egyptians a sporting club that compared with, and matched, the Raj-style institutions set up by the British during colonial occupation; that Al Ahly were populist and proud, that as they grew they found an alter-ego to be their foil, their rivals, Zamalek becoming the Inter to their AC Milan, the River Plate to their Boca Juniors. Al Ahly, meaning 'The National', have 45,000 paying members in the Cairo area and the more worldly among them do not mind being called the Real Madrid of Africa but tend to qualify it with a reminder that they are Egypt's people's team first. They became the country's dominant club not from a history of privilege – although the Egyptian state, with its grants and tax-breaks, is now helpful to them financially – but because they rouse.

In post-colonial Egypt, Zamalek had played the part of royalists against the working-class Al Ahly: Zamalek even bore the name of King Farouk for a period. In republican Egypt, Zamalek then took the name of the moneyed Nile island of Cairo where both clubs have their headquarters. And in modern Egypt, the joust of the two clubs has been played out at the very summit of African club football. Al Ahly had won their fifth African Champions Cup in 2006, which gave them as many such triumphs as Zamalek and ushered them into their centenary year with the opportunity to direct some forceful bragging at their neighbours. They also stuck on their medalled chests another gleaming badge. As African champions, Ahly had voyaged to Tokyo in December to take part in the World Club Championship, a Fifa jamboree with six-figure prize-money that brings together the champions of each continent and so claims to represent the very pinnacle of world football's pyramid. At the 2006 version, Africa finished in the medals. The South American champions, Internacional of Porto Alegre in Brazil, defeated Al Ahly in the semi-final and went on to beat Barcelona, the European champions, in the final. Al Ahly then overcame the Central American champions, América of Mexico, to take the bronze and the right to talk of themselves for the next 12 months as the third best club team on earth.

It was not a boast likely yet to stimulate great consternation at Manchester United or at AC Milan, but for an African club to rank itself just behind Barcelona in the most serious global tournament counts for something. When, four months later, Al Ahly met Sundowns, the club from a township outside Pretoria on a Friday evening in the third round of the 2007 African Champions Cup, the Egyptians knew they were being regarded as heavyweights. It was a contest to which all sorts of labels would be attached: North versus South; the establishment versus the nouveau riche. Some called it the wealthiest football match in the annals of African history, not because of the prize-money available, but because of the budgets of the contestants. Sundowns are often dubbed the Chelsea of southern Africa, bankrolled as they are by a billionaire, their chairman Patrice Motsepe, who made his money from drilling for natural resources and did very good business in the years immediately after the fall of a totalitarian regime. Motsepe is to post-apartheid South Africa something like Roman Abramovich is to post-glasnost Russia.

Motsepe's generous distribution of some of his wealth from platinum mining into football goes a long way beyond arranging for 50 supporters to travel with his team all the way from Pretoria to Cairo. In a good month, his very best players can take home 400,000 rands in wages and bonuses, more than 10 times what an average South African mineworker might earn in a year.

Sundowns wear Brazil's colours, canary shirts, cobalt-blue shorts and have as their emblem an open palm, index finger pointed upwards, their slogan The Sky's The Limit. They have come up a long way, through a story not as long as Al Ahly's, but as dramatic and feisty. Under apartheid, they were underprivileged. Next to Kaizer Chiefs and Orlando Pirates, the giants of Soweto, they were outsiders. Under Motsepe, they have usually eclipsed their domestic competitors in the local league. They recruit as many good local players as Chiefs and Pirates and sign better ones from as far away as South America. They attract the best sponsorship deals from companies who like to see Sundowns venturing into African club competitions and across frontiers. In Cairo, the front of their jerseys bore the brand of the mobile phone network, MTN. Al Ahly's scarlet tops carried Vodafone. There's a clue here to a vigorous corporate appetite for a vast market: Africa's mobile phone base grows faster than anywhere in the world, by over 900 per cent in the first five years of the new millennium and counting. Al Ahly also had Coca Cola emblazoned on the tails of their shirts, competing rudely with Pepsi's perimeter advertising around the pitch: Al Ahly against Sundowns is the sort of spectacle businesses want to put their name to, a game beamed live to dozens of the continent's countries, and most watched in two of its biggest economies, South Africa and Egypt.

After a 2-2 draw in Pretoria in the first leg it was nicely poised, too. By the end of the night, Africa's club of the century had imposed the might of tradition over the upstart pretensions of their guests, the noise of the vuvuzelas drowned out. An Al Ahly crowd on the scent of victory makes quite a sight and a sound, from the woman in a headscarf banging her outsized, scarlet-rimmed tambourine, to the great red flag that covers the space of 10,000 seats behind the goal where the Ahly ultras like to stand, let off their flares and sing verses about Zamalek being the club for foreigners and immigrants. When Al Ahly captain Shady Mohammed converted a second-half penalty to put Ahly ahead in the tie the same area turns into a bouncing red and white blancmange, flags waving, arms stretched upwards. Shady Mohammed encouraged them by clenching his fist around the Al Ahly badge on his red jersey and kissing it.

His team had been much the savvier competitors, quick to spread the ball to the wide positions. Once Mohammed Aboutrika, tricky as a sphinx, burst from a challenge to hoist a measured chip, while running at full pelt, over the Sundowns goalkeeper, ticker-tape rained from the upper tier. Ahly, 2-0 winners, had disposed of the upstarts from the south. By the end of the year, they would be in the third of four successive African Champions League finals. By the following February, they would be supplying most of the players for Egypt to retain the African Cup of Nations and extending their record in the continent's principal international competition beyond the immediate reach of any challengers, a sixth win for The Pharaohs. Aboutrika, known as 'The Smiling Assassin' would be named runner-up as Africa's Footballer of the Year for 2007 and 2008, the first time in nearly a quarter of a century that a player employed in Africa, and not in Europe, placed so high in the rankings.

All of which put Egypt, approaching the second decade of the new millennium, at the vanguard of football in Africa. The

Egyptians have never been too far from that position, although the national XI has been the continent's most conspicuous absentee from all but two World Cups. Egypt went to the 1934 tournament, though the invitation was extended not to them as Africans but as winners of a Middle-East play-off against the country then known as Palestine. They played only one match at the final tournament in Italy, lost it and concentrated their best efforts after that on Olympic tournaments. Only some 56 years later did Egypt return to a World Cup finals, again in Italy. Spearheaded by the ageless striker Hossam Hassan, who won the 43rd, 44th and 45th of his 169 international caps, they drew with Ireland, took a point from a gifted Holland team, and held a genuine prospect of making the second round, until a narrow defeat against England in the final group match. They returned home resolved to fortify their domestic game. Professional football, with salaries for full-time players, was introduced to the Egyptian league in 1990, at the behest of the national coach, Mohammed El Gohari. Led by Al Ahly and Zamalek, the wealthier clubs began to recruit from across Africa, particularly West Africa. By 20 years later, they were proudly fending off offers from European clubs and retaining footballers like Aboutrika in the face of competitive offers from across the Mediterranean.

That makes them unusual. There are few clubs in Africa who can aspire to navigate the global market for good footballers and hold their own and they come from a small group of countries: Egypt, Tunisia, and South Africa. For that, they like to think they are championing, protecting the African game. A few days before the match against Al Ahly, I had met Gordon Igesund, Sundowns' South African head coach at his office at Sundowns' highveld training centre between Johannesburg and Pretoria. He explained how his club, like the serial champions of Egypt, were trying to stem the flight of the best players abroad. 'You look at Al Ahly, they hear many offers for their players to go to Europe and they hold on to them,' said Igesund. 'We want to be like that. We don't want to have to sell our players, we want to keep them and improve our team and become a world class club. When clubs make an offer for our players we want to be in the situation where the player does not automatically say, "I want to go abroad for the money" but says "No, I really want to be here, I don't want to travel, I am comfortable where I am and I'm getting paid well".' Even with the millionaire Motsepe's backing, and the capacity to pay its best footballers a basic of R50,000 a week, Igesund acknowledged this was some way off: 'We have a long way to go to match the salaries of the English league. But we want to keep growing, and I think the gap is definitely closing, not just on the financial side but also because we are serious about wanting to become the best team on the continent.' The closest Sundowns had been to that was the Champions League final of 2001. There they were beaten by, naturally, Al Ahly.

■ ■ ■

In the months after they met in Cairo, and Aboutrika's Al Ahly again knocked Sundowns out of the Champions League, both clubs invited the European champions, Barcelona, to Cairo and to Pretoria for exhibition matches. They both paid Barcelona around $1m for the privilege and they both put up decent performances. In each case, they drew bigger crowds for a friendly against the Spanish team than they had for the competitive games against one another. Africa's club football still struggles to catch non-partisan interest in the same way as a Barcelona or a Manchester United. In that, the African Champions League, the competition for club sides, pales next to the African Cup of Nations, which is for countries. The Nations Cup, the concentrated three weeks of football that brings the best African players back to stadiums and audiences in Africa, begrudgingly released by their club employers in Europe, gets broadcast to more parts of the world now than any other international sporting festival other than football's World Cup, its European championships and the Olympic Games. People who have never been to Africa tune in with such enthusiasm because they expect to see a football played that is distinct from what television usually provides them, a football with some daring about it, some improvisation.

Africa's club football, by contrast, suffers large areas of neglect. The point was made rather poignantly to me during the 2008 African Cup of Nations in Ghana, in the Atlantic coast town of Cape Coast. Football in West Africa situates its year zero here, on a space now tiled over in concrete, overlooked by the bust of Queen Victoria, where an expatriate teacher gathered his pupils into teams and formed a club, Excelsior, in 1903. This is the settlement where a Ghanaian princess's grandson, Arthur Wharton, played the sport with his school friends, refining the skills that made the goalkeeper good enough to play for money in England in the 19th century. It is where the shabby Robert Mensah stadium remembers in its name Africa's finest goalkeeper of the 1960s, who was murdered in a row outside a bar when he was still at his peak. Here, twice a season, the Ghanaian league stages the derby between clubs whose names alone used to sell the fixture to curious locals, Venomous Vipers against Mysterious Dwarves. The Dwarves (they became Mysterious in an era, the 1930s, when several teams in the area had dwarves in their titles and they needed to be different) have since the turn of the millennium been strong enough to travel to as far away as Egypt in Pan-African Cups, but have fallen on hard times, relegated to

Ghana's second division. Market forces and the flight of talent are largely to blame.

Cape Coast can reasonably claim to have nurtured one of the finest African footballers of the last decade. Not far from the Robert Mensah arena stands Saint Augustine's College, a handsome schoolhouse with tall white columns set on grassy playing fields, where the player Michael Essien was educated, to be fast-tracked not into a life as a Viper or a Dwarf but to a career playing football outside Africa, later to be celebrated at Chelsea in the English Premier League as the epitome of the modern, multi-skilled footballer. Essien, naturally, was Ghana's pin-up while they hosted the Nations Cup, his beatific smile beaming from posters across the country. In the place where he learned his football, he was simply a famous alumnus. The Nations Cup had barely touched Cape Coast, scheduling its matches elsewhere. In Accra, Sekondi, Tamale and Kumasi, new stadiums had been constructed for the event, built, like many projects in modern Africa, by Chinese contractors. Cape Coast and the clubs with the strange, gothic names felt left behind.

In sub-Saharan Africa's major cities, ancient club rivalries still animate big crowds. Games like Chiefs against Pirates in Johannesburg, Hearts of Oak against Asante Kotoko in Accra and Kumasi. But these have carried with them recent troubles. Within a month of one another in 2001, overcrowding at stadiums where Chiefs played Pirates and Hearts met Kotoko took the lives of 169 spectators. Africa's safety record at football grounds is dreadful. Ahead of the qualifying matches for the 2010 World Cup, Fifa undertook a broad inspection of the principal stadiums across the continent. Some good it did. On the first weekend of the final phase of that qualifying tournament, in March 2009, 19 people died in crushing at Adidjan's Houphouët-Boigny arena as they tried to watch Ivory Coast play Malawi.

Club football suffers a lack of trust, too. Standards of refereeing at domestic games in Africa are generally low, allegations of crooked officials high, and incidents of corruption in the management of football frequent. At the top of the club pyramid, the African Champions League models itself on its European equivalent; it has considerable obstacles to overcome. The distances teams are required to travel is one, the difference in resources another: from the corrugated earth of the best playing surface in N'Djamena, Chad to the manicured pitch of the Stade El Menzah in Tunis. A team playing a home and away leg a fortnight apart in December in the Champions League might play one of the matches in temperatures close to freezing and the other in hot summer. Away victories in Africa are notoriously hard, wherever you come from. Even watching away games on television can be tricky. An international broadcaster who in 2007 bought the rights to show Nigerian league games found their camera crews prevented from entering a stadium by local 'area boys', gangsters who wanted the guaranteed bias of the referee to be witnessed only by the spectators in the ground, not by an inquisitive television audience.

Move down the pyramid, and attendances in many of the mightier football cultures in Africa have slid in the last 20 years. In Cameroon, whose clubs once set the sorts of standards in the Champions Cup that the Egyptians and Tunisians now maintain, the flight of the best players to European football has altered the habits of weekend afternoons in cities like Douala and Yaoundé. The national team's matches, the occasions that return stars like Samuel Eto'o to the country's arenas, still draw capacity crowds, but fewer domestic fixtures fill the larger grounds. Televised European football has become a more widely available and an increasingly attractive alternative. Subscriptions to the channels that carry overseas packages are affordable to a small minority across most of the continent, but 'TV clubs' and bars bring Eto'o, Essien or Emmanuel Adebayor in the colours of Barcelona, Chelsea or Arsenal to the screens of their urban compatriots each Saturday or Sunday. Local leagues in parts of Africa have begun to alter the kick-off times of their domestic fixtures to try to avoid clashes with televised matches beamed from England, Spain, Portugal, Italy or France and encourage spectators back into stadiums.

In 2009, The Confederation of African Football launched a Pan-African scheme to revive the local game. The African Nations Championship is an international, country-versus-country tournament like the African Cup of Nations, except that its players are chosen only from among those employed by clubs in Africa. As a pioneering example of African self-sufficiency, it had a tepid start. Wealthy South Africa, drawing players from the most moneyed league on the continent, were beaten in the qualifiers by hard-up Zimbabwe. Neither Nigeria nor Cameroon, countries most affected by the exodus from domestic football of the most skilled, made it to the finals in Ivory Coast. The Democratic Republic of Congo, formerly Zaïre, emerged as the winners of the inaugural African Nations Championships, a gratifying fillip for a troubled country but not an indication that they might regain the punch Zaïre brought to African football in the 1970s. As for Egypt, they simply withdrew before the qualifiers began, snootily explaining that Egyptian football needed no help in encouraging its most talented individuals not to leave the country. As champions of each of Africa's elite competitions, for clubs and for nations, they, the fabulous Pharoahs, believed they had more important projects to see to.

EPILOGUE

Lindiwe Matshikiza waves an imaginary stick. 'This,' she says, putting on a merchant's voice, 'is the 2010 magic wand! It eliminates poverty and crime!' In front of Matshikiza, an audience of a couple of hundred hoot and giggle, and one of South Africa's finest comediennes moves on to the next gag in her virtuoso stand-up show. For several weeks, Johannesburg's Market Theatre, in the downtown district of a city where some folk worry about venturing out after dark, has sold out for 'Bafana Republic', a 90 minute series of light-hearted skits on Africa's first World Cup and all the baggage the lead-up to the tournament has assumed. On stage, Matshikiza is a brilliant mimic, and her satire cuts close to the bone. One minute she plays 'Jorge', the obscure foreign head coach hired for a mammoth salary from overseas to take charge of a national team in which he speaks no common language with any of the players. Then she is 'Chardonnay', footballer's bimbo wife, delivering puns about 'fine white whines' in a country of productive vineyards and a pale-skinned minority notorious for complaining how the nation has gone to the dogs since it found democracy.

Next, Matshikiza assumes the brogue of a weasely scam-artist, making money on the back of black market tickets and fake World Cup memorabilia, like the 2010 magic wand. She switches to the persona of Martina van Schalkwyk, a hapless Afrikaaner tour guide welcoming European fans to a country of 'safaris and soccer', full of exotic wildlife and 'white elephants', vast new stadiums with no obvious purpose once the World Cup charabanc has passed through. Matshikiza then caricatures the priggish representative of the imaginary, sinister PAHAD, People Against Heretics And Detractors, who forbid cyncism or humour at the expense of the biggest sporting event ever to be staged in Africa.

Happily, laughter and wit are natural, unbannable instincts in Africa. On the topic of the transforming power of the continent's first World Cup as hosts, a healthy scepticism exists as an antidote to too much hype. In the period since Nelson Mandela delivered his persuasive words to the executives of Fifa in Zurich, and it chose to take the event to Africa's southern tip, 2010 has become an obsession for South Africans. Mostly, it is anticipated with joy. Sometimes it is taken as a panacea to solve all the country's difficult challenges. The event has altered the very landscape. If you take the boat now from Robben Island, Mandela's old abode, into Cape Town's main harbour, one feature distinguishes the view from the outlines he peered at in March 1982, when he was ferried away from his cell there to a prison on the mainland. The sheer, flat summit of Table Mountain still takes the breath away, as it has for sailors for over 600 years, but, now, catching the eye as you approach is the super-futuristic, bright white form of a huge, oval arena. Lit up at night, the Green Point stadium, with its gently undulating lines, becomes the dominant architectural beacon. On 6 July 2010, it will be the focus of at least 250 million people around the globe, the stage for a semi-final.

Billions of rands of public money have been channelled into the 2010 World Cup, invested in stadiums whose principal purpose is to stage three or four matches during a festival that lasts for a month. It will draw the world's attention to the continent like no sporting event since The Rumble in the Jungle, when athletes from outside Africa came, conquered and left without glancing too long over their shoulders at a country, Zaïre, that would tumble into chaos for the next thirty years. Much of the rest of Africa has changed for the better since then. The landmark that is Cape Town's shimmering new arena was to be called The African Renaissance stadium, and if the name has not quite caught on, it is a phrase which has currency. Africa's maiden World Cup aspires to celebrate a continent in renaissance, where democracy triumphs in more states than it ever has done, where there are fewer armed conflicts, and where dozens of countries' economies were booming until the global slowdown of late 2008, where even the flight of skilled individuals out of Africa has shown signs of dipping and even of reversing. At its most optimistic, the 2010 World Cup promotes itself as a celebration of Pan-Africanism, an event that will touch the entire continent, almost as relevant to Nelspruit, near the South Africa-Mozambique border, as to Nouakchott in Mauritania.

There is no 2010 magic wand. Sport does not eliminate poverty and crime. Yet football can and does affect real lives in Africa. It acts as lightning conductor in periods of storm. If Zaïre put itself on the map through sport in the 1970s, so did Algeria with its World Cup impact in the early 1980s. Violent civil conflict between government and Islamists overcame the country over the next decade. In 1995, it claimed the life of 'Yamaha', the famous fan whose cheerleading and mischief were extinguished by a fundamentalist's bullet because he brought an irreligious frivolity into stadiums. His death roused the nation's youth as his praise-singing had animated their game. At Yamaha's funeral procession, thousands of mourners shouted slogans like 'Algiers is not Kabul', brought a liberating impulse to an oppressed time. The same year, Mandela saw the unlikely event of a rugby World Cup victory in Johannesburg genuinely unite South Africans across colour lines. He knew then that football, the people's sport, might do a great deal more. In Liberia, football made of George Weah a leader around whom a nation rallied legitimate optimism about its future. Liberians found peace where there had been none. A classy centre-forward played his part.

Liberia will not be winning a World Cup imminently. Nor will Algeria, still edgy, though a better place than it was. Nor will the Democratic Republic of Congo, once Zaïre. South Africa will not lift football's World Cup trophy on their own soil in July 2010 but their team will bring together the people of a country with enduring fractures at least as long as they last in the competition. Another African side should go further, perhaps reach a World Cup final, say, before the third decade of the new millennium. Various sages, captivated by a football that is thrilling, imaginative, muscular, have since the 1960s foreseen as much. Their predictions are not so much wrong as a little delayed. Mandela called African football 'a giant that has been dormant for too long'. If so, the waking-up will be spectacular. The dormant years have been anything but sleepy.

BIBLIOGRAPHY

Akpabot, Samuel *Football in Nigeria* (Macmillan, 1985)

Alegi, Peter *Laduma!* (University of KwaZulu-Natal Press, 2004)

Al Rouh, Djallal 'L'Homme qui portait un nom de moto, portrait de Yamaha', *Monde Arabe Maghreb-Machrek* (1996), 154.

Auf der Heyde, Peter *Has Anybody Got a Whistle?* (Parrs Wood, 2002)

Azikiwe, Nnamdi *My Odyssey* (C Hurst and Co, 1970)

Baker, William J and James A Mangan *Sport in Africa* (Africana, 1987)

Batukezanga, Zamenga *Sept frères et une soeur* (Édition St Paul-Afrique, 1975)

Belayachi, Nejmeddine *Style et Identité du Football Africain* (L'Harmattan, 1989)

Boer, Wiebe 'Football, Mobilization and Protest', *Lagos Historical Review* (2006), 6, pp. 39–61.

Bongers, Michel *Clemens Westerhof* (BZZTôH, 2002)

Chauvenet, Jacques *Larbi Ben Barek* (Les Presses de Midi, 1994)

Clignet, Remi and Maureen Stark 'Modernisation and Football in Cameroon', *The Journal of Modern African Studies* (1974), 12, 3, pp. 409-421.

Correia, Fernando *Matateu* (Sete Caminhos, 2006)

Coréa, Massiré *Weah* (Amphora, 1997)

Darby, Paul *Africa, Football and Fifa* (Frank Cass, 2002)

Dioumé, Fatou *Le Ventre de L'Atlantique* (Éditions Anne Carrière, 2003)

De Melo, Alfonso *Viagem em redor do planeta Eusébio* (Prime Books, 2004)

Deville-Danthu, Bernadette *Le Sport en Noir et Blanc* (L'Harmattan, 1997)

Domingos, Nuno 'Football and Colonialism, Domination and Appropriation', *Soccer & Society* (2007), 8:4, pp. 478–494

Drogba, Didier *C'était pas gagné . . .* (Éditions Prolongations, 2008)

Ébodé, Eugène *Le briseur de jeu* (Éditions Moreaux, 2000)

Ernaut, Gérard *Dahleb* (Calmann-Lévy, 1977)

Gyan-Apenteng, Kwasi (ed.) *Pride and Glory* (Total Africa Communications, 2006)

Hamel, Hédi *La Légende de la CAN* (Tournon, 2008)

Harris, Nick *England, Their England* (Pitch, 2003)

Herrera, Helenio *Yo Memorias* (Editorials Planeta, 1962)

Liwena, Ridgeway and Monde Sifuniso *The Gabon Disaster* (Ridgeway Liwena Publishing, 1997)

Luthuli, Albert *Let My People Go* (Collins, 1962)

Mahjoub, Faouzi *Le Football Africain* (Jeune Afrique, 1988)

Martin, Phyllis 'Colonialism, Youth and Football in French Equatorial Africa,' *International Journal of the History of Sport* (1991), 8 (1), pp 56–71.

Mazwai, Thami (ed) *Thirty Years of South African Soccer* (Sunbird, 2003)

Meredith, Martin *The State of Africa* (The Free Press, 2005)

Milla, Roger *Une Vie de Lion* (Éditions Duboiris, 2006)

Mokoso, Ndeley *Man Pass Man & Other Stories* (Longman, 1988)

Ntonfo, André *Football et Politique du Football au Cameroun* (Éditions du CRAC, 1994)

Oke, Adedayo *From UK Tourists to Super Eagles* (Okestra, 2000)

Pelé, Abedi *Ballon D'Or* (Solar, 1992)

Raath, Peter *Soccer Through the Years* (P Raath, 2002)

Ricci, Filippo Maria *Scusate Il Ritardo* (Limina, 2006)

Saadallah, Rabah and Djamel Benfars *La Glorieuse Équipe du FLN* (ENAL, 1985)

Scotch, N.A 'Magic, Sorcery and Football among the Urban Zulu,' *Journal of Conflict Resolution* (1961), 5, 1, pp. 70–74

Sello, Sekola *Chiefs, 21 Glorious Years* (Skotaville, 1991)

Vasili, Phil *The First Black Footballer: Arthur Wharton 1865–1930* (Frank Cass, 1998)

Vasili, Phil 'Colonialism and Football', *Race and Class* (1995) 36, 4, pp. 55–70

Wilson, Jonathan *Inverting the Pyramid* (Orion, 2008)

AFRICAN CUP OF NATIONS FINALS 1957–2008

	Venue	Champion	Runner-up
1957	Sudan	Egypt	4-0 Ethiopia
1959	Egypt	Egypt	2-1 Sudan
1962	Ethiopia	Ethiopia	4-2 Egypt (aet)
1963	Ghana	Ghana	3-0 Sudan
1965	Tunisia	Ghana	3-2 Tunisia (aet)
1968	Ethiopia	Zaïre	1-0 Ghana
1970	Sudan	Sudan	1-0 Ghana
1972	Cameroon	Congo	3-2 Mali
1974	Egypt	Zaïre	2-2 Zambia (aet)
		Zaïre	2-0 Zambia (replay)
1976	Ethiopia	Morocco	1-1 Guinea (group format)
1978	Ghana	Ghana	2-0 Uganda
1980	Nigeria	Nigeria	3-0 Algeria
1982	Libya	Ghana	1-1 Libya (7-6 on pens)
1984	Ivory Coast	Cameroon	3-1 Nigeria
1986	Egypt	Egypt	0-0 Cameroon (5-4 on pens)
1988	Morocco	Cameroon	1-0 Nigeria
1990	Algeria	Algeria	1-0 Nigeria
1992	Senegal	Ivory Coast	0-0 Ghana (11-10 on pens)
1994	Tunisia	Nigeria	2-1 Zambia
1996	South Africa	South Africa	2-0 Tunisia
1998	Burkina Faso	Egypt	2-0 South Africa
2000	Nigeria/Ghana	Cameroon	2-2 Nigeria (4-3 on pens)
2002	Mali	Cameroon	0-0 Senegal (3-2 on pens)
2004	Tunisia	Tunisia	2-1 Morocco
2006	Egypt	Egypt	0-0 Ivory Coast (4-2 on pens)
2008	Ghana	Egypt	1-0 Cameroon

AFRICAN TEAMS AT WORLD CUP FINAL TOURNAMENTS, 1934–2006

1934	Egypt	First Round	P1 W0 D0 L1
1970	Morocco	First Round	P3 W0 D1 L2
1974	Zaïre	First Round	P3 W0 D0 L3
1978	Tunisia	First Round	P3 W1 D1 L1
1982	Algeria	First Round	P3 W2 D0 L1
	Cameroon	First Round	P3 W0 D3 L0
1986	Morocco	Last 16	P4 W1 D2 L1
	Algeria	First Round	P3 W0 D1 L2
1990	Cameroon	Quarter-Finals	P5 W3 D0 L2
	Egypt	First Round	P3 W0 D2 L1
1994	Nigeria	Last 16	P4 W2 D0 L2
	Cameroon	First Round	P3 W0 D1 L2
	Morocco	First Round	P3 W0 D0 L3
1998	Nigeria	Last 16	P4 W2 D0 L2
	Morocco	First Round	P3 W1 D1 L1
	Cameroon	First Round	P3 W0 D2 L1
	South Africa	First Round	P3 W0 D2 L1
	Tunisia	First Round	P3 W0 D1 L2
2002	Senegal	Quarter-Finals	P5 W2 D2 L1
	Cameroon	First Round	P3 W1 D1 L1
	South Africa	First Round	P3 W1 D1 L1
	Nigeria	First Round	P3 W0 D1 L2
	Tunisia	First Round	P3 W0 D1 L2
2006	Ghana	Last 16	P4 W2 D0 L2
	Ivory Coast	First Round	P3 W1 D0 L2
	Angola	First Round	P3 W0 D2 L1
	Tunisia	First Round	P3 W0 D1 L2
	Togo	First Round	P3 W0 D0 L3

AFRICA'S OLYMPIC FOOTBALL MEDALS

1992	Ghana	Bronze
1996	Nigeria	Gold
2000	Cameroon	Gold
2008	Nigeria	Silver

AFRICAN CHAMPIONS CUP FINALS 1964–2008

1964	**Oryx Douala** (Cameroon)	2-1 Stade Malien (Mali)
1966	AS Real Bamako (Mali)	3-1 Stade Abidjan (Ivory Coast)
	Stade Abidjan	4-1 AS Real Bamako
1967	Asante Kotoko (Ghana)	1-1 Tout Puissant Mazembe (Zaïre)
	TP Mazembe	2-2 Asante Kotoko*
1968	**TP Mazembe**	5-0 Etoile Filante
	Etoile Filante (Togo)	4-1 TP Mazembe
1969	TP Mazembe	2-2 Ismaily (Egypt)
	Ismaily	3-1 TP Mazembe
1970	**Asante Kotoko**	1-1 TP Mazembe
	TP Mazembe	1-2 Asante Kotoko
1971	Asante Kotoko	3-0 Canon Yaoundé (Cameroon)
	Canon Yaoundé	2-0 Asante Kotoko
	Canon Yaoundé	1-0 Asante Kotoko**
1972	**Hafia** (Guinea)	4-2 Simba FC (Uganda)
	Simba FC	2-3 Hafia
1973	Asante Kotoko	4-2 AS Vita Club (Zaïre)
	AS Vita Club	3-0 Asante Kotoko
1974	**CARA Brazzaville** (Congo)	4-2 Ghazl El-Mehalla (Egypt)
	Ghazl El-Mehalla	1-2 CARA Brazzaville
1975	**Hafia**	1-0 Enugu Rangers (Nigeria)
	Enugu Rangers	1-2 Hafia
1976	Hafia	3-0 Mouloudia Algiers (Algeria)
	Mouloudia Algiers	3-0 Hafia (4-1 on penalties)

1977	Hearts of Oak (Ghana)	0-1	Hafia
	Hafia	3-2	Hearts of Oak
1978	Hafia	0-0	Canon Yaoundé
	Canon Yaoundé	2-0	Hafia
1979	Hearts of Oak	1-0	Union Douala (Cameroon)
	Union Douala	1-0	Hearts of Oak (5-3 on penalties)
1980	**Canon Yaoundé**	2-2	AS Bilima (Zaïre)
	AS Bilima	0-3	Canon Yaoundé
1981	**JS Kabylie** (Algeria)	4-0	AS Vita Club
	AS Vita Club	0-1	JS Kabylie
1982	**Al-Ahly** (Egypt)	3-0	Asante Kotoko
	Asante Kotoko	1-1	Al-Ahly
1983	Al-Ahly	0-0	Asante Kotoko
	Asante Kotoko	1-0	Al-Ahly
1984	**Zamalek** (Egypt)	2-0	Shooting Stars (Nigeria)
	Shooting Stars	0-1	Zamalek
1985	**FAR Rabat** (Morocco)	5-2	AS Bilima (Zaïre)
	AS Bilima	1-1	FAR Rabat
1986	**Zamalek**	2-0	Africa Sports (Ivory Coast)
	Africa Sports	2-0	Zamalek (4-2 on pens)
1987	Al-Hilal (Sudan)	0-0	Al-Ahly
	Al-Ahly	2-0	Al-Hilal
1988	Iwuanyanwu (Nigeria)	1-0	ES Sétif (Algeria)
	ES Sétif	4-0	Iwuanyanwu
1989	**Raja Casablanca** (Morocco)	1-0	Mouloudia Oran
	Mouloudia Oran (Algeria)	1-0	Raja (4-2 on pens)
1990	**JS Kabylie**	1-0	Nkana Red Devils (Zambia)
	Nkana Red Devils	1-0	JS Kabylie (5-3 on pens)
1991	**Club Africain** (Tunisia)	6-2	Villa SC (Uganda)
	Villa SC	1-1	Club Africain
1992	**Wydad Casablanca** (Morocco)	2-0	Al-Hilal
	Al-Hilal	0-0	Wydad Casablanca
1993	Asante Kotoko	0-0	Zamalek
	Zamalek	0-0	Asante Kotoko (7-6 on pens)
1994	Zamalek	0-0	Espérance (Tunisia)
	Espérance	3-1	Zamalek
1995	**Orlando Pirates** (SA)	2-2	ASEC Mimosas (Ivory Coast)
	ASEC Mimosas	0-1	Orlando Pirates

1996	Shooting Stars	2-1 Zamalek
	Zamalek	2-1 Shooting Stars (5-4 on pens)
1997	Goldfields (Ghana)	1-0 Raja Casablanca
	Raja Casablanca	1-0 Goldfields (5-4 on pens)
1998	Dynamos (Zimbabwe)	0-0 ASEC Mimosas
	ASEC Mimosas	4-2 Dynamos
1999	**Raja Casablanca**	0-0 Espérance
	Espérance	0-0 Raja Casablanca (4-3 on pens)
2000	Espérance	1-2 Hearts of Oak
	Hearts of Oak	3-1 Espérance Tunis
2001	Mamelodi Sundowns (SA)	1-1 Al-Ahly
	Al-Ahly	3-0 Mamelodi Sundowns
2002	Raja Casablanca	0-0 Zamalek
	Zamalek	1-0 Raja Casablanca
2003	**Enyimba** (Nigeria)	2-0 Ismaily
	Ismaily	1-0 Enyimba
2004	Etoile du Sahel (Tunisia)	2-1 Enyimba
	Enyimba	2-1 Etoile du Sahel (5-3 on pens)
2005	Etoile du Sahel	0-0 Al-Ahly
	Al-Ahly	3-0 Etoile du Sahel
2006	**Al-Ahly**	1-1 Sfaxien (Tunisia)
	Sfaxien	0-1 Al-Ahly
2007	**Etoile du Sahel**	0-0 Al-Ahly
	Al-Ahly	1-3 Etoile du Sahel
2008	**Al-Ahly**	2-0 Cotonsport Garoua (Cameroon)
	Cotonsport Garoua	2-2 Al-Ahly

*Asante Kotoko failed to attend replay.

**Third leg abandoned; goal difference not applicable over first two legs.

AFRICAN FOOTBALLER OF THE YEAR

	Player	Country	Club
1970	Salif Keita	Mali	Saint-Etienne (Fra)
1971	Ibrahim Sunday	Ghana	Asante Kotoko (Gha)
1972	Chérif Souleymane	Guinea	Hafia (Gui)
1973	Tshimimu Bwanga	Zaïre	Tout Puissant Mazembe (Zai)
1974	Paul Moukila	Congo	CARA Brazzaville (Cog)
1975	Ahmed Faras	Morocco	Chabab Mohammedia (Mor)
1976	Roger Milla	Cameroon	Canon Yaoundé (Cmr)
1977	Tarak Dhiab	Tunisia	Espérance Tunis (Tun)
1978	Abdul Razak	Ghana	Asante Kotoko (Gha)
1979	Thomas Nkono	Cameroon	Canon Yaoundé (Cmr)
1980	Jean Manga Onguene	Cameroon	Canon Yaoundé (Cmr)
1981	Lakhdar Belloumi	Algeria	Mascara (Alg)
1982	Thomas Nkono	Cameroon	Espanyol (Esp)
1983	Mohammed Al Khatib	Egypt	Al-Ahly (Egy)
1984	Téophile Abega	Cameroon	Toulouse (Fra)
1985	Mohammed Timoumi	Morocco	FAR Rabat (Mor)
1986	Badou Zaki	Morocco	Mallorca (Spa)
1987	Rabah Madjer	Algeria	Porto (Por)
1988	Kalusha Bwalya	Zambia	Cercle Brugge (Bel)
1989	George Weah	Liberia	Monaco (Fra)
1990	Roger Milla	Cameroon	Saint Denis (Reunion)
1991	Abedi Pelé	Ghana	Olympique Marseille (Fra)
1992	Abedi Pelé	Ghana	Olympique Marseille (Fra)
1993	Rashidi Yekini	Nigeria	Vitória Setúbal (Por)
1994	Emmanuel Amunike	Nigeria	Sporting (Por)
1995	George Weah	Liberia	Milan (Ita)
1996	Nwankwo Kanu	Nigeria	Ajax (Hol)/Internazionale (Ita)
1997	Victor Ikpeba	Nigeria	Monaco (Fra)
1998	Mustafa Hadji	Morocco	Deportivo La Coruña (Spa)
1999	Nwankwo Kanu	Nigeria	Arsenal (Eng)
2000	Patrick Mboma	Cameroon	Parma (Ita)
2001	El Hadji Diouf	Senegal	Lens (Fra)
2002	El Hadji Diouf	Senegal	Lens (Fra)/Liverpool(Eng)
2003	Samuel Eto'o	Cameroon	Real Mallorca (Spa)
2004	Samuel Eto'o	Cameroon	Real Mallorca/Barcelona (Spa)
2005	Samuel Eto'o	Cameroon	Barcelona (Spa)
2006	Didier Drogba	Ivory Coast	Chelsea (Eng)
2007	Frédéric Kanouté	Mali	Sevilla (Spa)
2008	Emmanuel Adebayor	Togo	Arsenal (Eng)

ACKNOWLEDGEMENTS

This book would have been impossible without the help and enthusiasm of hundreds of people. As most of them were in or from Africa, help and enthusiasm were guaranteed. It is nothing new to praise the continent's hospitality and generosity; it is equally hard to imagine how that reputation could ever be overemphasised.

It also needed the confidence of David Luxton, of Luxton Harris, to push the idea and of Tom Bromley, who commissioned, expertly guided, and edited the manuscript. Malcolm Croft and Matthew Jones, of Portico, took the project on and galvanised it. It also benefited from the rigour of Chris Stone. Its flaws are mine, not theirs. Nor are any errors the responsibility of anyone listed below.

The grounding came from my good luck to have worked under three inspiring sports editors at two great newspapers. Most of all, I'm grateful to Alex Butler, of *The Sunday Times* in London, a clairvoyant who predicted how football's appeal would grow beyond national borders and who backed that judgement with a commitment to reporting from abroad. I'm also indebted to Edward Griffiths, once of *The Sunday Times* in Johannesburg, who sent a novice to remote places and still points him in wise directions, as does Nick Pitt, formerly of *The Sunday Times* in London.

Apart from sources and interviewees cited in the text, knowledge, time, hints and advice have been provided by: Souleymane Aboubakar, Mario Albano, Carlos Amato, Peter Auf der Heyde, the late Doc Bikitsha, Billy Cooper, James Copnall, Jermaine Craig, Amadou Diallo, Fatou Doukouré, Paul Doyle, Julian Dube, Calistas Ebare, Boeti Eshak, Ahmed El Faki, Mark Gleeson, Ousmane Gueye, Gérard Houllier, Danny Jordaan, Lesika Keatlhotletswe, Moussa Khassoum, Bareng-Batho Kortjaas,

Isidore Kouadiou, Ahmed Al Kout, Patricio Kulemeka, Amy Lawrence, David Legge, Anthony Locke, Sy Lerman, Jonty Mark, Tony Mashati, Roy Matthews, Louis Mazibuko, Kgomotso Mokoena, Ivan Modia, Rob Moore, S'bu Mseleku, Alain Niyungeko, Shabani Nonda, Wedson Nyirenda, Brian Oliver, Tunde Orebiyi, Yazid Ouahib, Mark Palmer, Kosta Papić, Hervé Penot, Barnaby Phillips, Patrick Phiri, Webonga Piouhiri, Ronald Reng, Arlindo Rodrigues, the late Gavin Schmidt, Jacqueline Shipanga, Frank Simon, Alex Simpson, Madeleine Soppi, Cynthia Tshaka, Richard Wasswa, Jonathan Wilson, François Yenguere and Mohammed Zitouni. To any I mistakenly left out, apologies. To those who spoke to me requesting anonymity, I trust you find your mystery preserved, your points fairly represented.

Special thanks to Sonia Hawkey for her sensitive transcription of acres of interviews in French and to Michael Clarke for his meticulousness doing the same in English. Thanks also to the reading of Luke Alfred, Stephen Burgen, Emma Hawkey, Alex Hudson and my parents, who all helped lift the text closer to the standard at which they write. I'm grateful to the archives and helpful staff at: *El Moujahid* (Algeria), *L'Opinion* (Morocco), *The Vanguard* (Nigeria), *The Daily Graphic* (Ghana), *O Brado Africano* (Mozambique), *The Sunday Times* (South Africa), *The Times* (Zambia), *L'Auto/L'Equipe* (France) and *News International* (Great Britain); to the Atlético Madrid museum, and the national libraries of Britain, Egypt, France and Zimbabwe and the African Studies Department, Leiden University.

Thanks also to my family for keeping me company through this interest: My parents for first introducing me to west and south-east Africa; my mother for showing me north Africa and for the sort of indomitability that once dared tell the Cameroon team of the 1980s to turn their music down (it was loud, and they did); to my sister, Emma, for being around from Kano to Cape Town, and regularly agreeing that there'd be no better way to spend a Saturday than, say, watching Swaziland play a World Cup qualifier at the Somhlolo; and to my son, Michael, for his expertise in the behavioural patterns of chameleons, his enthusiasm for our big trip to the desert and his flexibility over whether we start it in Windhoek or end it in Tamanrasset.

PICTURE CREDITS

Larbi Ben Barek © Universal/TempSport/Corbis; Nigeria Fans 1949 © Popperfoto/Getty Images; Eusebio © Kent Gavin/Getty Images; Salif Keita © Universal/TempSport/Corbis; Algerian FLN team (x3) © Offside; Zaïre 1974 World Cup squad © Colorsport; Algerian fans, 1982 © Colorsport; Nkono/ Maradona © Offside; Roger Milla © Bongarts/Getty Images; Kalusha Bwalya © Gideon Mendel/Corbis; George Weah © Christian Liewig/Tempsport/Corbis; George Weah at election rally © Chris Hondros/Getty Images; Nigeria Olympic football team © Jerome Prevost/TempSport/Corbis; Mandela and South Africa team, 1996 © Mark Thompson/Allsport/Getty Images; Senegal players, 2002 © Jacques Demarthon/AFP/Getty Images; Mali supporter, 2002 © Jonathan Wilson; Togo fetish market © Author's collection; Nkono and policemen © Frank Fife/AFP/Getty Images; 'Right to Dream' football academy, Ghana © Jonathan Wilson; Mandela with Fifa World Cup trophy, 2004 © Andreas Meier/Reuters/Corbis; Nigerian fan with Bible © Gavin Barker; Ghanaian fans, 2006 © Gavin Barker; Al-Ahly fans © Gavin Barker; Mohammed Aboutrika © Koichi Kamoshida/Getty Images; Samuel Eto'o © Ben Radford/Corbis; Emmanuel Adebayor © Gavin Barker; Michael Essien © Ben Radford/Corbis; Didier Drogba © Ben Radford/Corbis; Orlando Pirates fan © Gavin Barker; Green Point stadium under construction © David Rogers/Getty Images.

INDEX